In Search *of the* PERFECT BREW

In Ontario and Quebec

. . . The Saga Continues

IAN BOWERING

GSPH

Published by

GENERAL STORE
PUBLISHING HOUSE INC.

1 Main Street Burnstown, Ontario, Canada K0J 1G0
Telephone (613) 432-7697 or (613) 432-9385

ISBN 0-919431-80-1
Printed and Bound in Canada.

Layout and Design by Mervin Price
Cover Illustration by Bill Slavin

General Store Publishing House gratefully acknowledges the assistance
of The Ontario Arts Council.

Canadian Cataloguing in Publication Data
Bowering, Ian, 1951-
In search of the perfect brew: In Ontario and Quebec
2nd ed.
Includes index.
ISBN 0-919431-80-1

   1. Beer – Ontario – Evaluation. 2. Beer – Quebec
(Province) – Evaluation. I. Title.

HD9397.C22B69 1993   641.2'3'09713   C94-900063-9

First Printed December 1993

"Our English houses consisted of three roomes a peece
& as many severall floors. The Cellar held ye beer
...together with the Beefe Pork and Butter."

Thomas Gorst describing Charles Fort on James
Bay at the mouth of the Rupert River, in 1670.

No book is ever the result of the efforts of one person, this work is
no exception. I would particularly like to thank advanced
brewerianist, beer aficionado and homebrewer
GORDON HOLDER
of Toronto for the use of his collection of historic Canadian
beer labels, and his comments and support.
I would also like to thank homebrewer extraordinaire and
President of the Canadian Amateur Brewers Association
PAUL DICKEY
also of Toronto for his continued support and
encouragement and the Members and Executive of the
CANADIAN AMATEUR BREWERS ASSOCIATION
for so kindly permitting to reproduce their winning recipes,
and glossary of brewing terms.

THANK YOU.

Table of Contents

CHAPTER 1

INTRODUCTION

My first enjoyable experience with a cold, refreshing bottle of beer took place during a spring high school field trip, when my friends and I happened upon a couple of fishermen willing to sell us a six pack of "Golden", to further our studies.

I had tried beer before, but never enjoyed it as much as I did that day under a tree in a pasture, while the rest of the class was investigating various forms of natural history.

Having had my first successful encounter with the product of the noble hop at school, it is logical that my next experience came about in the hallowed halls of North Park Collegiate in Brantford. An indifferent scholar at best, my only hope of escape was through history. In reading about Ontario's and Canada's glorious and heroic past, I discovered that French Canada was founded on the fur trade, the French language, the Catholic Church and sustained by beer.

Similarly, I learned that modern Ontario was established by Loyalist soldiers and their families, and that if Napoleon's armies marched on their stomachs, the British marched with their mugs full.

The same held true with the opening up of Hudson's Bay and the West. One of the first things the thirsty would be fur traders did upon landing on the Bay was brew beer.

Further studies revealed that beer was an integral part of the Canadian diet. No less of a figure than the "Godmother" of Canadiana Catharine Parr Traill wrote, there was simply no other refreshment, then as now, like beer to provide "...some cooling and strengthening beverage ...much required by men who have to work out in the heat of the sun."

Naturally, I had to try to replicate this beer. Remember this was in the 60s when all most homebrewers had to work with were the rather primitive malt extract kits. Always game, my Dad an Englishman, who longed for a pint of "real ale" helped me set-up my "brewery".

Ever mindful of tradition, I decided to brew porter. Six weeks later my thick, dark, pungent brew was ready. One sip was enough for Dad, but not for me, I was hooked on the trail of discovering the real pioneer beverage. Why? Because I couldn't believe that our forbearers could have possibly drunk anything so appalling.

Eventually I graduated from high school, and ended up in University. Logically when faced with a Master's thesis in history and museology (museum curator training), at the University of Toronto and the Royal Ontario Museum, I abandoned the study of politics, economics, and all assorted social ills in search of the traditional brew, and I found it - brewing a three gallon barrel for my dissertation.

Graduating, and to the relief of all concerned, giving up brewing, I did not lose my interest in consuming and learning about beer. Eventually in 1988 my first book, "The Art and Mystery of Brewing in Ontario", the history of Upper Canada's brewing industry appeared. Coincidentally, the first brewpubs and microbreweries were beginning to have an impact on the beer world. Both my publisher Tim Gordon and I thought that, what Canada needed was a beer guide, and I set out to write, "In Search of the Perfect Brew - the brewpub and micro-brewery guide to Canada", not as a beer expert or judge, but as an enthusiast.

And these are my qualifications. Twenty-five years researching and consuming beer, several years of making bad beer, and many, many days, weeks, and months of interviewing and sampling the best products Canadian brewmasters can produce.

Still I am not an expert. There are only a handful of "experts" in Canada, and they are the Masterbrewers, and a small number of certified beer judges. You can, however, be a beer aficionado the moment you open your taste buds to something new. And if you want to enhance your appreciation of your favorite tipple you can enroll in the beer judging course sponsored by the Canadian Amateur Brewers Association.

Never forget though, we are talking about beer, and shouldn't take ourselves too seriously. Let the "wine boys" raise their pinkies with every glass, and spit out the disagreeable samples, if they want to - its too bad for them that they have chosen the wrong beverage - as beer drinkers - with our mugs full and firmly in hand, we must always remember "there is really no bad beer, just better". In this exploration, unless noted, I have sampled everyone of the beers discussed, and if possible talked to the brewmaster. Throughout my saga I came to believe that "NO ONE'S TASTE WAS WRONG". In part because of this, and partially because Jamie MacKinnon in his "opinionated" guide to Ontario beers did such a commendable job dissecting, praising, lampooning and rating Ontario's beers and listing their ingredients, this book does not analyze each beer as minutely. Instead I have chosen to describe the brewery, talk to the brewmaster and discuss each brew according to its style. In this manner my personal bias towards British ales was curtailed, and I was able to more fairly assess the numerous brews and styles now available to the consumer. If, however, you like to read unbridled opinions, turn to "The Tastings", where various panels of enthusiasts waded through any number of samples in a dozen nights of tippling to record their remarks.

And of course I expect you to disagree, and invite you to write in your comments to me, through the Publisher.

In response to numerous requests, I have also enclosed a lengthened glossary and a new homebrewing section. Compiled with the generous assistance of the Canadian Amateur Brewers Association, this section provides brewers with

Canada's award winning amateur recipes for 1991 and 1992. If you are serious about the beer you make, you really should join the CABA.

I did not discuss brew on premises locations, however, as the industry is in a state of flux due to new Ontario tax laws, and as it really deserves a book of its own.

And finally because I am a historian I have included an update on Canadian Brewing heritage and a section on the Brewer's Retail.

I hope you enjoy the "Saga" and I invite you to watch for the history of Brewing in Canada sometime before the next century!

BEAVER AND BEER

Civilization and brewing go hand-in-hand. Some historians claim that human's gave up their roaming way of life for their brew to ferment, rather than for their bread to rise. It makes sense to me, as it takes longer for beer to rise than bread. And just recently officials at the Royal Ontario Museum in Toronto, discovered traces of beer in a clay jar form the Sumerian city of Godin Tepe, dating back some 5,000 years. According to Cuyler Young, ROM director emeritus, as reported in the March 1993 edition of "On Tap" published by the Brewers Association of Canada, "beer represented the easiest way to preserve barley.' If you leave it (barley) as grain, dry rot gets at it, or the mice eat it. But if you turn it into beer, mice and rats don't get into it, and drinking a bottle of beer gives you about the same amount of carbohydrates as eating a couple of slices of bread".

Despite such authoritative comments, we will never know what happened conclusively, but we can say British North America, French Canada, and Native Canada were all nourished by beer.

While it is well known that French Canada was founded for beaver, the church, and the crown, it is not as well known that during the winter of 1535-36, that Jacques Cartier and his men staying near the Indian village of Stadacona, (Quebec City) would have all perished of scurvy if the Natives had now shown them how to brew spruce beer to counteract the disease.

The good Jesuit Fathers also appear to have enjoyed their beer. In 1646 "The Jesuit Relations" recount that Brother Ambroise made some homebrew, and that a year later the Jesuits' brewery in Sillery, near Quebec went into operation. It is just one of those happy coincidences that Ellen Bounsall's St. Ambroise beers are named after the good Father.

Having taught the French how to brew a century earlier, the Iroquois are now found trying to burn the Montreal Brewery down. Fortunately "four Frenchmen" staved off the assault.

While beer sustained and nourished French North America, the need for fresh beer can be claimed to be the reason for the selection of Plymouth by the Pilgrims as their landfall. From the "Log of the Mayflower" we learn that "For we could not now take time for further search (to land our ship), our victual being much spent, especially our beer".

It is interesting to not the number of "Brewsters" on the "Mayflower", the old English word for female brewer.

To the North along the shores of Hudson's Bay, the British continued their search for new lands and beaver and their passion for beer. In 1668, as soon as the crew of the "Nonsuch" carried their provisions ashore for their first winter, they "brewed Ale and beer and provided against the cold which was their work". Their trials continued with the building of Charles Fort under the directorship of Thomas Gorst in 1670. Constructing two houses of three rooms with several floors the records continue "The Cellar held ye beer were brewed therefor our daily drinking, together with the Beefe Pork and Butter".

The records of the Hudson's Bay Company for 1679-82 continue with the Chief Factor complaining about the quality of the beer. He wrote (original spellings.)

"There is one thing which I writ of to yow. That I must call back, and that is concerning youre malt, for by experience I have found since we removed house, to live by oure selves, we can make good beare for such a quantity of malt as we put in. the mistake was this, when oure men brewed, Capt. Walkers men and they being confederates together, they durst not, or would not hinder them, so much that they drunke up the most parte of the first running of sweet woorte, and we were faine to drinke the washings of the graines".

If malt was lacking the lads apparently enjoyed spruce beer. A Company clerk noted "firr trees, which last kind of tree hath an excellent turpintine (as they call it), on its bud, which boiled in their beer they found very wholesome, and restoring them to strength and vigour when they looked pale, and were sick and weak". Apparently they could enjoy this elixir or prunes and raisins to fight off scurvy.

In 1688, head office in London thoughtfully dispatched a supply of hops. The records relate: "Wee have sent you a few hopps which will better preserve your Beere and save you the Trouble of Brewing soe often. If this arrive before Capt. Youngs Departure, Wee desire you to spare him some few men for his better defence & Strength in his voyage homewards The Seas being Dangerous thro. French Privateers, when he approaches our Coast, or that of Ireland". This is the only reference I have ever seen of good English hop beer being used as protection against the French. You can be assured I have sent a copy of this extract to Preston Manning.

In the 1740s the men on the Bay celebrated Christmas with anything potable at hand. A Company clerk noted:

"For the Christmas celebrations, which lasted twelve or fourteen days, Middleton decided to "give our people strong beer and brandy every day all the time", and when the English beer was all expended by Christmas Eve the issue was changed to "spruce beer" and brandy, the only means used here to prevent the scurvy".

Appreciating the heartening qualities of good barley wine, the Royal Navy contracted Allsopp's of Burton-on-Trent to brew 540 gallons of hight gravity ale to withstand Arctic temperatures for Captain Edward Belcher on his rescue mission for Franklin's lost expedition in 1842.

Belcher reported:

"By experiments made at a temperature of 42°F on deck, it was found to stand +12°F before affording any symptom of congelation. Very good and very important."

When the brew ran-out during the second winter the lads were forced to rely on homebrew made with essence of malt, and hops.

In his final report to the Admiralty, Belcher related that the ale had truly helped the sick and kept very well.

Moving south to Quebec, "The Red Barrel - The History of Watney Mann" printed in 1963, relates that over two thousand pounds sterling of strong beer was shipped from the Griffin Brewery, London to Quebec in 1763 to provide the British garrison with their beverage of choice. This trade apparently kept up for the next three decades until Anglo-Quebec brewers, such as the Molson's and the Dawe's could serve the market.

In Upper Canada, beer followed the Loyalists, the British Army, and the fur trade.

Sometime before 1793, the Loyalist Finkle brothers started Upper Canada's first brewpub and tavern in Ernesttown Township (Bath), west of Kingston.

Governor Simcoe seconded this activity. From letters by an unknown author printed in "The Canadian Antiquarian and Numismatic Journal" for the July-October, 1912 issue of the magazine we learn that in 1793 Simcoe

"...had taken some steps towards the establishment of a brewery, in the hope that the use of a wholesome malt liquor might be substituted by the lower classes, in the place of ardent spirits...It would no doubt be a most desirable circumstance, that this substitute could be brought about, as tending to the improvement of morals, by cutting off so fruitful a resource of delirious excess, as the intemperate use of drams."

The introduction of malt liquors, into general use, would have other good effects, by its encouragement of husbandry, as opening a market to the farmers, for the sale of barley, and further, by retaining those sums of money in the country, which must be annually disbursed for the purchase of the foreign article'.

To further his plan Simcoe advertised in the April 18, 1793 edition of the "Upper Canada Gazette".

"Notice is hereby given, that there will be a BREWERY erected here (Niagara-on-the-Lake) this Summer under the sanction of HIS EXCELLENCY the Lieutenant-Governor, and encouraged by some of the principal Gentlemen in this place, and whoever, shall sow barley and cultivate their Land so that it will produce grain of a good quantity, they may be certain of a Market in the Fall at one DOLLAR a Bushel on delivery".

The brewery was apparently never constructed, but as events turned out, the industry took off without formal government support. Like most events in early Canadian business history, the arrival of our first major commercial brewery seems to be linked to the activities of the fur trade, in this case, North West Company agent Joseph Frobisher, who was instrumental in backing what would eventually become Kingston's famous Bajus Brewery sometime in the 1790s, to satisfy the palates of the thirsty garrison.

As the heart of British military power in Upper Canada, the opening of a brewery in Kingston was almost a natural event, as after 1792 every British soldier was entitled to "6 pints of small beer per day" when "billeted with an innkeeper, or five when quartered in barracks".(H. de Watteville, "The British Soldier", 1954, pp. 81, 92.)

If the garrison was unable to brew its own beer, it was necessary to contract the service out. More than usual dissatisfaction about the abysmal quality of the beer, provided to the troops, led the War Office in London to cancel the daily ration, and give-up brewing, and replace it with "beer money" after 1800. For his penny a day, a soldier could purchase five pints of beer. To meet the demands of the thirsty recruits an industry was born!

Beer as a regular part of the diet, however, was not restricted to the Army. In 19th century Britain Parliament required the master of immigrant vessels to see to it that all passengers had 2/3 pound of bread; 2/3 gallon of beer; 2/3 pound of fresh meat; 3/4 pound of vegetables; 2/3 ounce of cocoa; 3/4 ounce of sugar and 1/4 ounce of tea per day. The beer ration translated into a healthy five Imperial pints of beer per day for everyone aboard.

While the English immigrants, Army and officialdom may have favoured beer, brewers could not initially keep up with the demand.

In 1831, stout-hearted nationalist, English beer drinker and journalist William Catermole advised that immigrants coming to Upper Canada should bring a good stock of barley "for malting... this is an article more wanted than any other grain, and if persons emigrate take seed-barley, it will repay them the carrying, and will operate powerfully when breweries are planted, to improve the taste of the Canadians and the Anglo-Americans from the use of whiskey, which is simply the raw corn spirit, as sold to rectifiers in England'.

Catermole goes on to note:
"If any person with a competent knowledge of brewing would commence in York, or on the Lake, within 10 or 20 miles, it would be an absolute impossibility not to succeed, all are anxious to obtain the beverage they have been accustomed to, added to which, it is a well known fact to everyone, that all who have commenced, even without knowledge of it, have not merely succeeded, but have actually saved fortunes". (It's amazing how accurately Catermole forecast the future, look at the fortune Canadian Breweries' E.P. Taylor made with his various no name products!) Maltsters also much wanted, there being a great difficulty to obtain malt, which is chiefly made by the brewers for their own use, the recent

immigrants would brew if they could get malt. Hops are very inferior to England, from the little care paid to the growth of them, and are chiefly imported from the United States."

(Wm. Catermole, "Emigration. The Advantages of Emigration to Canada," 1831, London, pp. 62, 81, 94.)

Eventually the brewers did arrive, founding more than 750 breweries, while Prince Edward County became the hop centre of Ontario, but that's another book.

Brewing Traditions of Ontario and Quebec

Most microbreweries to one extent or another proclaim that they brew their beers according to tradition.

After you read what traditional Canadian brews were, I think you will agree with me that you are glad they don't!

Spruce beer for instance is fairly difficult to make palatable, while traditional maple beer is often a waste of good maple syrup and beer. Catharine Parr Traill for example wrote that:

"Maple beer...made with sap, boiled down as vinegar, to which a large handful of hops boiled and liquor strained in, is added with barm to ferment it, some add sprigs of spruce, others bruised ginger. To four gallons of boiling water, add one quart of maple syrup and a small tablespoonful of essence of spruce. When it is about milk warm, add a pint of yeast; and when fermented bottle it. In three days fit for use".

Now I am sure with practice you could learn to enjoy this beverage, but I am not sure you could ever warm to the early French Canadians first beer, which was a "bouillon" made from a ball of raw dough left to ferment in a solution of spiced water. If barley malt and hops were not available our forbearers might make their beer "...from fruit, herbs, or seeds by the aid of some kind of fermentation". As late as 1825, Alexander Peddie in "The Hotel, Inn-Keeper, Vintner and Spirit Dealer's Assistant" wrote:

"Herb Ale is made by infusing the herbs among the ale into the cask, (or boiling them among a little water, and pouring as much of the water among the ale to be drunk, as will give it a degree of bitterness requisite) such as horehound, quassia, wormword calomel, gentian root, etc., or part of each; by adding a greater quantity of herbs the ale can be brought to any degree of bitterness required...

Note:

- A herb ale requires to be drunk warm, if a greater quantity be heated than will be drunk at the time, it will not keep, but will turn sour. To prevent this, have a shallow broad pan, fill the pan with water, keep it on the fire, and have a few jugs, it will heat, when called for, in three minutes..."

And don't think that "chili beer" is new either. Not strictly a beer, Frank Dickens, the son of the famous Charles, while serving with the North West Mounted Police described one of the drinks that incapacitated the west.

Dickens penned:

"A glass of bootlegger Yeast Powder Bill's whisky cost 50 cents. Almost a day's pay for a constable. At such an exorbitant price one might justifiably expect a Highland dew blended by angels fallen from the peatiest parts of heaven. Not so. As an innkeeper you will want to write down the de facto recipe for what they call "The Paralyser", no doubt in honour of John Palliser, an Irishman mad enough to explore this region before there were pubs.

- one quart of alcohol

- one pound of overripe black chewing tobacco

- one handful (large handful) red peppers

- one bottle Jamaican ginger (or failing that, one bottle of mare's sweat)

- one quart of black molasses (treacle), poured slowly

- water to taste

Mix and boil the ingredients in a cauldron that has been abandoned by a coven of witches because they ran out of Tartar's lips. The concoction is allowed to mature for five minutes, no longer, as after that it begins to eat a hole in the surface of the Earth".

Dickens along with providing us with this recipe threatened to write a book about the Canadian West to be called "Thirty Years Without Beer".

Obviously these are extreme examples, and brewers did strive to make palatable beverages, however, even as late as 1833 a journalist in York complained "that local brewers were found wanting in part because the barley was adulterated "with buckwheat, oats, peas, rye and chaff".

Once the industry began to settle down, Quebec's and Upper Canada's first brewing traditions after the French, followed the tastes of the United Empire Loyalists and the British. This was essentially a dark ale market. With officers and gentlemen favouring porters and stouts. The popularity of the last two beverages was reinforced with the arrival of the Irish during the 1830s, slowing down the gradual change to India Pale Ales with the introduction of clear drinking vessels.

Reflecting the tastes of some British immigrants, John Brain favoured barley wine and stated "Anything under 30% content wouldn't be fit to drink". The development of lager quickly followed German settlers across the Atlantic with George Rebscher of Berlin (Kitchener) claiming the title of Canada's first lager brewer.

The taste for crystal beers, brought about by the use of clear-glass drinking vessels, the development of lager, and temperance advocates who seemed to equate clearer beers with lower alcohol, saw the growth of the British cream ale market and start of the lager tide. Bolstered by the huge German population to the south, lager soon became available across Ontario, while ale remained more firmly associated with Quebec. Capitalizing on this "new" product Eugene O'Keefe became one of Canada's first large-scale lager brewers around 1879. While the Molson's, following the trend for lighter more sparkling ales, took the idea of Export India Pale Ale to develop "Export" Ale during the first decade of the 20th century.

And while many Canadian beer drinkers lament the fact that our beer has been Americanized, believing this to be a new abomination, Copland's of Toronto first introduced Budweiser to Canadian palates around 1908.

Technology played a large part in the development of the brewing industry. Refrigeration made it possible to brew year round, and lager in particular. Pasteurization made transportation across long distances possible with the product now stabilized against the elements. Steam beer, somewhat of a fad in California today, however, was only a way of advertising beer brewed at a factory powered by steam.

In terms of taste, and homogenization of flavour, the real turning point can be marked with the dry years decreed by temperance, roughly from 1916 to 1927 in Ontario, 1919 to 1921 in Quebec and in the United States from 1919 to 1933, when the Volstead Act was finally amended. Apart from closing the breweries down, prohibition lumped beer with all other alcoholic beverages, ending the concept that many Europeans held that beer was a natural, healthy beverage, if enjoyed in moderation. Temperance also changed the taste of beer when brewers were forced to sell 2.5% "near beer", derisively known as "Fergie's Foam", after the Ontario Premier of the same name. With the taste for beer lost, the public perception of beer low, and the residual lager market, all it took was an E.P. Taylor, to buy up all of the small community breweries, to apply advances in brewing technology to homogenize the product, and then to ship it across Ontario to begin changing the taste of beer. This trend towards homogenization and lighter fizzier beers was reinforced with World War II, when the young recruits first became introduced not only with real British ales, but the lighter lagers provided in abundance by the Americans, along with soft drinks. Remember pre War boys turned into the post War "Pepsi" generation. For many, beer had become a light, cool, bubbly, refreshing beverage. Even though there were a few attempts to reintroduce porter after the war, it was lager that took over. With the technology there to produce millions of gallons of characterless suds, all it required was the teaming-up of the brewing industry with the growing power of the ad man to create our modern designer brews.

So what is the traditional brew?

From this short foray into the history of the development of Ontario and Quebec's beer styles, you can see it can be practically anything a brewer wants it to be. Fortunately, the microbrewers have decided the traditional brew is a quality product.

By the 1960s beer lovers began to question the suds the Big Brewers were offering them. A small, but hardy group of beer drinkers gave up the brew altogether, tired of the adjunct ladened beer that chemically induced a "little" pickaxe wielding man inside their skulls the morning after. Some started making their own brew; all of them began the quest for something different. Canadians began to travel and discover that there were alternatives! Imported beers began to filter into Canada. Often they were mass produced, but they were new. With some of them you could even discern a distinct aroma and taste. And interestingly enough, in a market that began to stagnate and shrink in 1982, the imports showed real growth.

At this point the microbrewery and brewpub movement stepped onto the stage. In the United Kingdom disgruntled beer drinkers who had never even heard of the Reinheitsgebot, formed an organization known as the Campaign for Real Ale (CAMRA), to resist pasteurized, carbonated suds and promote traditional brewing, which led to the revival of cottage breweries and brewpubs; the movement's influence first showed up in North American in California.

In Canada the Federal government first allowed cottage brewing in 1982, leading John Mitchell to open the Horseshoe Bay Brewery, brewing for the Troller Pub in Vancouver. Opened in the same year and operating until 1987 and then reopened two years later, it was Canada's and North America's first modern brewery to produce cask-conditioned ale.

The first step taken, it was not long before the word spread, and once microbrewing and brewpubs gained a toehold they increased rapidly. Today Ontario and Quebec have nearly 20 microbreweries, 30 brewpubs and numerous brewers ready to show anyone interested how to start-up.

According to the Department of Consumer and Corporate Affairs a Cottage Brewery is a brewery that produces 25,000 hectolitres a year, a microbrewery 75,000 hls, followed by the regional brewers, and then by the Big Two. While the temptation exists to define or include only those microbreweries that make real ale in the purist English tradition with 100% barley malt, yeast, hops and water without preservatives,or pasteurization, or strictly according to the Reinheitsgebot - such restrictions would make this a very slim volume, and might soon eliminate those micros that are diversifying as they grow rapidly.

Size of a brewery should not indicate quality, the brewing philosophy and process dictates this. A brewpub until a few years ago was a licensed establishment that produced and served the beer brewed on premises or from an adjacent brewery. With the development of the wort delivery system, where the yeast is pitched at the pub, the rules have changed, and I think a pub that does this may be called a brewpub even if they do only pitch the yeast. Again the purists may disagree, but the proof will be found in the pint.

I will discuss the trends in mircrobrewing and the industry as a whole again, but for the present just want to note the fact that the micros have forced the Big Two to rethink their brews as witnessed by the introduction of Labatt's Duffy's Dark and Molson's Rickard's Red.

Significantly, one brewer, Lakeport has tried to take on the Big Two with a premium taste alike product sold at a discount. Tellingly Lakeport's President's

Choice expanded to three labels within a year, while we all saw the Big Two respond in part, with their own lower priced beers.

As for the direction our modern brew will take. Well we have survived draft in a bottle, almost always consumed cold-filtered beers, and have been familiar with ice beer since Niagara Falls Brewing produced their first bottle of Eisbock several years ago. As for Dry beer, despite the best efforts of the ad men, we all seem to have given this one a pass, as for Lite - well some trends are hard to beat. All the above really shows, however, is that the Big Two will continue to develop new labels and feed the ad agencies and serve the general market, while the micros will continue to make their finely crafted beers. And maybe, just maybe, the Big Two will begin to return to the brews that made them famous - don't hold your breath though - rumour has it that Miller in the United States is already planning a clear beer, believing that its very clarity will convey purity and wholesomeness!

Before leaving this topic though, I will suggest that there are no hard and fast brewing traditions, whether you favour Native Spruce Beer, French Canadian Bouillon, English Real Ale, Irish Stout, German Lager, or Japanese Dry beer, the choice is yours, and with the advent of the microbrewing industry the selection is now there.

Brewing For The Year 2000

Where is the microbrewing industry going? While we know in Ontario that the homebrewing on premises industry is headed for a decline, since the Provincial government decided to tax it, I won't be able to answer the question about the microbrewing industry with any certainty until the year 2001. I will, however, bet a few pints on the following comments, and make some observations and predications based on my recent research.

First of all I will state the obvious, the brewing industry in Ontario and Quebec is alive and well, despite beer sales falling off by 7.4% in Ontario and 1.9% in Quebec last year - the microbrewing segment according to the comments made by the brewers, and verified by the activity at their breweries, is growing by leaps and bounds, as the nearly 50 micros and brewpubs demonstrate. Appreciation for good beer is up. Boredom with expensive, tasteless "ad" beer is up. Now we contribute 53% of the cost of a pint to the government, making our beer the most heavily taxed in the world, Canadian drinkers are turning to alternatives to get something for their dollar.

In southern Ontario one of the most pleasing trends is the dramatic increase in keg draft sales, despite the best efforts of the Big Two, particularly in Eastern Ontario, to convert us all to the bottle. This trend is being capitalized on by London's Thames Valley and Mississauga's Great Lakes, which at the time of writing produced keg draft beer only.

Staying with draft, the English 20 ounce pint "sleeve" glass can now be found nearly everywhere. Some pubs even offer a slightly smaller "pound" glass for those with less capacity.

Brewpubs have also found a following, and have begun to edge out the "Empire" chain of ersatz English pubs. In response to the desire for a Canadian pub, the Neighbourhood Pub Group, based out of Guelph have appeared to serve micro products and Ontario foods. And Real Ale, can now be enjoyed from Carp to Guelph. Finally, if you are sick and tired of electronic games, and are not very good at darts, the pool table is making a definite comeback. The industry has also given birth to several prophets. When I began writing about beer in 1988, most editors and publishers thought I was joking. Now there are four English books about the industry and one French one, with another English tome appearing this winter. And better yet, the "Toronto Star", Canada's largest circulation newspaper now has a regular columnist. And for the future, a Canadian beer magazine is in the works.

In Ontario the industry has been able to embarrass the Provincial government into easing up the law to permit Sunday sales, to earn tourist revenue, if for no other reason. In Quebec micros still can't sell at the brewery. No one seems too worried about it though, and it probably won't alter, meaning Quebeckers will have to travel to Ontario to sit in attractive hospitality lounges such as the one found at Brick overlooking the brewkettles, and Sleeman's with its historic memorabilia collection.

In order to maximize their space, put all of their equipment to work, and prevent the risk of infection from two types of yeast in one brewery, the micros will continue to pool their resources. In Quebec they have already moved towards an efficient distribution system. In Ontario, breweries that basically brew ale have used the facilities of lager brewers to prevent yeast contamination, while it is not unknown for micros to share canning and possibly in the future, packaging lines.

Since the Ontario Provincial government permitted off premises brewing for brewpubs, you are sure to see more places such as the Jame's Gate, that could not possibly brew their own for their size, on site. As for the wort suppliers, they will survive providing the tax man is paid, and not too many brewpub owners complain that it is unfair that they had to pay $100,000 plus, while these systems can be installed for less than 10% of their outlay. Similarly, more contract brewers will appear to turn the products of the brewpubs into potable beverages.

And while there have been closures of such places as Mash McCann's in London and the Madawaska in Arnprior, two pubs that should have never opened; and Sculler's in St. Catharine's, a brewery that produced a fine lager, but was underfunded from the first, both micros and brewpubs will continue to flourish. I have no doubt that we will see a dramatic increase in the number of brewpubs across Ontario and Quebec. Microbrewery growth will, however, be much slower, as the ones we have are already expanding their product lines to meet customer demands. Look for Belgian style beers in Ontario soon.

To sustain their growth, the micros will continue to produce and bottle under licence. Brick has already tried this to break the interprovincial barriers to enter B.C. St. Ambroise, is trying the tried and tiresome route through the Vintages section at the LCBO. The licence programme will also strengthen the regional brewer's market and their ties with the brewpubs as they produce local beers like

Hart's Dragon's Breath for the Kingston Brewing Company, reinforcing the Eastern Ontario connection.

Others will use it to earn extra profits and eat up excess capacity as Upper Canada has done by bottling for Canadian Pacific Hotels. Who would have believed we would have "house beers" several years ago? This trend will continue, and will be good news for drinkers stranded in places that once served "Classic" as an import.

Brewing "handcrafted" products, brewed from the bottom up, with all natural ingredients, the micros have an immediate advantage when it comes to flavour and quality over the Big Two high gravity brewers, without ad men, the micros are able to spend the extra money on the beer. Their will to do so, makes their choice obvious.

How is the micro industry doing? How will it do in the future? In 1990 the micros were hoping to capture 1% of the market. If the micros that moved up to become regional brewers are considered in the figures, it seems that they have achieved their goal. Jamie McKinnon in "The Ontario Beer Guide" noted that the small brewers already had 5-6% of the market and that their sales were increasing in Ontario. Yet for all of this optimism the whole microbrewery output for Canada was less than 10% of Labatt's production for Blue and Blue Light for 1991-92. With such competition, and such distances to cover, its no wonder the micros can only look forward to going up the sales ladder.

The potential for growth is there, the selection and variety is now available, as it has never been available before. I hope that this guide, along with the works of my fellow "prophets", helps to stimulate this industry and aids you in discovering your perfect beer. The yeast is now in your wort!

Stop The Press ! This November Molson's returned to making the beer their grandfather brewed. Try the New Cream Ale & Amber Lager – You may never drink a high priced European, import beer again.

CHAPTER 2

SETTING UP

The construction and location of a microbrewery, and or brewpub, is unique to each situation. They may be found in strip malls, heritage buildings, abandoned "art deco" warehouses, former bakeries, or specially designed buildings, to name a few options.

The brewery might be custom made, "turn key", combination of the two, or the newest development - a collection of fermenting and conditioning tanks - that are filled with wort prepared at another location.

Here are some of Ontario's leading microbrewery and brewpub consulting firms.

Please note I did try to obtain more information about these and other outfits, but with a few noted exceptions they seemed unwilling to spend much time furnishing me with details.

Calgary, Alberta,
CASK BREWING SYSTEMS INC.,

5925 #225, 12th St. S.E.,
Calgary, Alberta, T2H 2M3
403-640-4677;
FAX: 403-640-4680.

(with an office in Montreal at)
5785 Sherbrooke St. W.,
Montreal, Quebec, H4A 1X2
403-514-485-MALT;
FAX: 514-485-MALT

Founded: Started as a representative of Inn Brewing Ltd., of the U.K., Cask installed the first malt extract brewing system in Canada at The Terminal in Nanaimo in 1984.

Production Capacity: Some 19 Canadian and American micro- breweries and brewpubs and 43 brew on premises systems.

(Logo courtesy, Cask Brewing Systems Inc.)

Writing before the Ontario Provincial government "fined" homebrewers for using on premises or brew your own systems, Cask President J. Peter Love wrote:

"...You can see that our focus has changed quite substantially over the past 24 months. The expansion of the beer industry in Canada has been in the Brew on Premises industry. I suggest, based on the lobbying efforts across the country to various provincial liquor control boards, that you will see continued growth in the years to come."

Peter seems to have forgotten the counterlobby! He continues "All of our brew on premises systems are either six or eight, twelve Imperial gallon kettle designs."

Mississauga, Ontario,
CONTINENTAL BREWERIES INC.,

100 Matheson Blvd. E., ste 101,
Mississauga, Ontario, L4Z 2G7
613-890-1373.

President: Allan Calford.

Founded in 1984, and building their first prototype brewing system in 1985, they were fully operational by January 1986.

Responsible for Canadian brewpubs and microbreweries from Lennoxville, Quebec to Miami, they did not care to disclose any more additional information.

Woodbridge, Ontario,
HANWELL'S BREWING,

9330 Pine Valley Drive,
Woodbridge, Ontario, L4L 1A6
416-832-9689

Brewmaster-Consultant: Doug Warren, 2 years training Upper Canada Brewing

Started by: Alan Knight

The business is now operated by Doug Warren, who just let me know of the changes 4 hours before press time!

Woodbridge, Ontario,
MR. BREW,

20 Hanlan Road, unit 23,
Woodbridge, Ontario, L4L 3P6
416-850-5893

Brewmaster-Consultant: Stephan Riedelsheimer

Trained in Munich, Stephan, known as Mr. Brew, provides the full grain, unfermented lager wort to both the Blind Duck at the University of Toronto's Mississauga Campus, and Quinn's in Toronto.

Mr. Brew also operates several brew on premises locations.

Toronto, Ontario,
W. IMPORTS,

33 Laird Drive,
Toronto, Ontario, M4G 3S9
416-422-1484; FAX: 416-425-4858.

President: Bill Wickham

Representative: David Slichter, 416-393-6378; FAX: 416-393-6503.

If you have a taste for the great Belgium beers such as Duvel, Douglas Scotch Ale, Maredsous, Mort Subite, La Trappe, and La Chouffe to name just a few, and your local LCBO Vintages counter is "out-of-stock", you can try ordering your favourites, either individually, or by the case from W. Imports, Ontario's only supplier of these beers.

CHAPTER 3

THE BEER - GUIDE TO BREWPUBS,

MICROBREWERIES AND BETTER BEER BARS IN ONTARIO AND QUEBEC.

With good planning it should be possible to travel around Ontario and Quebec without ever having to go without a pint of good beer. Before you set off on your quest for liquid pleasures, a few words about how this guide is organized will help.

Starting with Ontario and then Quebec, each province is broken down alphabetically by City, and where there are two or more pubs in one location they are listed alphabetically by name. If all of this is too much after savouring a few pints, go to the index.

And one word about the brewpubs and pubs, at the time of printing all of them listed were open, however, for any number of reasons a brewpub may stop producing, to avoid disappointment and futile detours, call ahead. The same caution also applies to microbreweries.

If you are interested in history and beer, see the section titled "Gone But Not Forgotten", this way you can get your fill of Canadian heritage while enjoying the best beers available.

And of course if you don't agree with what I have written, if I have left some noteworthy pub out, or if you just want to make yourself heard, write-in your comments.

RATING YOUR FAVOURITE BREWPUB AND PUB.

"Beer is one of those things like bread. You can only take so much white bread and then you want rye bread."

D.L. Geary, D.L. Geary Brewing Co., Maine.

The question of rating pubs is difficult, to say the least, no matter how pleasurable it may have been. Obviously the beer must be good, but there must be more. Drinking in Canada has been legal for more than 60 years. Temperance is dead, our rough and tumble pioneers habits have been refined, and Canada is no longer a frontier society. Happily gone are the days when men huddled around a small sticky table, in a dark smelly room pushing down their pints as quickly as possible.

This guide is premised on the fact that moderate drinking, in pleasant surroundings is part of everyday life, and can even be included as part of a family outing in the European tradition. Accordingly, the test of a pub is not only the beer, but in the whole presentation. My judging is based on the most demanding criteria I know of -the mother-in-law. Putting it succinctly, would you take your mother-in-law there? This being the yardstick, a low 'mug' score does not mean that the beer is off, even though it might be, or that you might not find the pub a pleasant retreat from family responsibilities, but that it is not a family establishment. For this reason alone, many of Quebec's pubs, located in retrofitted taverns do not receive high ratings. Conversely, however, if the pub has good beer, and a wide selection of imports, or micro products, there is every chance it will receive the four mug mother-in-law rating.

While you may agree with some of my selections, you are sure to note that I have probably missed a well loved watering hole, please accept my apologies, and do let me know about it; with all of the good new pubs opening, this guide is of necessity only a sampler!

BREWPUB AND PUB RATING GUIDE

Good food, or good beer, but not both. Marginal surroundings, probably not suitable for your mother-in-law. Likely a great place to have a pint with your friends.

Reasonable food, and reasonable beer, but basically a tavern, not really family oriented. Not a place to impress your date. A good place to have drinks with your friends.

Good food, good beer. Pleasant surroundings and atmosphere. Suitable for everyone.

Great food and great beer, your search is nearing its completion. Pleasant surroundings and comfortable for everyone. These pubs often have very wide selections of imports, or Ontario or Quebec micro beers, and two personalities; one for the day and dinner trade, and one for nightclub clientele. The four mug rating is usually reserved for brewpubs only.

PLEASE NOTE:

The ratings and comments are merely the opinion of the author, and neither the author nor the Publisher imply or accept any legal responsibility whatsoever should these ratings be made public or be used in any fashion whatsoever without the express permission and under the conditions set down by the author and Publisher.

Finally, I would like to thank all of the brewers, brewpub and pub owners, and microbrewery enthusiasts and entrepreneurs. I would like to offer a special tip of the mug to collector and beer aficionado Gordon Holder for his suggestions and the use of his beer memorabilia collection, and to Paul Dickey, President of the Canadian Amateur Brewers Association for his continued support. Without the heroic pioneering efforts of all of the above people and groups, it would not have been possible to continue the SAGA, "In Search of the Perfect Brew".

Cheers,

Ian Bowering,

Cornwall, June 1993.

Chapter 4

Ontario

Bowmanville, Ontario,
Lighthouse Brewpub And Restaurant

In the Flying Dutchman Hotel, Liberty St.
at Highway 401 Interchange 432,
Bowmanville, Ontario, L1C 2W4
416-623-3373

145 Duke St.,
Bowmanville,
Ontario, L1C 2W4

Rating: While the restaurant is adequate, without the brewery in operation and lacking any interesting micros or imports, you may as well keep driving.

General Manager: Christopher Mendes

Founded: 1990, equipment breakdown October 1992, may not reopen.

Production Capacity: Continental Malt Extract System, the manager/ brewer was trained by Jon Downing.

Occupying the hotel's former swimming pool area, I once hoped that the Lighthouse would provide an oasis for the beer lover on their way between Kingston and Toronto. Unfortunately the equipment broke down, and when I visited it, the staff seemed amazed I would care if the brewery ever reopened, and would I like a Blue?

Call before stopping!

Brampton, Ontario,
Tracks Brewpub

60 Queen Street East,

Brampton, Ontario, L6V 1A9

416-453-3063

(the heart of old downtown Brampton, near the library, and just south of the railway tracks.)

Rating: Unable to get here before press time. I tried to obtain some information from the pub, unwilling to take part, I am able only to provide the following.

Manager: Jimmy Floris

Brewmaster: Doug Warren (contract brewer)

Founded: July 1987.

Production: They started with a three vessel Continental Malt Extract System, with a 1,000 litre capacity now converted to full grain by Alan.

Alan told me that he brews a copper coloured, hoppy, yeasty German style lager, from a single fermentation. While the brewpub offers the usual run of imports, it does not serve the products of other Ontario micros.

Burlington, Ontario,
Pepperwood Bistro

Formerly Suds International; Formerly a Luxembourg

1455 Lakeshore Road,

Burlington, Ontario, L7S 2J1

416-333-6999

Brewmaster: Geoffrey Mallard. A malt extract system to be converted to full grain. First brews: Cream, Pale and Red Ales.

Too new to rate for publication

Your Turn; send your opinions to:

Beer Saga

c/o General Store Publishing House

1 Main Street, Burnstown, Ontario, K0J 1G0

or FAX :613-432-7184.

Carleton Place, Ontario,
Hart Breweries Limited

175 Industrial Ave.,

Carleton Place, Ontario K7C 3V7

613-253-4278; FAX: 613-253-3705

President: Lorne Hart

Brewmaster: Keith Hart, trained at McAuslan's in Montreal under Ellen
Bounsall, and the Wild Goose, Maryland, under startup consultant Alan
Pugsley.

Founded: Evolving out of the proverbial campfire chat, work started on the new
brewery on June 10, 1991. On August 8, the same year, general partners
Lorne Hart, Leo Richer, Gary Lawton, and Frits Bosman hosted a party
for the 24 limited partners marking the completion of the brewery.
On September 15, 1991, the first batch of Hart Amber Ale was made.

Production Capacity: Starting with 5,000 hl the 7,000 square foot brewhouse
will soon grow to 12,000 hl (more than 3 million pints). Custom designed
under the direction of brewmaster- consultant Alan Pugsley, startup costs
were $750,000.

Using a gas-fired copper whirlpool (brewkettle), carmalization is avoided by
using a "whirling" pump. A traditional brewhouse, they use open fermenters.
Wisely breaking with some traditions, the automated bottling line can fill 120
bottles per minute.

*For half a century the stag or hart,
an adult male deer, adorned the labels
of Ottawa's Brading Brewery, it is
reassuring to see it once again
gracing the labels of fine brews made
in Eastern Ontario for Ottawa and the
Valley.*

(Logo courtesy, Hart Breweries Ltd.)

Conceived while friends Lorne Hart, Leo Richer and Gary Lawton "...were
sitting around a campfire enjoying one of Lorne's excellent brews" after a day

of whitewater rafting, it took three years for the idea to mature. Full of idealism and adventure, the trio first investigated the possibility of resurrecting the century old stone brewery in Neustadt. After talking with numerous people in the business and John Wiggins of Creemore fame in particular, they refined their ideas and became committed to the project.

Circumstances now intervened to push the project ahead, when Nepean's Ottawa Valley Brewing Co., formed in 1986 closed in July, 1990 due to "...an overwhelming debt load."

Acquiring a fourth partner, Ottawa contractor Frits Bosman, they purchased a two acre site in Carleton Place's industrial park because of its proximity to Ottawa, the reasonable land costs coupled with good serviced lots, helpful civic officials and the tasteless, hard water essential for good ales.

With the necessary capitalization well under way, they began to build their new brewery.

Interested in "...seeing many people drink a few glasses of beer, than see a few people drink many beers" Hart's Brewery wants to be known for producing "High quality, distinctive ales. Brewed simply and traditionally without computers and unnecessary gadgets. To operate a brewery that doesn't require an engineer to understand it."

For the future, the Brewery plans to establish itself as Eastern Ontario's Brewery, selling its products from Ottawa to Kingston to Cornwall. Once this is done, they will look more seriously at Toronto, and then if interprovincial boundaries fall, Quebec, and export to New England.

Establishing a name as an ale brewer, they plan to explore a wide range of ales over the next few years.

Vital Statistics - The Brew
Cream Ale, 4.5%

A golden cloak covers this well laced brew, which possesses a gentle aromatic balanced nose, leading to a smooth, malty, caramel like body derived from the carastan malt. Finished with a nice malt and bittering, a second sip is inevitable. It is easy to see how this style originally met the lager challenge.

I have always enjoyed cream ales, and didn't think it was possible to exceed what was already available on the market, I was apparently wrong. For a gruelling, but eminently rewarding experience compare Hart with Sleeman.

Dragon's Breath Pale Ale, 4.5%

The first microbrewery beer brewed for a brewpub and sold at the Beer Store, (see the Kingston Brewing Company). In Quebec it is not unusual for micros to produce "housebrews", Hart has refined this trend by actually producing a separate recipe for a restaurant, and brewpub at that. It also labels or housebrew for Ottawa's Elephant and Castle.

Hart Amber Ale, 5%

Bottle and draft. For a real treat try it cask-conditioned at the Swan in nearby Carp.

Cloaked in copper and capped with a rocky, peaked, long lasting and well laced foam, the nose is flowery up-front, and then followed by malt. Enticing in a word, it is definitely not balanced, but who cares? Now you are this far you can savour the exceptionally, light, whipped cream foam, and enjoy the smooth warm taste rife with hops, hops and more hops, which lead to an earthy, malty aftertaste that blossoms.

Winner of a gold medal in the bottled dark ale category at the 1992 International Food, Wine and Beer Show held in Toronto.

Hart Hardy Stout, 5%

To be released in the fall of 1993.

Beer available from Kingston east to the Quebec border, and in some select Toronto locations, and at the brewery.

Souvenirs may be purchased at the brewery, and tours may be arranged.

Carp (pronounced Kerp), Ontario,
THE SWAN AT CARP,

Falldown Lane,

Carp, Ontario

613-839-SWAN

Rating: 🍺🍺🍺 - 🍺🍺🍺🍺
The fact that it is the only pub in Eastern Ontario serving Real Ale, makes the Swan an exceptional experience!

Publican: Stan Dugdale

Founded: 1987

Regally perched on top of a small hill overlooking the village of Carp, at the end of Falldown Lane in a Victorian Presbyterian Manse, The Swan is not a pseudo British pub, but the real thing.

Presided over by former Staffordshire Publican Stan Dugdale, who came to Canada to help prepare for his

(Logo Courtesy, The Swan at Carp.)

Canada to help prepare for his daughter's wedding, Stan "...felt at home here, but not with the beers." Finally over a period of four years, and three return trips, he decided that "Canada was in dire need of a Real Pub with Real Ale" and he immigrated to fill the void. And at least in Carp, and by extension the rest of the Ottawa Valley he has done just that. A visit to The Swan, where real beer is lovingly cared for, served, enjoyed and talked about in the British tradition, is all any beer lover can ask for. And indeed, the only pub like accoutrement missing is a brass footrail for the bar.

Vital Statistics - The Brew
Hart's Cask - Conditioned Best Bitter.
If you have never tried a "real ale" and you think that you like beer, you owe it
   to yourself to make the trek to Carp. If you have sampled it before, you
   don't need any convincing. In the words of Publican Stan Dugdale
   "Brewed in Carleton Place by Hart Breweries, this Best Bitter is a unique
   'living ale' that completes its fermenting in our beer cellar beneath the
   bar. Additive-free and unpasteurized, it is drawn with a hand pump once it
   reaches its peak of perfection...a light, refreshing flavour comparable to
   the best ales available in England." And Stan is right. The brew achieves
   a smoothness that might make whipped-cream seem harsh. Extremely
   well hopped, and packing a full taste, words are not enough to describe
   this elixir.

Menu - beer: With not a single German beer in sight, The Swan is a draft pub,
   which features, John Smith's Bitter, Fowler's Mild, Strongbow cider,
   Guinness, Smithwick's and if you must Tennent's Lager. Bottles include
   Hart, Upper Canada, Bass and DD. and if you really press, you can order
   a Coors Light. But if you come here for that you are lost. The bar also
   carries a small selection of single malt Scotch.

Menu - food: Even though they have fish and chips with mushy peas on the
   menu Stan assures me that the fish is "cod and not carp".

Appetizers: chicken liver paté, deep-fried breaded mushrooms, Scotch Egg.
   Entrées: Guinness Stew, Bangers and Mash with a Canadian twist baked
   beans, Shepherd's Pie, my grandmother's favourite - Sausage, Eggs and
   Chips, Cornish Pastie, Steak and Kidney and Steak and Mushroom pies,
   ploughman's lunch with real pickled onions, vegetarian menu, and dessert
   pies. Also a menu for children 12 and under.

Lunch for two with beer under $25.

Dinner for two with beer under $35.

Credit Cards: All major credit cards.

Atmosphere: Look as hard as you might there is not a television in sight. A traditional British pub that plays classical music, has a dart board, and is located in the old Presbyterian Manse. An outdoor patio. A piano for entertainment, special jazz nights. "A Real Pub with Real Ale."

Parking: Ample parking lot.

Hours: Seven days a week.

Cornwall, Ontario,
THE TOWN HALL RESTAURANT

169 Pitt Street,
Cornwall, Ontario
613-932-3322

Rating: 🍺🍺 - 🍺🍺🍺
A beer and fish house.

Publicans: Ray and Clara Henstock

Founded: 1992

(Photo courtesy, Inverarden Museum, 91-27.6)

Old Cornwall Town Hall, Pitt Street north of 3rd, 1863 - 1968, the building has now been replaced, the pub does not occupy this site.

Believing that a pub should be a community centre, in the English tradition, and not just a place to "swill ale, but a place to come and talk," Publican Ray Henstock named his establishment The Town Hall. Located in a former greasy spoon, at Pitt and Second Streets, in the heart of old Cornwall, this pub is your only hope for good beer and fish. A former publican from around Leeds England for 16 years, Ray cares about how his beers are served, and pumps them into eager mugs with the "beverage mix" instead of CO_2, to prevent artificial carbonation. Believing that "flavour is first and foremost" in beer, Ray's operation is basically a fish and chip house. Taking his fried fish seriously, Ray has one of only two imported English frying ranges in Canada. Using 50 pounds of fat, rather than the standard 150 used in North American ranges, makes the fried food less greasy, while the range is faster and more economical to operate.

Divided into the "Snug" with the long bar, graced by a television which is often mercifully silent, and the dining lounge; The Town Hall may not be the most elegant eatery described in this book, but it is one of the least pretentious, where hearty food and well cared for beer are liberally dispensed.

Vital Statistics

Menu - beer: On tap: Guinness, Smithwick's Ale, Harp Lager, Bass Ale, Tennent's Lager, Stones' Best Bitter, and DAB. No Ontario micros available. No bottled imports, of course there are products from the Big Two.

Menu - food: The Town Hall serves what I describe as the best plate of 'Eastern Ontario ethnic" available - perch rolls. You can get steaks, hamburgers, etc. anywhere, but in Eastern Ontario the lowly perch has been raised to new gastronomic heights. I must admit it, that when I first heard about perch rolls I guffawed. Why would anyone bother even keeping perch I thought. And when I saw them served up in hot dog buns covered with white sauce I was convinced it was a joke, and then I tried one - that was 14 years ago, and now when anyone comes to town I make sure they don't leave without sampling our local delicacy. Along with the rolls and perch plates, there is a daily homemade soup, salads, shrimps, salmon, halibut, trout, sole, frogs legs, pickerel, lobster, and if you must steak, chops, hamburgers and daily specials. For the adventurous side orders include mushy peas and poutine.

Lunch for two with beer around $20.

Dinner for two with beer under $35.

Credit cards accepted.

Atmosphere: A beer and fish house. Weekend traditional entertainment.

Parking: Ample on the street, and off street parking lots. A quarter still buys an hour in Cornwall.

Open seven days a week.

Creemore, Ontario,
CREEMORE SPRINGS BREWERY LIMITED

139 Mill Street, (P.O. Box 369)

Creemore, Ontario, L0M 1G0

705-466-2531 FAX: 705-466-3306

(from Toronto an hour-and-a-half drive north along Airport Road, or north on Hwy. 400 to Barrie exit Hwy 90 west to County Road 10 north, and then west to County Road 9, 48 kms from Hwy 400.)

President: John Wiggins

Brewmaster: Kurtis Zeng, (trained in microbiology at the University of Guelph, apprenticed at Wellington County Brewery. Diploma in brewing technology, Wisconsin, sponsored by Master Brewer's Assoc. of America.)

Founded: 1987

Production Capacity: 1987 - 2,000 gallons per week growing to 7,000 hectolitres per annum in 1989. The final expansion to take place in 1993 will bring the brewery's capacity to 18,000 hectolitres a year.

Showing a profit in the first year of operation, Creemore is the exception to the rule in the Ontario micro brewing industry. Located away from the Toronto market, and producing only one brand, their secret is an all natural, traditionally brewed quality lager.

Nestled amongst Central Ontario's rolling hills, Creemore Springs beer is produced according to John Wiggins "...with all the good stuff," pure spring water, Canadian two row and six row barley, imported malts, European hops, select yeast "and lots of tender loving care."

Leaving the self-importance and bustle of Toronto and southwestern Ontario to others, the men behind Creemore Springs selected the village of Creemore, with a population of 1,200, its residual late Victorian charm, and unassuming nature, for its direct link to the past and tradition of hand craftsmanship. They are proud of the fact that they are 100 years behind the times.

Acquiring the May Hardware Store for the brewery and retail outlet, the new proprietors were determined to return the building to the Victorian elegance of the 1890s, while installing the finest brewing equipment available. They succeeded in their dual goals; the cash register is the same one used by William A. May in 1902, while the lights above the sales counter, and in the upstairs office are the ones used until the store was modernized after World War II. To turn the structure into a brewery, the interior had to be gutted and ten 1,200 gallon fermenting tanks and a 20 barrel (240 gallon) copper brew kettle squeezed through the front window. In the process, manager and retired hydraulic equipment designer Russ Thornton, who came to the area to ski, exclaimed, "You know, I think the brewery is going to happen." And several months later, before a thirsty crowd of 2,500, the brewery opened, selling its entire stock of bottles in less than 30 minutes.

Initially promoting the local aspect of their premium lager, and their traditional brewing techniques, along with the product's profitability and quality to licencees, Creemore is now available in more than 140 Beer Stores, and the initial ten bars have grown to over 225.

To attract so many taverns and restaurants, Creemore embarked upon a direct sales campaign that emphasized their local premium beer could be a house specialty, rather like some wines. To encourage patronage, they offer hints on ways to improve service, and profitability through the use of the now standard Sankey 30 and 50 litre draft kegs. They also offer their clients product knowledge seminars.

These efforts, coupled with what many people believe to be Ontario's best lager, have enabled the brewery to make plans for its final expansion. Even though they have a waiting list for clients, they do not plan to go beyond the confines of the old hardware store by spoiling a good thing and getting too big. With gross sales of $2 million in 1991, and 14 full time and six part time people, the brewery is well on its way to being the village's largest employer.

Vital Statistics - The Brew

Made according to the dictates of the Reinheitsgebot under an open fire copper kettle. Available in bottle and draft.

A beer both the critics and general public alike enjoy, amazing.

Creemore Springs Premium Lager, started at 4.9%, now 5%.

In designing this beer, the brewmaster met Catharine Parr Traill's requirements for the perfect Canadian elixir. She might have penned "there is simply no other refreshment as Creemore lager to provide...some cooling and strengthening beverage...much required by (Canadians) who have to work out in the heat of the sun". This carefully hopped, dark orange lager, with a dry, light, slightly bitter palate, is the perfect antidote to the summer heat. To suit my tastes, it only requires a pinch more malt to be perfect. Made with Canadian two and six row barley malt, two imported malts and Czechoslovakian Pilsener (Saaz) hops.

Aged three weeks.

Publications: "Froth Talk - Brews News and Views" for the Loyal Order of Frothquaffers. The Loyal Order is Creemore Springs official fan club. Membership in $13. by writing to the brewery (you receive a T-shirt), and the following attestation to your sobriety before leaving a bar, for home, by quickly repeating "Frothquaffer" three time without becoming tongue twisted.

Retail outlet with souvenirs, no hospitality lounge. Closed Sunday.

"The brewery offers everybody a tour by just stepping in the front door. Customers can stand at a railing and look down on the brew house in operation; or look through a large window into the refrigerated fermenting room."

Elora, Ontario,
THE ELORA MILL COUNTRY INN & RESTAURANT

77 Mill Street West,

Elora, Ontario, N0B 1S0

519-846-5356; FAX: 519-846-9180

Innkeeper: Tim Taylor

Rating: While it would be impossible not to give the Inn a high rating, I will wait until the products of the neighbouring brewery are on tap.

Having dragged your family this far from home, you have been saved by the presence of The Elora Mill. Sure to please any mother-in-law, the view from the five storey 30 metre high stone mill overlooking the "Tooth of time", an outcrop of rock and trees, dividing the Grand River as it plunges into the Elora Gorge, should be enough to keep any conversation going.

Providing Sunday Brunch and an international and traditional menu, micros on tap include Creemore, Sleeman, Brick and Upper Canada. And if you find you are enjoying yourself too much, you can stay overnight, if there is space, as reservations are recommended.

I should warn you though, this establishment is on the higher end of the scale.

Elora, Ontario,
TAYLOR AND BATE BREWING CO. LTD.

Mill St.

Elora, Ontario, N0B 1S0

Not open at time of printing, call before you go.

President: Crozier Taylor

Brewmaster: Doug Warren

Founded: September 4,1993.

Production Capacity: 9,000 Imperial Gallon (697) keg Cask Brewing and Malt Extract System, converted to full grain, from the former Taylor and Bate Brewpub in Stratford. When it opens it will probably be the smallest brewery in Canada.

(Winter, 1993)

Bringing the family back to brewing in 1988 when he opened a brewpub in Stratford, Crozier Taylor is a direct descendent of the Taylor and Bate Brewing Company operating in St. Catharines from 1834 until 1935, when its operations were moved to Hamilton by Canadian Breweries.

Ever mindful of tradition Taylor will be teaming up with brewer Doug Warren to revive another brewing legacy lost just this spring- and will reintroduce India Pale Ale.

This high gravity, well hopped ale was originally brewed for the British garrison in India. clean, light and bitter - with lots of hops acting as a natural preservative and providing bushels of aftertaste, the style's crystal clear complexion, coupled with its lighter taste, gained instant popularity throughout the 1830s, over the dark porters and stouts, now glass was replacing stone and pewter mugs.

Once made by nearly every major brewery in Canada, Labatt's was the last Canadian brewer to produce it commercially.

A traditional IPA is a sparkling clear, premium ale 5 to 5.5% in alcoholic content, fruity and well hopped, with as many as 40 bittering units.

Planning to follow John Labatt's pronouncement made in 1901, Doug's "Ale will not be artificially charged with gas (carbonated) as are some ales, but will be allowed to mature in the natural way. Not pasteurized, it will retain the delicate flavour and aroma of the hops and malt. Taken before meals, (I trust) it will stimulate the appetite and prevent constipation. Pure wholesome, palatable beverage."

(adapted by the author from a 1901 Labatt's ad for their ale)

In other words, after consulting with a number of beer enthusiasts, Doug is brewing a real IPA using Goldings' hops with 35 to 40 bittering units.

For special events and festivals he also hopes to brew bottled conditioned limited editions, turning the old stone warehouse brewery into a sure destination for beer lovers.

Vital Statistics - The Brew
Elora Pale Ale
Golding's Hops, 5.5% made with pale malt and 10% caramel malt.

For British comparison try Double Diamond and Bass.

Etobicoke, Ontario,

GREAT LAKES BREWING CO. INC.

30 Queen Elizabeth Blvd.,
(on the north side of the Queen Elizabeth on you way into Toronto.)
M8Z 1L8
416-255-4510

President: Peter Bulut

V.P.: Peter Bulut Jr.

General Manager: Anetta Bulut

Reception: Dagmar Bulut

Brewer-Operations Manager: Bruce Cornish. Trained under Viv Jones of Upper Canada fame before being inducted into the "Art and Mystery" of brewing Bruce was an auto mechanic. He has been brewing professionally since 1988.

Quality Control: Former 30 year Tennents and Molson veteran John Kerr

Founded: Reopened February 1992.

First opened in Brampton in 1988 as a malt extract plant, the business voluntarily closed in November 1990. Reopening again over the summer of 1991, it was mothballed again to seek refinancing. With new owners the brewery moved to its present larger location, and reopened as a full grain draft brewery.

Production Capacity: 1992 - 10,000 hectolitres with plans to reach 50,000 hectolitres with a year. While sales generally are down throughout the industry, Great Lakes' are still strong. Plans for bottling in 1993.

(Logo courtesy, Great Lakes Brewing Co. Inc.)

Producing a quality lager, that often rivalled Creemore in tastings, microbrewery fans will once again be able to have the pleasure of becoming reacquainted with Bruce Cornish's full bodied European style lager.

Previously always strapped for cash, Bruce approached construction contractor Peter Bulut to takeover the brewery. Not even a homebrewer but rather an entrepreneur who had defected from Yugoslavia in the 1950s, meeting his wife Dagmar in East Germany, the couple fled from the Iron Curtain together. At first Peter was skeptical about the brewery. Bruce persisted, and finally his enthusiasm convinced the Buluts to take the project on as a family business. Setting up in the Remington Fire Arms Company's machine shop and firing range, built in 1954, the brewery is ideally situated just north of the Queen Elizabeth, providing free advertising. Moving into the facility in January 1992, the Buluts have put some $2 million of their own money into converting this 35,000 square foot firing range into a brewery. It is outfitted with the brewhouse from Brampton's defunct York Brewing Co., equipment from Conner's Don Valley plant, and storage tanks from Molson's old Fleet Street location.

With 20 employees and still only brewing draft, Anetta Bulut relates that they are continuing to conduct market research before developing an image. Anetta continued that the family views the brewery as an "exciting, interesting, opportunity" and plans to produce quality beers that will compete head to head with the beers made by the large brewers, leaving 'niche' and specialty brews to others.

Hoping to eventually develop their own North American style ale, lite, and European lager, in draft and bottle, Anetta summed up her family's ambitions when she said they were "Looking forward to being part of the Ontario brewing industry, and if the time comes, part of the industry Canada wide".

Vital Statistics - The Brew

When asked about his beer, brewmaster Bruce Cornish said that he was "...striving for a quality North American style lager, that would appeal to a majority of the consumers". To this end he wants to brew a "...softer lager, not as bitter or as heavy as European lagers".

Great Lakes Lager is full grain, all malt, unpasteurized beer with Northern and Hallertau hops. Bruce uses Swiss Hürlimann yeast.

Great Lakes Lager, 5%
Draft only, to go to bottles
Bruce may have done it again, and may be far too modest to own up to it. Admittedly I tasted the beer at the brewery, but in my opinion the full balanced flowery and malt nose, soft body, and crisp finish remind me of draft Pilsner Urquell.

In order not to be to enthusiastic about the beer I tried a container of it six weeks later, and was surprised and pleased to find that it still retained its wonderful aroma, and tasted as good as any of the best lagers.

Beer available on tap throughout Metro Toronto, Hamilton and Niagara. They do not retail it at the time of writing in bottles, but they are planning to.

Tours and a souvenir stand are also in the works.

Etobicoke, Ontario,
MARCONI'S RESTAURANT AND BREWERY

262 Carlingview Drive/Dixon Road,
(in the Journey's End near the Toronto International Airport.)
Etobicoke, Ontario M9W 5G1
416-675-6854

Rating: 🍺🍺
Proprietors: Larry and Lisa Marconi
Brewmasters: Alda and Gord Slater
Founded: December 1, 1989.
Production Capacity: Cask seven vessel malt extract system.

If trendy motif, mainstream beer and Italian food appeal to you, it may be worthwhile visiting Marconi's. Unfortunately, I would not visit for the beer alone.

VITAL STATISTICS - THE BREW
A sampler table is located in the front hallway. I didn't go any further.

Dry Lite
A typical wet lite.

European Lager
A pleasant well balanced example of a Euro lager; golden amber in colour, and faintly hopped. The most flavourful of the house brews.

Superiore Lager
Light in colour, with some hops in the nose and a hint of malt. Smooth mouthtaste, syrupy aftertaste.

La Birra Superiore, European Lager 5%
Bottled under licence by Algonquin Brewing. From a family recipe, a Euro lager. I did not sample.

Menu - beer: Small selection of popular imports.

Menu - food: Antipasto salad bar, Italian Sausages, Grilled Halibut Italiano, Veal Marconi Scallopine, Linguine and Clams, Fried Calamari, Peel & Eat Shrimp, Mexican, sandwiches, Banana Fudge Delight, Raspberry Swirl - you get the idea.

Lunch for two including beer around $25.

Dinner for two including beer around $45.

Credit cards accepted.

Atmosphere: Slick. The bar area has been turned into a "Mexican" something or other, with hanging Mexican souvenirs replacing ferns. Loud, large screen for sports.

Tours and collectibles available.

Parking: adjacent to the Hotel, free.

Open daily.

Formosa, Ontario,
ALGONQUIN BREWING COMPANY LIMITED

(formerly) The Northern Algonquin
  Brewing Co. Ltd.)

1 Old Brewery Lane,

Formosa, Ontario, N0G 1W0

519-367-2995

FAX: 519-367-5414

(Head Office,
1270 Central Parkway
West, ste. 301,
Mississauga, Ontario,
L5C 4P4.)
416-949-0790;
FAX: 416-949-1076.

President: Evan Hayter II, partnership with Ignat Kaneff Properties Ltd., and Eric McKnight.

Master Brewer: Jack Massey. After receiving a Bachelor of Science in Microbiology from the University of Guelph, Jack joined Canadian Breweries six year long apprenticeship programme, receiving a Diploma from the British Institute of Brewing. Remaining with Canadian Breweries (Carling-O'Keefe), he rose to become the Director of Brewing until he retired after the amalgamation with Molsons to join Algonquin as head of brewing operations. Throughout his career he has won The Brewer's Guardian Challenge Cup, a Silver Medal in the British Commonwealth Bottled Beer Competition, and Gold and Bronze Medals at the Olympiades de la Biere, Cologne, Germany.

Marketing and Sales V.P.: Drew Knox.

Founded: 1988 (started brewing for the U.S. market in October 1987 under contract with Carling-O'Keefe).

Production Capacity: 70,000 hectolitres. According to figures released for 1991, Algonquin held first place in the micro market with 16.9% of the sales.

(Logo courtesy, Algonquin Brewing Company Limited.)

In 19th century Ontario, A German community without a brewery was incomplete.

Before the enthusiastic population of the Village of Formosa (Northern) Algonquin's President Evan Hayter proclaimed that his brewery was the reincarnation of that brewery that should have never closed down.

Drawing fame because it was the only brewery not turned off by the 1969 Ontario beer strike, the venerable old Formosa Spring Brewery, first opened in 1870, and was not acquired by Benson and Hedges until 1970. In the '70's the trend was towards growth, and as the brewery could not expand it was closed within a year, and the name moved to a new plant in Barrie. Three years later the Barrie facility was purchased by Molson's and the Formosa name apparently disappeared.

The new wave of microbreweries, however, has given this old brewery a new lease on life. Taking aim at the specialty beer market, the new proprietors planned to become the largest micro in Canada, a position they attained in 1991, but have to keep working hard to maintain.

Housed in the old brewery that was made famous because of its natural pure spring water supply fed by an aquifer, the new facility incorporates the traditional with the modern to make a "state of the art cottage brewery". As the only micro housed in a historic brewery, Algonquin is unique.

At Algonquin marketing is also a specialty, and if you think that you have seen the birchbark canoe on the label before, you have. It is a replica of the canoe on the old Canadian silver dollar. Aimed partially at the American market, the promotion of good Canadian beer worked and it is now available in more than ten States with sales increasing monthly.

Initially brewing the beer under contract with Carling-O'Keefe, Algonquin went looking for a plant once they had a market.

Marketing, familiarity with the beer industry, sound financial backing - along with their beer, are the four elements that make up Algonquin. Founded by former Carling-O'Keefe marketing men Evan Hayter and Drew Knox and independent Allen Sneath, the firm received financial assistance from entrepreneur Eric McKnight, and Peel Region's property management giant and multi-millionaire, Iggy Kaneff. Famous for his business sense, Kaneff backed Algonquin because he believed that they were simply going to be the industry leaders.

Eventually hoping to reintroduce the old Formosa names, once an agreement is reached with Molson's, and offering plant tours that will turn this historic factory into a tourist site, it is good to see that this old German community will once again be "complete".

VITAL STATISTICS - THE BREW

Their goal is to brew the same style of beer that originally made the brewery famous. The most "mainstream" of the small brewers, Algonquin still produces some interesting products, that attract those looking for something different, but not too challenging. Their first place position (1991) in the microbrewery market confirms the soundness of their direction. A good introduction to beers with taste.

Like all of the other microbrewers, Algonquin does not do any high gravity brewing, and provides unpasteurized cold-filtered products.

Algonquin Ale, 5% (Special Reserve)

A very pleasant, orange, well laced, interesting English style brown ale with hints of chocolate and fruit. Nicely balanced, a fine introduction to microbrewery product. Grande Gold Medal at the Brussels, Monde Selection.

Algonquin Light, 4%

A light pine beer with a short foam, sweet nose and balanced mouth.

Banks Beer, 5%

Once made by Upper Canada, I did not try this Caribbean lager.

Bavarian Style Bock, 6%

Returning to a style of beer that made the original Formosa famous, this brew is a fine understated introduction to the style. This brilliant amber orange beer with a smoky, nutty-sherry-like aroma, is well balanced with a nod again to sherry-like qualities in the taste. Leaving a pleasantly bitter, gently lingering aftertaste, this is a delicate beer, that only misses a longstanding head, to be a great beer.

Bruce County Lager, 5%

Ostensibly only available in the Bruce County, the brewery's home turf, it is a lightly hopped, balanced, fruity lager.

Country Lager, 5%

A clear golden lager, with a short aerated foam, light, subtle nose, and sweetish mouth finished with a super puckering, sweet aftertaste.

Formosa Lager, 5%

On tap only this is a traditional lager.

Formosa Springs Draft, 5%

According to the brewery this is a "Traditional draft lager, golden colour, original recipe, 100% Canadian barley malt, cold filtered, no additives or preservatives, natural carbonation". But apparently not a lot of taste. Gold Medal at the Brussels Monde Selection.

Formosa Springs Light, 4%

Almost oak in colour, this may be the lightest of the lights in colour. A short foamy head, sweet nose, followed by a tingly sweet mouth and aftertaste.

Marconi Beer, 5%

Brewed and bottled and sold through the Brewer's Retail for the brewpub of the same name, it is made according to a family recipe, and is a good example of a techno-Euro lager.

Royal Amber Lager, 5%

Billed as an "old-fashioned glass of beer", I agree with the p.r. department about this all malt pleasantly hopped beer. When a glass of this brew was handed to me, I was completely baffled. At first I thought it was an ale. I certainly couldn't place it, to the joy of the laughing publican. A lager full of character, I happily joined in the joke and had another, and yes then another until they finally told me who my new friend was. I wasn't able to compare it with some of Ontario's other leading lagers, but can easily recommend that you give it a try.

P.S. It was the carastan malt that initially threw me off the scent.

Also various contract housebrews for the "Owl's Roost", the "Golden Valley Inn", and "The Feathers".

Available throughout most of Southern Ontario, the brewery has a hospitality room, and offers tours by appointment, and of course retails beer.

Guelph, Ontario,
SLEEMAN BREWING AND MALTING CO. LTD.

Silver Creek Brewery,

551 Clair Road West,

Guelph, Ontario N1H 6H9

519-822-1834

(exit Highway 401, 295 - Highway 6 to Hanlon Parkway, and Guelph, on the east side).

President: John W. Sleeman.

V.P. Marketing and Sales: J. Kevin Meens.

Brewmaster (V.P. Operations): Al Brash, formerly of Labatts and Conners. The man who developed "Blue".

V.P. Finance and Administration: Doug Berchtold.

Founded: 1988.

Production: 1989 100,000 hectolitres; 1994 capacity 250,000 hectolitres.

(Logo courtesy, Sleeman Brewing & Malting Co. Ltd.)

Following the credo laid down by George Sleeman in 1911 that "We cannot wait for good things to come to us; we must go after them", Sleeman's quickly broke the microbrewery barrier to become Ontario's major regional brewery. On Friday, October 14th, 1988 the first bottle of Sleeman beer to be filled since 1933 came off the assembly line. Using a closely guarded, slightly modified recipe first formulated by George Sleeman on January 5, 1885; Sleeman's Cream Ale is nothing short of a reincarnation of an exceptional traditional pale. The English brewer's answer to the lager tide engulfing North American beer market during the last years of the 19th century.

The Sleeman's originally started brewing in 1834, two years later Cornishman John Sleeman opened a brewery in St. David's near St. Catharines. From here he ended up in Guelph where he worked at the Silver Creek Brewery, finally gaining control in 1859. In 1867, John's son George took over the family concern. George wrote that his beer was "Endorsed by millions of sensible, thinking men as the most palatable and healthsome of beverages when judiciously used."

Marketing their products across Ontario, the Sleeman's owned the Silver Creek, and Spring Bank Breweries. Prohibition forced the family, however, to cease brewing. With the end of temperance, Henry O. Sleeman incorporated the Spring Bank Brewery in 1927, but the time was not right, and the business was sold to Jockey Club Brewery Ltd. in 1933, marking the end of Sleeman's beer, until 1985 when Sleeman Brewing and Malting was once again incorporated by John Sleeman's great, great grandson John W. Sleeman.

John W. Sleeman combined with Stroh's Brewery, America's third largest, to reopen Sleeman's doors. Aiming at capturing 2% of Ontario's beer market, with the backing of Stroh's who hold 19% ownership in the concern, this modern 30,000 square foot brewery on a 3.2 acre site cost approximately $7,000,000.

Pleased with the firm's growth that witnessed sales increasing by about 25%, when the industry was down approximately 10%, John Sleeman said the success is due to "the product, the packaging and the fact the business is essentially family owned". Al Brash said that the brewery is expanding to be prepared to enter Quebec, British Columbia, Michigan and the American West Coast with their Cream Ale, once the interprovincial trade barriers go down. This growth is underwritten by the fact that the brewery now employs 100 people, up from the 30 it started with.

Backed by Manulife Financial of Toronto, who own 10% of the brewery and Stroh's, the alliance with the Americans is not strictly financial, as the firm not only uses original recipes and copper kettles, but fire brews the same way their partners do. According to world beer authority Michael Jackson in his "Pocket Guide to Beer", the flames create hot spots in the kettle offering the brew "the briefest flirtations with carmelization."

Whether it is the fire brewing instead of the more common steam heating, or the recipes, Sleeman's are not just other beers. To my mind, one leg in the quest for the perfect beer ends here!

VITAL STATISTICS - THE BREW

Following the original century old family recipe, Sleeman's uses corn grits and pasteurizes some of their products. They only use adjuncts for Stroh's products to meet their specifications.

Sleeman Cream Ale, 5%
Still the number one seller, this beer was first created in 1885 to appeal to the lager drinker and possibly women, making it one of the first target market beers in Canada.

(Photo courtesy, Sleeman Brewing & Malting Co. Ltd.)

A crisp golden ale, with a well hopped nose offering a hint of malt. The warm body is tinged with bitterness trapping you into a second sip.

Brewed with an ale yeast, the addition of carastan malts, gives it a slightly caramelized flavour. The English Fuggles and Goldings hops account for the British orientation of the aroma. The beer also has Cascade and Chinook hops.

When originally developed by George Sleeman, he added corn flakes (grits) to make it a milder, more "lively" product over English bitter. In other words the grits were added to make a creamy head and lighten the complexion.

When I asked Al Brash what the major differences were between this ale and the 1885 version he said the development of "20th century varieties of malt and hops".

If you wonder what the "64" means under the cap, it refers to the page the recipe is found in Sleeman's diary.

Gold medal Brussels, 1992.

Sleeman Cream Draught Ale.

Sleeman Silver Creek Lager, 5%
A golden pine, well hopped, flowery, well balanced European style lager protected by a creamy foam.

With Hallertau and Saaz hops how could this be anything but a European lager? A warm smooth mouth, and an enticing aftertaste. Again the corn aids the creamy head.

Sleeman Silver Creek Lager Draught-Gold medal winner at the 1992 Toronto International Food, Wine and Beer Show. Grand Gold Brussels, 1992.

Sleeman Premium Light, 4%
An original brew not a cutdown version like many "lights".

It has a pleasant nose created by the Styrian and Goldings hops. The Yugoslavian and Canadian two row barley malt provides a light taste. Possessing only 96 calories, there is a mild aftertaste.

Sleeman's licenced brews.
While Sleeman's products are not "high gravity" brewed, the American brews are made following American specifications.

Schlitz, 5%
Brewed about 1/2% higher in alcohol for Canadian tastes with Galena and Cascade hops, what can I say except it is sweet.

Stroh's, 4.4%
Styled a "Bohemian" Lager, and made according to the "exact same recipe as the one used by the Stroh Brewery Company of Detroit" the authentic Bohemian (think Pilsener Urquell) recipe appears to have been waylaid between Europe and Detroit. A very light nose created by Cascade hops, the sweetness from the corn syrup pervades the aroma and takes over the taste.

Stroh's Light, 4%

I plead guilty. I did not try it!

Cascade hops, corn syrup added, and high gravity brewed, it would be a pretty fair guess to say that this is a watery product.

Beer sold at the brewery with collectibles. Open seven days a week. Also sold throughout Ontario. Plans to ship to Michigan, and Quebec?

An interview with Masterbrewer, Al Brash.

One constantly enjoyable aspect of putting together this book was the opportunity to speak to people as knowledgeable and enthusiastic as Sleeman's Al Brash.

After the repeal of temperance quality control over the brewing process came to the fore as a problem. E.P. Taylor of the newly formed Canadian Breweries saw it as a challenge, that if overcome would put his products ahead of the others. In order to address this issue he established a brewing school-apprenticeship programme in conjunction with the British Institute of Brewing. To fill this training course Canadian Breweries' production chief Major F.N. Ward

"...was looking for good scholastic standing, and much more; he wanted men of good character who could learn to get along with the workmen in the plants, were physically fit and had the necessary imagination to appreciate and cope with the many complex processes and problems involved in the large-scale production of beer."

(A.A. Shea, "Vision in Action," pg. 94)

Al Brash was one of these young apprentices.

Starting at Canadian Breweries' O'Keefe Simcoe Street plant, Al worked at the firm's various Toronto locations. He related it was a "...five year programme, every nine months, the various trainees came together to discuss technical papers concerning various problems the brewery faced, and were then assigned to their next brewery."

Training "British Brewers", Ward only hired college graduates, while E.P. Taylor saw to it that "everything was first class...nothing shoddy."

After completion of the course, Al left Canadian Breweries, joining Calgary Brewing and Malting. Soon acquired by Canadiana Breweries, Al now entered the MBA programme at the University of Western Ontario.

After this he joined Labatt's Ontario Region. Dominated by recently cancelled IPA, and still popular "50", Al in his early 30s was soon promoted over the older, conservative ale producing British brewers. With only 14% of the market at that time, management believed that they had nothing to lose by innovation, accordingly Al was put in charge of improving the Pilsener Lager first introduced in 1951. With too much diacetyl (caramel buttery) character, he changed the yeast and hops using Old Vienna as his reference point. In 1958 Pilsener won the "Prix d'Excellence" at the World Beer Competition in Brussels.

Soon to become known as "Blue" in deference to Manitoba drinkers who called for it by the colour of its label, Labatt's Pilsener became the first Canadian beer to receive national advertising attention. (Who said ad men don't listen to the public?) Catching the lager wave embracing Canada, Blue became the country's best selling beer.

Leaving Labatt's, Al abandoned brewing altogether until the opportunity to help develop Sleeman's came along.

When I asked him about the bugaboo of pasteurization, Al harked back to his early training "...originally beer was not clean, there was a lot of air in it leading to oxidization and staleness. Pasteurizaton remedied this...Brewing procedures have improved now, and only light pasteurization is needed."

Commenting on lite beers Al said "...lite beer was aimed at the female market. Everything about it was lighter - colour, taste and aroma. Originally it was a watery product because of high gravity brewing. It was simply cut across the board with water. If brewed properly though (not high gravity), lite can have flavour".

On Dry, Al was less generous. "Dry is not a brewer's beer, it was made for marketing men, it is not balanced. When you think of dry remember it was developed in Japan, and then think of sake, the Japanese palate does not like sweetness, and Dry was developed to remove the sweetness. It is made by brewing out the residual sugars, that is fermenting out all of the sugars, this creates the dryness".

At this point we both reached for a glass of Cream Ale, put away the note pad, and savoured the aftertaste.

Guelph, Ontario,
WELLINGTON COUNTY BREWERY LIMITED

950 Woodlawn Road,
Guelph, Ontario, N1K 1B8
519-837-2337

President: Philip Gosling
Head Brewer: Michael Stirrup.
Founded: October, 1985.
Production Capacity: 8,000 hl, 5,200 square foot brewery.
Equipment purchased from Hickey and Co. of London England for $750,000. Gas fired, stainless steel brewkettle with a heat recovery system.

(Logo courtesy, Wellington County Brewery Ltd.)

A traditional English style brewery producing cask conditioned real ales, in the time honoured, unpretentious British manner - Wellington County has lived up to the predictions of its first brewer Charles MacLean, and has almost become too successful.

Loyal supporters of these beers keep the brewery producing to capacity by simply drinking it all, an activity that sometimes causes shortages. And no wonder, when I first hoisted a sleeve of draft County Ale, in the heart of Toronto's fizzy quaffing Yonge Street strip, I was immediately transported to another realm.

Continuing to brew "real ale", which is smoother and fuller due to the fact that it is not filtered, and cask conditioned, these beers are only made from the pure water provided locally by Arkell Springs, malt, hops and British yeast.

Neither carbonated, nor pasteurized, the beer is placed in casks after primary fermentation where it undergoes a second fermentation. Developing a natural carbonation, it matures at its own pace. Still "live" and "working" when it reaches the pub, the cask is placed on a stillage in a cool room, and is vented to permit the escape of carbon dioxide. Within 48 hours the yeast has settled and the keg may be tapped, and hooked to a hand pump engine to yield a pint of real ale. Believing that the public should be able to enjoy this treat at home, President Philip Gosling related in the July/August 1992 issue of "Kegs and Cases."

"...when we first entered the Brewers Retail system with a one-gallon box of Real Ale. What a time we had! One-gallon plastic bags were painstakingly filled by hand, placed in a specially-made box and then delivered to the store where they were stacked wherever space was available. This may sound simple enough, but on a warm day after a long, bumpy ride, the Real Ale - which contains live yeast - would start fermenting and internal pressure turned the square boxes into the shape of a football. Believe it or not, the driver had to "burp" each box before they could be stacked one above the other!"

These days are gone, but the beers live on "...to rival Britain's Best." Head Brewer Michael Stirrup shares Phil's desire to win an award of excellence in the United Kingdom.

Striving to brew the best English style beers in North America, Mike claims that the authentic flavours are enhanced by the use of crystal malts. He goes on, "Real ale is the brewery's real strength."

A "typical" new brewer because of his eclectic background, Mike was on the Canadian National Junior Champion Swimming Team in 1982.

From a family of English publicans, Mike's interest in winemaking and brewing came from his dad. This interest in the noble hop resulted in Mike securing a training position at England's famed Ringwood Brewery. Before he entered this programme, however, an apprenticeship position at Wellington Count opened up. Taking 5-1\2 years, he started as second assistant, and worked his way through Quality Control and the lab., and everything else, until he became Head Brewer early in 1993. On his way up he became a Member of the Institute of Brewing and of the Brewer's Guild in the U.K.

As a brewer, Mike is attracted to the "craft". He said "Quality before quantity is the goal."

As the Head Brewer in the only craft brewery still producing the only commercial Real Ale in North America, he would like to expand the market and appreciation for this product, and looks forward, like everyone else in the brewing industry, to seeing the removal of interprovincial barriers on trade. He also hopes to see the Beer Store open a Microbrewery only outlet for all North American craft brews. As a brewer he underlines how necessary it is to "maintain the quality of the product and hygiene." While holding onto these basic principles, he said that the brewery is gearing up to increase production for expansion, by making a concentrated effort to bring Real Ale to pubs.

And when all the efforts of a typical 12 hour brewing day are done, I asked Michael where he derives his job satisfaction.

He replied:

"...the biggest high anyone can get in microbrewing, is finding a beer they made at 6 a.m. in the morning, and then seeing 100 people enjoying it a week later at the Woolwich Arms."

Vital Statistics - The Brew

Wondering just how authentic Wellington County's brews were, I applied them to an acid test, a Cockney with an Oxion accent - my dad. Having given up beer for a quarter of a century because he couldn't find a Canadian beer he liked, after introducing him to Wellington, he is once again in the habit of taking a pint at noon hour for his "digestion". Having reacquainted him with the "medicinal" and soothing qualities of fine ales, when I visit I better not leave without depositing a few thank you litres in the refrigerator.

Most products are available on tap if you are lucky enough to find them.

Arkell Best Bitter, 4%

This beer puts a lie to idea that lower alcohol doesn't possess any taste. Brewed with Fuggles and various Goldings hops, this brew has a well balanced nose underlined by a warm body. While the mouth has a full, smooth, nutty, malty taste, it ends with a fine, dry, puckering flourish.

County Ale, 5%

In draft form an unfiltered real ale, that makes it totally unnecessary to visit the U.K. unless you are visiting relatives. (Yes, I have to admit I am one of those who only travelled overseas to drink beer.)

In bottle

The company's most popular brew, When I first sampled it, I thought I had been transported back to England.

A beer to talk about, it is reddish amber in colour, with a rich complex nutty, hoppy, fruity, burnt sugar bouquet reminiscent of autumn, and a rich full malt taste, followed by a puckering, malty sweet aftertaste, making a second sip inevitable.

Let this beer warm, and you will begin to experience everything it has to offer.

Imperial Stout, 5.5% to 8% seasonal

Again too low to be an "internationally" recognized Imperial stout, it has a fine silky mouth and tastes of roasted malt. Northern Brewer hops have replaced Progress to make the stout a little dryer.

Iron Duke, 6.5%

Perhaps the closest a Canadian brewery comes to producing a barley wine, or strong beer best associated with Thomas Hardy, this warm, deep, malty brew is my beer of choice to get through the cold, dark days of winter. A word of caution though, drink it slowly, a litre is more than enough for an evening's enjoyment.

And if you can do as Jamie MacKinnon suggests and compare it with Niagara Falls' Olde Jack Strong Ale, be sure to have the next day off!

Premium Lager, 4.5%

When an ale brewery tries its hand at a lager, you know you are going to encounter something interesting. The right colour, it is brewed with Fuggles, Tettnanger, Cascade and Saaz hops. A pleasant alternative to the others.

SPA - Special Pale Ale, 4.5%

A buckwheat cloak belongs to this brew with a warm, honey sweet, delightfully hopped aroma. Tasting like a "round vowel" the mouth is effervescent and reminiscent of honey graham crackers. While the aftertaste is short and light, it adds accent to this fine persuasive elixir.

Or if you would prefer:

A perfectly balanced, delightfully hopped, golden ash brew - a real treat.

Three types of Goldings hops - Whitbread, East Kent and Goldings.

Available throughout southern Ontario.

This brewery is only open on weekdays, tours by appointment only, limited souvenirs.

Guelph, Ontario,
The Woolwich Arms

176 Woolwich Street (Corner of Yarmouth and Woolwich),

Guelph, Ontario, N1H 3V5.

519-836-2875.

Rating: 🍺🍺🍺-🍺🍺🍺🍺(In a word, Genuine.)

President: Bob Desautels, part of the Neighborhood Pubs Group.

Managers: Don Stewart and Paul Jenkins.

Assistant Manager: Wes Harper

Founded: Bob Desautels opened a French restaurant in this location called "La Maison" in 1985, sold it in 1987 when it became a British style pub, and re-emerged as its owner again in 1990, operating it as a pub offering Ontario beers, wine and food, increasing sales from $385,000 to $800.000 in 1992.

*(Logo courtesy, Neighborhood Pubs
Group Inc. - The Woolwich Arms.)*

As the number one seller of cask-conditioned real ale in North America, a visit to the Woolwich Arms is a must.

Situated in Dr. Stewart's "Queen Anne" home built in 1895, the pub is divided into a bar and two living-dining rooms, that feel more like sitting at home than in a restaurant. With only 80 seats, The Woolwich Arms captures the slightly fuzzy ambience of a true British "local".

Comfortably ensconced in one of the dining-rooms talking with Bob and his wife Sue and daughter Emily, I enjoyed a hearty "Arms Classic" hamburger garnished with jalapenos and sweet Mango chutney, all washed down with carefully conditioned and well served County Ale.

Vital Statistics - The Brew

Menu - Beer: Wellington County cask conditioned real ale, we could stop here, plus nine other taps, one of which Bob "regretfully" admits is "Molsons". Imports. Single malt whiskies, featured Ontario wines.

Menu - Food: Varying from the other locations - burgers with either chicken or beef for adults and children are featured along with salsa pita pizzas and salad, tortière pie with pickled beets, sausage beans and chips. Tuesday curry night and desserts - pecan pie, New York Cheesecake, etc.

Lunch for two with beer under $25.

Dinner for two with beer under $40.

Credit cards: All major credit cards.

Atmosphere: Like sitting in your own living room except you don't have to pickup afterwards. As far away from a fern bar and the British look alike pubs as it is possible to be. In a word, Genuine.

Special Events: Occasional entertainment.

Parking: Ample off street.

Hours: Seven days a week.

Interview with Bob Desautels, founder Neighborhood Pubs Inc.

With three successful pubs in operation and plans for as many as ten across Ontario by 1995 - featuring Ontario micro beers and products for the "quality conscious consumer", Bob stands to become a real presence in the Ontario small beer market.

In search of the Canadian taste, and willing to travel Ontario's back concessions to find authentic local delicacies (I have bumped into him more than once in our joint quests) Bob may create a certain appreciation, while returning to our history by melding the best of our founding culture's beer, cheese and wine.

If I am beginning to sound like a copywriter for Neighborhood Pubs, all I can say in my defence is that I am not!

A former pro golfer Bob Desautels entered food administration, lecturing at the University of Guelph. Optimistically starting with a French restaurant, he quickly sold it in 1987. Turned into the Woolwich Arms, he took the operation back three years later. Doubling the draft taps to ten, and becoming one of the first in the region to carry Creemore lager, he attracted all segments of the University crowd, while breaking the slightly stuffy English mould that the pub had fallen into.

Searching like so many others for the "Canadian" pub, while maintaining the ambience of an English House, he introduced Canadian food, local entertainment, and most important of all, good Micro beer. He went towards the micros because "The small brewers are more interested in quality and taste, while the larger ones sell image."

Sales doubled and with half a million dollars of his own, $450,000 in Ontario venture capital, and three partners, Bob decided to market his formula - beer with aftertaste and "honest Canadian made food" through an association of "like minded pub owners" known as the Neighborhood Pubs Group. Stressing that this is not a franchise operation, each pub has a team of managers who when trained and experienced will have the opportunity to purchase the business.

Confident in his pubs, his staff, Ontario's beers and food, the "Group" deserves to succeed if it sticks to its motto of "serving up the best."

See Peterborough - The Peterborough Arms

Toronto - The Bow and Arrow

Plans to establish a pub in Kingston's 150 year old Bajus Brewery, and open a Mediterranean Café and Restaurant group.

Heidelberg, Ontario,
Olde Heidelberg Restaurant and Brew Pub

2 King Street,
Box 116, N0B 1Y0
519-699-4413

Rating: 🍺🍺 Go for the food. (The steady crowds and rave reviews of others, show just how subjective a reviewer's opinions can be!)

Owner: Bob Oberholtzer, Jr.
  Howie MacMillan

  Bob MacMillan
Founded: August 1986 (the hotel has been in operation since 1838).

Production Capacity: 10,400 gallons (approximately), Continental Malt Extract System.

Traditionally a German community was incomplete without its own brewery. Today, nestled amongst the rolling hills of southwestern Ontario, in the heart of old Order Amish and Mennonite Country, 12 kilometres northwest of Kitchener, visitors will have to share Regional Road 15 with horses and buggies to reach the Olde Heidelberg. Located in a stagecoach stop built in 1838, the brewpub offers a slice of living heritage. Owner Bob Oberholtzer took over the family business from his father in 1983, stating "...we are trying to earn a reputation for good food at reasonable prices." And they do.

Three years later Bob planned to upgrade this basic Ontario roadhouse tavern by installing $70,000 worth of copper plated brewkettles, and fermenters, in a glass enclosed $30,000 brewery.

Producing their own North American style beer, sold at prices less than the commercial brews, the Heidelberg features a Honky Tonk piano and sing along with Ozzie on Friday and Saturday.

Still maintaining its links with Ontario's dimmer tavern days, the pub also has a poolroom, shuffleboard and TV.

Ideally located for site seeing and visiting rural markets and antique fairs, travel editor David E. Scott of the "London Free Press" wrote that the Inn offered "...one of the best weekend package deals to come along in a long time." With a free standing 16 room motel and Fun Centre equipped with mini-golf, it is possible for two to eat, drink, sleep and site see for under $150 for the weekend. One warning, however, at these prices expect comfort, not luxury. And while I enjoyed the atmosphere of the tavern-brewpub, I would not take my mother-in-law here on her birthday.

Vital Statistics - The Brew

Heidelberg O-B Lager

Named O-B after the owner's nickname, the beer always seems slightly flat. With a mildly hopped, fruity nose, the body gives only the slightest hint of malt. There is, however, enough of a pleasant, lingering aftertaste to ask for another.

Menu - beer: A full range of beers from the Big Two, and the usual alcoholic beverages.

Menu - food: Traditional Germany daily specials with half portions for children. The menu features schnitzel, pigstails, sausages, pork hocks, sauerkraut and spare ribs, piled onto large platters at bargain prices along with sandwiches, and the ubiquitous onion rings, fries and hamburger. If you want something different for a snack - try a side order of Pigstails and bread for only $2.75, you will never be satisfied with a mere hotdog again!

Dinner for two including beer around $25.

Credit cards accepted.

Atmosphere: Basic 1960's Ontario's men's room with a difference, families flock here.

Souvenirs available.

Open seven days a week, but Sundays only from noon to 7:30 p.m.

Parking: Ample, free.

Kingston, Ontario

The Kingston Brewing Co. Ltd. (KBC)

---

34 Clarence St., K7L 1W9

613-542-4978

Rating: 🍺🍺🍺🍺 (Serving hand drawn cask-conditioned ale, save your fare to England and visit Kingston)

Proprietors: Richard Cilles, Paul Debenham, Van-Allen Turner.

Brewmaster: Rodger Eccleston

Founded: February 1986, first pint sold April 25, 1986. Ontario Brewpub licence no. 2, and with the demise of no. 1, Ontario's oldest brewpub. KBC also has Canada's first wine pub licence.

Production Capacity: 9,000 Imperial gallons per year (698 kegs), Cask Brewing and Malt

Extract System. Exploring full mash potential, but currently using imported malt extract, and hop leaves.

(Logo courtesy, The Kingston Brewing Co. Ltd.)

If ambience, real ale, comfortable food, and history make a great pub, then this is one of the best.

According to proprietor Richard Cilles "A growing demand for something other than light domestic lager inspired the owners of the (nearby) "Pilot House to a brewpub which would brew limited supplies of darker, more flavourful lagers and ales. The Pilot House, a popular fish and chip establishment, having served imported beers for many years, was in an ideal position to take the brewpub plunge when the regulations allowing brewed-on-premises beer appeared imminent."

The regulations changed in 1986, and starting with approximately $85,000 worth of equipment from Cask Brewing System, the brewpub opened to rave reviews. Making the beer originally from malt extract only, the KBC became the first brewpub in Ontario to have its recipe bottled under licence by a commercial brewer and sold at the Beer Store.

Now reporting 2/3s of its sales from its own products, and "In keeping with the owner's belief in total control over everything to its customers," in May 1992 the brewpub became the first winepub in Canada.

For most of us who make the trek between Montreal and Toronto, the KBC located near the harbour in downtown Kingston, takes the effort out of finding a place to stop for a break, and is an integral part of the trip. A definite must. And oh yes, if you find yourself enjoying your tipple too much, there are numerous reasonably priced hotels in the vicinity.

Vital Statistics - The Brew

Regal Lager, 5%

Produced with a blend of three hop varieties and imported yeast.

Dragon's Breath Real Ale, 6% draft.

In authentic British tradition the Dragon's Breath on tap differs from the bottled example. It has a smooth, creamy head, fine Belgium lacing, with a warm malty mouth balanced by some fine bittering. Simply refreshing. As it is cask-conditioned - served directly from the maturation vessel, in its glorious unfiltered, uncarbonated state by a traditional hand-drawn British beer engine - this is the one to go for. As brewer Roger Eccleston says the "only preservatives are hops!"

Dragon's Breath Pale Ale, 4.5% (brewed for KBC by Hart)
You know you have had enough of this brew, when the dragon on the label
    winks back!

It is fitting that Ontario's longest surviving brewpub should be the first one to
have its recipe bottled and sold at the Beer Store. The recipe profiled and
developed in Kingston delivers a "medium-bodied ale similar to an English
bitter with a nice fruity fresh aroma and crisp taste with a pleasant hop finish."
Slightly less pronounced than Hart Amber Ale, and the weighty St. Ambroise,
the beer's spring like fresh aroma and fruity apricot palate makes it a must try.

Rampant Rooster (cock ale, see glossary) a.k.a. Anniversary Aberration Ale

According to brewer Roger, this is a "clean-out" beer made from "...all
oddments of malt hops etc. collected from various sources, with a very heavy
original gravity!!!" To celebrate KBC's first anniversary they made a cock ale.
Roger continues, "We actually put four rock cornish hens (plucked, cleaned,
and partially cooked), in a muslin bag in the primary fermenter. The resulting
beer was terrific! Smooth, rich, strong and sold-out very quickly."

Other brews are produced whenever capacity permits, but Strong Autumn Ale
is an annual seasonal regular.

Other brews include Never Again Stout, Moby Pale Ale, Cobbler's Ale (the
original Dragon's Breath), Johanne Sebastian Bock etc. Look forward to Mead
in '93.

Menu - beer: On tap: Strongbow Cider, Guinness, Moosehead, Sleeman's Ale,
    Conners Special Draught. Rotated with the products from Ontario's
    microbreweries.

Bottled - St. Leonard, small selection of national brands, some Ontario
micros, Newcastle Brown Ale, Swan de-alcohol, etc.

And we can't forget the homemade wine.

Menu - food: Like all restaurants, the menu varies but the quality doesn't. Baked
    goods done on premises. Chicken and ribs smoked naturally with hickory
    and mesquite. Stressing that they don't offer alsoran "pub grub" they
    make their own desserts, "build and spice their own burgers and cut their
    own scalloped chips". With daily "theme" specials - example: Indian
    curries on Thursday, Mexican on Fridays. The portions are always more
    than generous. Also nachos, ploughperson's lunch, lamb burgers, Italian,
    vegetarian sandwich, salads and fish.

Lunch for two including beer around $20.

Dinner for two including beer around $40.

Credit Cards accepted.

Atmosphere: Located in a brick Victorian building amongst Kingston's
    limestones, this is probably as close to an English pub a you are going to
    find, with the added bonus of having its own brewery. Outdoor summer
    patio. Occasional special events and entertainment. Sunday brunch.

Tours of the brewery on request, collectibles available.

Parking: ample, metered street parking.

Open seven days a week.

Hamilton, Ontario,
Lakeport Brewing Corporation

201 Burlington St. E., L8L 4H2

416-523-4200;

FAX: 416-523-6564.

President: William R. Sharpe, President, Chief Executive Officer. Former President of Pacific Western Brewing.

Brewmaster: (Director of Brewing Services - Plant Manager) Adam Foye, PhD. in Biochemistry and Biological Sciences, Heriot-Watt University, Edinburgh. Member of The Master Brewers Assoc. of the Americas, Institute of Brewing and American Society of Brewing Chemists.

Learning his craft from "the floor up" at Wm. Younger's Ltd., and Wm. McEwan's Ltd., Adam Foye returned to University to obtain his PhD. In 1973 he came to Canada and started working at Henninger (in the brewery now occupied by Lakeport), and rose to become Head Brewer. Under Amstel's management of the brewery he remained in this position until he moved to Carling-O'Keefe where he introduced Foster's Lager to the Canadian market, and developed and designed Molson Special after the merger. At Carling-O'Keefe he became Manager of Brewing Projects, ending his tenure after the merger with Molson as Director of Brewing Services, involved in the rational downsizing of 16 plants to 10, "and the merging of three brewing philosophies."

V.P. Finance - Controller: Vince P. Lubertino

Founded: March 11, 1992. Located in the old Peller, Canadian Breweries, Henninger, Amstel plant, the brewery is 175,000 square feet, while the complex covers 7.5 acres along the Hamilton harbourfront.

Start-up June 4 with the "limited edition" 'Around Ontario', Canadian 125 lager sold only at the LCBO in former Amstel bottles.

Production Capacity: At the present time, the brewery could produce 330,000 hectolitres or 4.4 million cases of 24 a year. Objective for 1993, 3.2 million cases. When Amstel ran the brewery they employed 50 people, by the winter of 1993 there were 84 people working here with plans to go to 100.

Beer drinkers may not "hang out in Loblaws" (and apparently they don't eat), as Michael Palmer an analyst with Equity Research Associates quipped to

(Label courtesy, Lakeport Brewing Corporation.)

I wonder if the Big Two breweries are feeling the pressure, and have responded with their "friendly" priced beers, introduced for the 1993 summer beer drinking season? If so, they have changed their tune from the previous year, when Paul Smith a spokesman for Labatt told "Globe and Mail" reporter Scott Feschuk on December 7, 1992, that 'We're definitely not quaking in our boots. We've never shied away from competition in the past."

"Globe and Mail" reporter Scott Feschuk but they do seem to like the lower priced, premium quality mainstream beer Lakeport Brewing Corp. produces.

Defying conventional wisdom that states a new beer needs a massive advertising campaign to launch it, Lakeport's PC beer became a runaway success due to its identification with President's Choice, comparable quality and lower prices, without the ad men. In fact, Lakeport's only similarity with other small brewers is the fact it does not have an ad agency.

It does, however, have President Bill Sharpe.

Matching the Big Brewers' products head-on, Sharpe created Lakeport after 36 years in marketing, sales, distribution and management in the beverage trade. Starting out with Canada Dry, Bill entered the brewing industry in 1978 when he spearheaded a group of Edmonton businessmen to purchase the partially completed Uncle Ben breweries in B.C. The Richmond facility was sold in 1980. and Bill then became President of Old Fort Brewing Co. in Prince George, B.C. turning the brewery into a thriving regional operation with 7% of the market. Here he learned that success and reliance on a single brand would expose him to cut throat competition from the major brewers. True to tradition, one of the Big Brewers, Carling-O'Keefe met his opposition, by hiring Bill away as Executive to the President. From here he moved into the position of Vice President for Manitoba and Saskatchewan.

After the merger with Molsons, Bill found himself General Manager of Santa Fe Beverages Co. of Toronto, an arms length beer importer owned by Molsons. Here Bill visited the Amstel plant to negotiate a licence for Molson to brew Amstel in Canada once Heineken packed up and went back to Holland. Molsons who had direct control over Santa Fe, made the decision to downsize by closing Santa Fe, and transferring the import brands to Molsons. This left Sharpe with no immediate future with Molsons, so he took their "very generous" severance package.

Putting his "retirement" to good use, Bill now laid the groundwork for President's Choice Beer. Still out of work and without a brewery in December, he told "Globe and Mail" reporter Scott Feschuk, "I decided there was no point looking for work in the industry, so I decided to look seriously at the old Amstel facility, which after some 33 million dollars spent on improvements since 1981, was in good condition. His visit found him face to face with an auction firm preparing the brewery for sale, "Globe" reporter Feschuck wrote, "Realizing the urgency of the situation, (Sharpe) faxed Amsterdam at 9 o'clock that night, an offer to buy the plant."

"The next morning he woke to find a message on his fax machine."

"Offer accepted. Work it out with our lawyers."

Able to raise 30% of the purchase, within two weeks Bill teamed up with Cott Corp. for the balance. The producers of private label soft drinks, and President's Choice drinks in particular, this opened the door to Loblaw's Dave Nichol, but did not immediately sell the idea, as it was now necessary to convince Nichol "that he could make a premium product for the least amount of money," with the Loblaws name only for collateral.

Eventually Bill Sharpe did just that, becoming the first Canadian brewery to sell real beer for a Canadian grocery chain that was not sold at the store. In fact, President's Choice was such a success that Lakeport ran out of beer within days of its release, surprising everyone. Happily admitting his "shortsightedness", Bill Sharpe then took out ads across Ontario apologizing to teetotaler Dave Nichol and Loblaws for failing to keep up with the demand. Lakeport, however, is much more than the PC brands. In order to prevent being squashed to death with only one brand, Lakeport wants to specialize in "custom packaging". According to an interview in the October/November 1992 issue of "Kegs and Cases", Lakeport's Deborah Parker said that "this practice involves being a surrogate plant for breweries in other parts of North America (or the world) who want the option of having their beer brewed in Ontario".

As for Lakeport's plans, Bill Sharpe said his "first objective is to lay the groundwork for expansion. Too big to be a micro and too small to be in the Major League, this will take time." In many ways the Big Brewers even helped, as they did not look at Lakeport as a threat when he came in with a mainstream, quality product at reduced prices. However, to maintain the momentum, it will be necessary to have the "...same running capacity as a Big Brewer." Lakeport has the room for expansion, and ever increasing canning, draft keg and bottling lines.

To break even, Lakeport has to sell 120,000 hl a year, the company did this in its first year when the LCBO took a quarter of a million cases of the "Around Ontario" 125th anniversary beer, allowing the brewery to get up and running. The balance of 250,000 cases was then sold to Eastern Europe.

Planning to sell some 3.2 million cases of beer, or about 75% of the plant's capacity in 1993, Bill is looking into the production of non alcoholic beer. You "either sit on the porch or get off and run with the big dogs." Squarely aiming to take on Molson and Labatt, Bill simply said he "...did not buy the brewery to tear it down."

To keep a leading edge he plans to keep looking for corporate accounts like Loblaws, to "put out quality products, with good packaging at a good price."

"I can't take the Big Two head-on but I can market the product in an attractive package across the province, and diversify, into such areas as quality non-alcoholic beer."

As for the future of the industry, Bill said "people are willing to try, to experiment, they are going away from the corporate image". Brewing traditions and images are breaking, the micros helped to break this mould. The consumer has now moved away from the single choice label. With the opportunity to sample other flavours, he is doing it." Our new labels and pricing has made an impact." It certainly has with Molson and Labatt introducing lower priced beer to kick off the 1993 summer beer season with.

Growing rapidly, Bill wrapped up the interview by saying, "Once we hit 75% capacity, I plan to double the brewery in stages to 9 million cases a year."

Vital Statistics - The Brew

Initially beating the Big Two at their own game, Lakeport has shown that good mainstream Canadian beer can be brewed and sold at a lower cost to the consumer, if the brewery is prepared to forego big advertising budgets and accept lower profit margins.

Inheriting the old Heineken brewing system that allowed for liquid corn syrup, (syrup is Lakeport's only adjunct.) They also use cornflakes, (as do a number of micros). A modern brewery in the sense that it brews in large batches and uses the most advanced technology, Lakeport brews like a big brewer rather than a micro. Brewing high gravity beer, the same way the Big Two do, the PC products are triple cold filtered while all of the other brews are pasteurized.

Black Tap draft only.
Did not sample.
Laker Premium Lager, 5%
A clean golden amber lager, with a sweet, short, aerated foam, over a light nose. Refreshing yet sugar sweet, it has a sharp, tingly mouth, and pronounced bitter then sweet aftertaste.
Laker Premium Light, 4%
A honey pine brew with a short, foamy head, and light balanced aroma. A tingling mouth brings forth a fresh, sweet, taste gently hinting of honey. It is finished with a puckering, dry aftertaste.
Lone Star, 5%
Did not sample.

Pabst Blue Ribbon, 5%
Increased from the 4.7% found in the American product to 5% to match the
standard in the Ontario market, this small increase in alcohol does not
alter the beer's flavour profile. The most flavourful of the American
contract brews sampled, the most I will say about it is, it is sweet and
refreshing.

President's Choice, Premium Draft, 5%
For price and quality found in the European Saaz hops, this brew is as good as
anything the Big Brewers are making. As a North American lager, it is a
clean, refreshing, light, gold representative member of its style. The gentle
hopping, light but continuous foam, and sweet balanced mouth make it
eminently acceptable, the price has made it irresistible to many.

President's Choice, Premium Light Draft.
Did not sample.

President's Choice, Premium Strong Draft, 5.9%
Did not sample.

Near Beer:
Master's Choice, available at grocery stores.

Beer available at the Beer Store throughout Ontario, and at the retail outlet at
the brewery. Hospitality lounge.

London, Ontario,
THE CEEPS

(C.P.R. Tavern and Brew Pub)
671 Richmond St.,
London, Ontario, N6A 3G7
519-432-1425

Rating: 🍺🍺 (you might as well take your mother-in-law here as you may
very well have met her daughter here. A University pub, Barney's next door is
for those that graduated - I never made it!)

Publican: Rick Tattersall

Brewmaster: Charles MacLean, of Wellington County fame.

Founded: January 1991, started brewing. (In operation as a hotel since 1890,
licensed as a beverage room in 1934.)

Production Capacity: 4,000 hectolitres. Five vessel Continental full grain system
with a steam boiler.

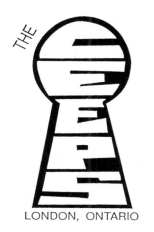

LONDON, ONTARIO

(Logo courtesy, Rick Tattersall, CEEPS.)

Anyone who spent anytime at Western can relate stories of pleasant hours at the CEEPS. My favourite has something to do with a deep conversation over some obscure historical point, that became dimmer and dimmer as the night wore on with my instructor. Fortunately for those of us who are afraid to return to old haunts because things just never look the same, I can report that after nearly a quarter of a century, that except with the addition of a patio, backroom and of course the brewery - the place is if anything, better than before.

Originally constructed in 1890, this 50' x 50' brick three storey hotel was described in "The Free Press" in September of the same year as containing an incredible "93 bedrooms...fitted and furnished throughout in the most approved manner."

Known as The Grand Pacific, the hotel located across from the CPR railway station was never operated by the railway. Charging a $1. per day to stay here, the London "Advertiser" for November 1907 took umbrage at the increase in the cost of a glass of suds. In a story headlined "Eight Ounces of Beer for Five Cents" the reporter wrote:

"The price of liquor is going up". Drinking is becoming more of a luxury every day, and it will soon be that none but the financially strong will be able to pick up "the white man's burden."

Yesterday a meeting of hotelkeepers was held and it was decided to raise the prices of liquor. "The price of beer will not go up. The glass will cost the same, but the good old-fashioned schooner has to give way and take its place along with the old brown jug and other relics of other boozing days. An eight ounce glass will be the vehicle of comfort now for the amber joy-producer which costs 5 cents."

After the CPR connected with Chicago before World War 1, the hotel's proprietors changed its name to the C.P.R. to capitalize on the location. Prohibition in 1916 closed the beverage room that was not reopened until 1934. To mark this event, the hotel celebrated New Year's with a seven course dinner.

Sold in 1948 for $150,000, the Tattersalls from England, took over in 1957. Owner Rick started working here in 1966 adding a brewpub for novelty, fun and to produce cheaper - interesting beers - after seeing the promotion at a trade show.

The CEEPS, as the largest dispenser of draught in London from 1970 to 1990, has still retained its University clientele and flavour.

Vital Statistics

Lager

A clean, shining amber main stream style lager, but with more of everything. This brew has an apricot nose, more malt, a smooth body, pleasing aftertaste and sparkling freshness.

Accounting for 25% of the pub's sales, the beer has become more mainstream over time to meet the habits of the public. Brewed three weeks, its produced with two row barley malt, cornflakes and Hallertau hops.

Menu - beer: Thames Valley Lager on tap, along with the Big Brewers and their bottles.

Food - Pub food: Soup of the day, salads, burger and hot dog platters, chicken pita, fries and natchos.

Lunch for two with beer under $20.

No credit cards.

Atmosphere: The University pub you learned to drink at is still there, except now they have windows, more games, a patio and a brewery.

Parking: Behind the pub and on the street.

Open seven days a week.

London, Ontario,

Thames Valley Brewing Company, Inc.

1764 Oxford St.,

Unit D12,

London, Ontario, 519-457-2023

Owners: An investors group including N. Blake Stoneburgh formerly of Tapsters Brewhouse and Restaurant in Mississauga.

Brewmaster: Steve Hannon, ex production manager for Amstel Canada, learned brewing the "hands-on" way-starting in 1973 with Heineken, then Henninger, and Amstel in Europe and North America.

Founded: Winter, 1993.

Production Capacity: 6,000 hectolitres. The brewhouse located at the rear of a strip industrial mall, has equipment made by Karl Jacobs of Germany, once used by New Brunswick's now defunct Hanshaus Brewery.

Additional equipment came from Charlottetown.

Is this the start of a draft brewery chain?

Producing draft only with 100% Canadian barley malt, a blend of North American and European hops that include the popular Saaz and Hallertau varieties, this Reinheitsgebot style lager is aimed at the mainstream drinker. Purposely not "too exotic", the owners at Thames Valley are keeping to draft according to brewer Steve Hannon because it "doesn't need expensive bottles or bottling lines and the Brewers Retail to sell it." In other

words, overhead is low. While keg draft tavern sales are under siege in Eastern Ontario by "bottled" draft beers, in Southern Ontario the product is doing well. When asked about future plans, Hannon said that, "If the beer takes, and the local market uses the brewery's capacity, the Thames Valley plant will act as a model for additional draft breweries across Ontario."

Vital Statistics - The Brew

Thames Valley Lager, 5%

You might well ask, who needs another taste alike lager? This might be a valid comment if this was not a well hopped, all malt product. When compared back to back with the corn syrup ladened beers, you will discover there is a difference.

It may be too early to fully comment on this beer, but it is worth tasting.

Only available in licensed establishments around London. No tours or souvenirs.

If you really want to test your tasting abilities, visit The CEEPS and try their brew, Thames Valley and a bottled draft and see if you can tell the difference.

Markham, Ontario,
Barb's Union Station Pub/Eatery

4396 Steeles Ave. East, Box 61 (Exit Hwy. 401 Kennedy Road north to Steeles, on the northeast side in Markham Village.)

Markham, Ontario, L3R 9W1

416-940-3131

Rating: Too early to rate.
Proprietor: Barb Stitt

Brewer: John Lippert contract brewer.

Founded: First opened in November 1989, fell into receivership in the Spring of 1990, and was eventually picked up by one of the investors to re-open January 1st, 1993.

Production Capacity: Cask Brewing Malt Extract using Edme Malts. 900 hl a year. One lager, and one 6% ale.

Changing orientation away from the younger crowd, the new owners are aiming their restaurant at families with music from the 60s and 70s. Open seven days a week they have a DJ for dancing, while the menu, which is still being developed features pasta, Tex-Mex, and pub food.

As for the beer - the draft taps dispense the usual line-up from the U.K., Sleemans, Conners, Moosehead and the mainstream Canadian.

There is ample parking and credit cards are accepted. Expect to pay around $25. for lunch and $40 for dinner.

P.S. The highlight of the visit could very well be the toy train "steaming" along a rail above the dance floor.

Mississauga, Ontario
C C's - Meadowvale Brew Pub

6981 Millcreek Drive
(Exit Hwy. 401 - 336 Erin Mills Parkway.)
Mississauga, Ontario, L5N 6B8
416-542-0136

Rating: 🍺🍺
Owners: John and Frank Pucci

Manager: Randy Mustatia

Brewmaster: Murray Voakes, B.Sc.

Founded: 1990. (The chain has six locations, but only one brewpub.)

Production Capacity: Five vessel Continental Breweries Inc., Malt Extract System converted to full grain.

A restaurant, nightclub, brewpub and sportsbar, "C C's" stands for "Cool Cats".

Seating 325, the brewpub was added as a novelty. Activities include special wing nights, sports trivia contests, casino nights, jam sessions, dancing, karoake and even a cigarette happy hour.

(Logo courtesy, C C's Brew Pub.)

Outfitted with a dance floor, pool tables and games, Manager Randy Mustatia says C C's has become a "second home for many regulars."

Arriving at 5 p.m., just in time to enjoy complimentary tortilla chips and salsa, I had no trouble getting comfortable while sipping my pint and admiring the brewery behind the bar.

Vital Statistics - The Brew

Accounting for some 75% of their beer sales, they brew their beer to please their customers. There are plans to introduce a dark ale.

Lager, 4.5%
Modelled after "Canadian", this creamy headed, well balanced, clean, crisp, lager has the advantage of being fresh, even if it is not adventurous. Cheaper than domestic draught.

Menu - beer: Products from the Big Two with a very limited import list. A full list of liquor and mixed drinks.

Food - menu: A full complement of popular items such as wings, burgers, finger food - gyros, mini burritos and tacos, breaded shrimp; finger food platters; kid's menu; sandwiches; and entrees including Souvlaki, perogies, Mexican, Italian, fish and steak.

Lunch for two with beer around $25.

Dinner for two with beer around $40.

Credit Cards: All major credit cards.

Atmosphere: A modern eating, meeting, and drinking emporium that strives to offer something for everyone.

Parking: Parking lot.

Hours: Seven days a week.

Niagara Falls, Ontario
Niagara Falls Brewing Company

6863 Lundy's Lane,
Niagara Falls, Ontario, L2G 1V7
416-356 BREW or 416-374-1166; FAX 416-374-2930.

Proprietors: Mario and Bruno Criveller 50%, other partners 50%

Brewmaster: Claude J. Corriveau, former wine taster and maker, turned brewer for a "real challenge". Harvey Hurlbut 39 year brewing veteran; consultant Tom Davey; assistant Wally Moroz formerly with Paul Masson Wineries.

General Manager: Claude J. Corriveau.

Founded: August 1, 1989.

Production Capacity: 10,000 hl., 1992 3 million bottles, hoping to peak at 4 million bottles. In the first two years of operation the brewery's capacity grew 66%. The brewery now employs 18 shareholders.

Eisbock, each year the label shows another historic "Falls" scene to mark the vintage.

(Label courtesy, Niagara Falls Brewing Company.)

"Always experiment, never let-up, never be complacent." With this attitude and the belief that the trend in microbrewing is to try something new all of the time, Niagara's brewmaster and General Manager, Claude Corriveau has introduced some of Ontario's most innovative and palatable beers. Trained originally by the Ontario government in wine tasting, Claude explains that tasting is "understanding", while judging is a matter of "palate". You must understand each individual component in a beverage's make-up, that is understand the raw materials, to understand the product." To be a brewer you have to know the functions of "the component parts."

Spending a total of 18 years in the wine industry, Claude said that he was inducted into it through his father-in-law Karl Podamer, the first Ontario winemaker to make champagne in the French method. Winning awards for these wines, Claude spent six years as a consultant for Barnes. He got involved in the microbrewery industry as a filtration system's trouble shooter, and is now brewing.

His goals are as simple to state as they are difficult to attain; "to be well recognized for award winning beers and wines."

Retailing his products as far west at Windsor and north to Peterborough and through the Vintages section at the LCBO, his specialty products are gaining a cult following.

Always striving to be in the forefront, Niagara Falls Brewing was the first microbrewery in the province to open on Sundays to sell to the tourist traffic.

As for his beer, he is striving to find the specialty market with quality products. "I want it to be known that if there is anything special or unique in brewing, that it will probably come from Niagara Falls Brewing. If there is something new or unusual, I want to be the first on the market. I want to be off the wall, without tying up a year with marketing.''

If Claude's premonition about Eisbock (known by the majors as Ice Beer) is any indication of things to come, I almost shudder to think what will happen if he brews a Morte Subite and Labatts and Molsons follow.

Vital Statistics - The Brew

50% of the sales are draft while the other half are in bottle. This even includes the "exotics" such as Eisbock.

Trapper Premium Canadian Lager, 5%

A light gold, lager, with a fleeting head, and nose of malt and corn. The creamy foam leads to a sweet, lightly hopped body, with a malty, hoppy, sweetish aftertaste. A typical well made North American cottage brewery lager, that has attracted an extremely loyal following as evidenced by the poem penned by Stan Lowe on his 80th birthday.

A couple of the boys were drinking beer

in one of the local bars.

The both of them ordered TRAPPER Beer,

They said it's the best by far.

The waiter said "you boys are right.

This TRAPPER tops them all,"

and it helps boost our economy,

it's brewed here in the Falls.

Some people buy American beer,

so they go across the line.

They want to beat the sales tax

and hope to save a dime.

But I drink beer for pleasure

I don't care about the dime,

and I pay my share of taxes

so it's TRAPPER beer for mine.

If you want to help your country

and enjoy the best of beer,

buy TRAPPER; MADE IN CANADA

and keep your money here.

Brewed with Canadian two-row and ground roasted malts, corn, Hallertau and
     Nugget hops.

Trapper Light on tap.

Gritstone Premium Ale, 5.8%

Barley wine in quality, this brew has a tawny complexion, with a malty, nutty,
     caramel - sherry like nose. With a rich barley wine taste, this well
     balanced ale has a lot of character for its alcoholic strength. The aftertaste
     is in turns, sweet, puckering and smoky.

Winner of a silver medal in 1992.

Olde Jack Bitter Strong Ale, 7.2%

Not an "English" bitter where the hops predominate, I believe that the bitter
     refers to the taste of bitter roasted malt. If you ever wondered what malt
     tasted like try this beer. This malty warmer can best be described as a
     chocolate bar with a kick. Ingredients include carastan, chocolate and
     ground roasted malts, Nugget and Northern Brewer hops.

Winner of a silver medal in 1992.

Brock's Extra Stout, 5.8%

Brewed in the Irish style, to be dryer and contain more alcohol, this brew has a
     wonderful sweet licorice nose. "Delightfully bitter", it was awarded a
     gold medal in 1992.

Eisbock, 8%

First introduced to Canadian palates in 1989-90, four years before the two other
     breweries thought of it, Eisbock is a tribute to the art of the master brewer.
     More like a wine than a beer, it is the perfect accompaniment to ham, and
     any formal dinner. Try aging it if you can. No I am not going to describe
     it, except to suggest you try it, and write in your comments. And please
     don't judge it on your experiences with the other two "Ice Beers".

Finally if you can do it, try an Eisbrock, a specialty of the brewery's
hospitality lounge. 2/3s Eisbock and 1/3 stout, this concoction had a creamy
head reminiscent of cold hot fudge Sunday, and gets better after this.

Maple Wheat, 8.5%, strongest beer in Canada.

Winner of a gold medal in 1992, Claude is very proud of this quintessential
     Canadian brew that he plans to sell at Florida's Epcot Centre.

Brewed with champagne yeast, Ontario Sunridge Maple Syrup, and Canadian
malted wheat, this is a beer unlike any other. A difficult beer style to make, one
that often wastes both beer and maple syrup, and is plagued with a sweet ginger
ale like taste, Niagara Falls Brewing has produced the best Maple beer I have
ever had, by fermenting out the residual sugars to eliminate the cloying
sweetness. With a good body, sweet smoked maple taste and powerful maple
nose, this beer is best enjoyed in a wine glass either as an aperitif, or after dinner
with your dessert. Try it!

Beer available in select restaurants, in over 150 Beer Stores and LCBO
outlets, and at the brewery.

Souvenirs may be purchased at the brewery.

Tours of the plant with a hospitality lounge overlooking the operations.

"We want (the tourist) to walk in, taste and see it all." This is without doubt the most inviting hospitality lounge in Ontario.

Orillia, Ontario,
Blue Anchor Restaurant And Brewpub

47 West St. South,
Orillia, Ontario, L3V 5G5
705-325-7735

Rating:
Proprietor: Barry Neil
Brewmaster: Rick Neil trained by consulting brewer John Lippert.
Founded: 1988.
Production Capacity: 2,400 hectolitres per year. Continental Malt Extract System.

(Logo courtesy, Blue Anchor Restaurant and Brewpub.)

"Who would have thought 'True Blue' Orillia would drink real beer?"

According to the CBC announcer who made this comment to me, not only do they like it, they keep going back for more.

Modifying a little to meet local tastes, the Blue Anchor is located in the heart of tourist land, where they usually call "Labatt's Classic" an import. Located in a 19th century building, the central, circular bar dominates this neighborhood pub that was designed after $500,000 of renovations.

Highlighting the brewery in the front window, the pub provides fresh beer and reasonable food.

Vital Statistics - The Brew
I have not sampled their products in the last year; Rick said there are seasonal variations. On the whole the beer is acceptable.

Light Lager, 4.5%

Light Ale, 4.5%

Bitter Amber Ale 5 to 5.5%

Menu - beer:

On tap: Harp, Creemore, Sleemans, Heineken, Smithwicks, Guiness. Various
    Canadian. Liquor and non alcoholic drinks.

Menu - food : Roadhouse, burgers etc.
    Lunch for two with beer under $20.

    Dinner for two with beer under $20.
Atmosphere: Pub.
    Credit cards accepted.

    Open daily.

    Parking: in the brewpub parking lot, free.

Ottawa, Ontario,
The Green Door Restaurant

198 Main St.,
Ottawa, Ontario,
613-234-9597

Rating: 🍺🍺🍺
Founded: 1988.

No I haven't lost it! If you care about natural beer, you will inevitably begin to
consider the food you eat. Logically then this can lead to a "vegetarian organic
natural food" restaurant.

I admit when my wife suggested we go here, and when I saw the place from
the outside full of St. Paul's University academic types, I said to myself "No
beer here!" Was I pleasantly surprised.

The first thing my eyes fell upon was a cooler full of Hart, Brick, Algonquin,
Upper Canada, Guinness and incongruently Black Label and Stroh's. (along
with wine) That settled I was ready to take a plate and line-up to ladle fresh
portions of spinach-tofu lasagna, curried lentils, leek and basmati casserole,
eggplant and potato curry, stuffed collard leaves and saffron rice for starters,
unto my plate. Followed by marinated mushrooms, quinoa tabouli, guacamole,
Greek salad, and whole grain noodles with pesto. And who cares if you don't
know what some of these things are, they are great. A word of warning though,
don't stack your plate too high, as you pay by the kilo. Desserts are equally
adventuresome and may include carrot cake, millet custard, blueberry pie,
almond-raisin squares and peanut butter cookies. And to cap it all off have an
organic coffee. This self-serve cafeteria style service, blends in with the
University atmosphere, which is complemented by the rotating art shows, and
punctuated by many animated conversations.

The emphasis is on informality and food preparation and taste. As the proprietors boast "Pies, cakes, and cookies are among the desserts that are baked daily, using local stone-ground whole-grain flours; wholesome sweetners such as maple syrup and brown rice malt are used exclusively. Yeast-free, sugar free, and dairy-free sourdough breads, as well as wheat-free sourdough rye."

If you are still one of the gastronomic dinosaurs who believe that meat and potatoes make a meal, and that vegetarian means beans, bury your prejudices, grasp a pint of your favourite brew and try it. You may even end up liking tofu.

Lunch for two with beer probably around $25., if you went on a regular basis. But if you live in a deep fried ghetto like Cornwall, and only visit once a month, its impossible not to sample everything.

Dinner for two with beer, once again probably around $25.

Credit cards accepted.
Atmosphere: Open University cafeteria style.
Parking: Ample street parking.

Hours: Tuesday to Saturday 11 a.m. to 9 p.m., Sunday 11 a.m. to 3 p.m.

P.S. If you really get into this there is a vegetarian grocery store and related bookstore next to the Green Door

---

Ottawa, Ontario,
Master's Brew Pub & Brasserie

(in the Citadel Hotel),
330 Queen St.,
Ottawa, Ontario, K1R 5A5
613-594-3688

Rating: 🍺🍺🍺

Owner: Tom Barton

Manager: Kelly Littlemore

Brewmaster: Martin Ruddy, studied Applied Chemistry at the University of Guelph, homebrewer since 1984, with the brewpub since 1988.

Founded: January, 1988.

Production Capacity: 10,000 Imperial Gallons (1,394 kegs). Cask Brewing and Malt Extract System now uses some grain in the recipes. This is a standard 7 vessel, seven barrel plant with two fermenting vessels allowing for the production of two continuous styles of beer.

(Logo courtesy, Master's Brew Pub & Brasserie.)

In the wasteland of food courts and chip-stands that litter the heart of bureaucratic Ottawa - there is only one hope of finding good beer. And that's at Master's, on the Queen Street side of the Skyline Hotel. Determined not to become a drinking hole or imitate the English pub, this slightly faded, yet comfortable "Miami Vice" style brewpub emphasizes generous portions of food and two interesting fresh brews.

The first brewpub to be located in a hotel chain in Canada, it is independently operated. Founded to offer something novel to the thousands of area civil servants and apartment dwellers, the owner also believed it was a sound investment.

With the brewery appropriately located in the hotel's old bakery, guests can view several maturation tanks while either sitting at the long bar or lounging in the comfortable chairs. Whenever I am in Ottawa, after a day of research at the Public Archives, I use Master's as my "office", and providing I miss the lunch and after work crowds, I have found it to be an ideal place to hold informal meetings.

Now priced to match domestic products, Brewer Martin Ruddy tries to create beers "...with a distinctive flavour, and more character than mainstream beers, but yet within the Canadian tradition."

Vital Statistics - The Brew

Here as in most brewpubs, the brewer makes continuous modifications to the recipe.

Master's Ale, 5%

A Canadian interpretation of a traditional English malt ale. Reddish amber in colour with a small foam, over an extremely well balanced aroma reminiscent of fresh flowers and fruit. The taste is predominated by the malt with a dash of hops. After the aroma, the real pleasure comes from the aftertaste which starts with the sweet malt, and expands into a lingering, pleasant bitterness.

Hops either Northern Brewer or Fuggles and Willamette.

Master's Lager, 5%

A Vienna style lager in colour, with a well formed head, assertive aroma from the Hallertau hops, backed with body. A creamy foam, leads to the fruity-malty taste with a pleasant hop finish. The aftertaste has a lingering sweetness underlined by the hopping. Cascade and Hallertau hops.

Menu - beer: Domestic draft, plus a full range of beers from the Big Two, and standard imports. House wines and the usual liquors and liqueurs.

Menu - food: Appetizers such as poutine, paté, stromboli, nachos, soups and salads. The open menu includes a lunch special, sausage sandwich, curry stir fry, croissants, baguettes, burgers, chili, Cornish pastry, Italian. Dinner entrées mixed grill, steak, veal schnitzel, breaded scallops.

Lunch for two with beer under $30. Lunch specials.

Dinner for two with beer under $45.

Credit cards accepted.

Atmosphere: Hotel style, and definitely not "British", yet there are comfortable corners to hide from the bureaucrats in. Unhurried, and you can even ignore the televisions. A nice long bar.

Parking: At last I can report that the recession has done some good! Four years ago parking might set you back $9., today it has dropped to a maximum of $6. Parking in numerous parking lots.

Hours:11:30 to 1 a.m. Weekdays; Saturday 5 p.m. to 1 a.m., closed Sundays.

Peterborough, Ontario,

The Peterborough Arms Pub and Restaurant

300 Charlotte St., (corner of Rubidge and Charlotte),

Peterborough, Ontario,K9J 2V5

705-876-0306

Rating:

President: Bob Desautels, part of the Neighborhood Pubs Group, see Guelph, Woolwich Arms.

Managers: Wendi Wood, Kendra Johnson

Founded: February, 1992.

Located in a 130 year old Victorian brick home, this is another in a series of pubs established by the Neighborhood Pub's Group, where Ontario micro beers are featured along with Canadian artisanal Cheeses. President Bob Desautels said they feature "...Oka cheese, maple syrup, gourmet pizzas, and the quintessential North American

(Logo courtesy, Neighborhood Pubs Group Inc. - The Peterborough Arms.)

food, the 'burger'...(along with) freshly made pasta, a selection of fresh seafood...and game dishes cooked in beers or wines."

Menu - Beer: Ontario classics such as Wellington County, Hart, Niagara Falls Brewing, cider on tap and many more.

Menu - Food: Sweet bell pepper soup of the day, salads, bruschetta, burgers -"the feta", "the Mexican Swiss", "The Bombay"; Chicken pot pie and Hunter's selection - venison and Maderia paté with choice of cheddar, and then desserts such as fresh fruit pie, etc.

Lunch for two with beer around $25.

Dinner for two with beer around $40.

Credit cards: All major credit cards.

Atmosphere: Comfortable family pub.

Parking: Ample street parking.

Hours: Seven days a week.

St. Catharines, Ontario,
Conners Brewery

(Don Valley Brewing Company (1990)
Limited operating as Conner Brewery)
227 Bunting Road, Unit J.
St. Catharines, Ontario, L2M 3Y2
416-988-9363, FAX: 416-682-4430

Headoffice:
544 Eglinton Ave. East
Toronto, Ontario, M4P 1N7
416-488-1406,
FAX: 416-322-1498

President: Glen Dalzell

Finance: Marc Bedard

Operations Manager: Dan Unkerskov

Head Brewer: Liam McKenna; restarted with consulting brewmasters Doug Morrow, and ex Amstel man Keith Armstrong.

Founded: The first Port Credit Conners was founded in 1986, and then according to the company "Early in 1991, Glen Dalzell and Marc Bedard purchased the Conners brands, recipes and trademarks when the Toronto microbrewery went into receivership."

"...(the working brewery was sold at auction November 6, 1990 for approximately $150,000., no where near the hoped for starting bid of $300,000.) Then the two former oil executives purchased the two-year-old Sculler brewery when it ceased operating after the former owner (Mike Driscoll) ran out of money."

The objective in reviving and integrating the two companies was to combine the marketing strength of Conners with the production strength of Sculler into one, profitable operation. The plan was to take Conners' four successful brands and produce them in the lower-cost St. Catharines facility."

March 11, 1991, the first keg of Best Bitter was launched.

Production Capacity: Brewing some 8,000 hl in their first "new" year of operations alone, the brewhouse has a 15,000 hl capacity. Refitting the old Scullers' plant into a British style brewhouse, the facility was modified with the addition of a whirlpool settling tank, mechanized mashing system replacing the traditional two 3 metre rakes, a new cooling system, fermenting vessel, aging tanks and mash tun malt delivery system, along with a micro filtration system for bottling.

At the time of writing they had a fulltime staff of four and part-time of three.

(Logo courtesy, Conners Brewery.)

Almost doubling their capacity in the first two years of their latest reincarnation, Head Brewer Liam McKenna said "They were back in the market as strong as ever, and growing while the industry as a whole was going down." In fact finding space to expand may be a real problem, as Liam in the best British brewing tradition, is uncomfortable with brewing lagers in an ale house.

Continually "fine tuning his products" Liam entered brewing through his teenage fascination with the microscope. Like many of us he then started homebrewing and winemaking in his later teens. In his second year at the University of Guelph co-op programme he entered the Ontario government's winemaking course, where he discovered that he did not want to continue "...with wine as it was fairly easy". The real craft laid with the vinculturists. Still interested in the production of alcoholic beverages, Liam then went to Sleeman's with the co-op programme again. Here he gained his appreciation for the art and mystery of brewing and spent his time learning all he could. When he was finished he went to Conners first as a Production Assistant, and then went on to brewing and lab. work.

As a brewer Liam considers himself a craftsman. He wants to "Buck the trends and get back to basics of brewing. The Germans proved with the Reinheitsgebot how good beer could be, if you stuck to the essentials, and only did the necessary."

As a brewer Liam is intense, and "in search of excellence."

He continued that the "...key ingredients in brewing are: 1. water, as it dictates the style, that is hard for ale. 2. Yeast, which activates the fermentation process, and adds the estery or fruity taste found in ales. 3. Hops - the spice or seasoning imparting flavour and aroma. And malt, a distant 4th which adds colour and establishes the base palate."

With these thoughts in mind, I was interested to hear what Liam had to say about pasteurization.

He said, "Pasteurization negates the food value of beer. One of the most important cultural ingredients in beer is Vitamin B. For example in World War 1, the Allied Naval blockade of Europe meant that barley had to be rationed in Germany reducing the amount of beer brewed, leading to a lack of Vitamin B in the diet and became a cause of adult pernicious anaemia."

And if this isn't enough Liam continued, "Pasteurization if not done properly leads to a cooked biscuit flavour to the beer."

One of the younger brewers Liam responded that "...it takes young people to look at old ways to find and lead change."

Looking at the future of the micro industry he "...would like to see a lot of new styles of beers being produced. To see us get out of the rut of brewing German lagers, and English ales."

He would like to see "more co-operation between small brewers and brewpubs and exchange of information." (this has already started, the small brewers have found co-operation particularly important in the area of distribution, and sharing some facilities such as bottling lines.)

As for the present Liam will keep experimenting with beer and beer styles, and promoting the idea of the sharing of information. Ultimately he would like to see the major brewers establish an Ontario Brewing Training Institute, similar to the Master Brewer's Association's Chair of Brewing Studies at the University of Wisconsin.

Vital Statistics - The Brew

Basically brewers of Ales, Conners introduced a Premium Lager in the spring of 1993 which I did not have the opportunity to properly evaluate before press time. In a test brew, however, I was impressed by its balance, and learned that it possessed Chester and Hersbrucker hops.

As to be expected the brews are not pasteurized.

Ale, 5%

A tawny brew with a very long tasting whip cream like rocky head; a pleasant fruity nose, and rich malty body. The hops come through along with the malt again in the warm - puckering aftertaste. Aptly described as a lively ale, it has the brewery's hallmark balance.

Carastan and black malts along with Canadian two row barley, and Fuggles and Cascade hops.

Best Bitter, 5%, No. 1 in bottle sales.

A fine representative example of an English Best Bitter. Unlike other Canadian beers in this style, Conners has a well balanced flowery, full hop nose, underlined by an earthy, malty warmth. Smooth to the taste, it has been pleasantly bittered with Chester and Cascade hops, leaving a pleasant slightly puckering aftertaste, while the carastan malt probably accounts for the slight residual sweetness.

Awarded a gold medal at the 1991 International Beer, Wine and Food Show in Toronto, for a Draft Ale.

Special Draft Ale, 5%, No. 1 in overall sales.

The only Ale draft in a bottle made in Ontario.

The brilliant golden pine body, exceptionally creamy tasting head is covered by a well balanced nose. Starting with a smooth malty earthy mouth, it develops the characteristics of a Bitter and is capped off with a nice malt start and hop finish that some might find a little too puckering.

Chester and Hersbrucker hops.

Imperial Stout, 5%

Too weak to be an "Internationally" recognized Imperial Stout, the brew has a silky mouth, and offers the taste of chocolate along with its full roasted palate.

Nugget, Cluster and Cascade hops.

Beer and collectibles may be purchased at the brewery, where tours can be arranged, and where you can view the operations from the second floor hospitality lounge.

Available in restaurants and beer stores throughout southern Ontario.

Sault Ste. Marie, Ontario,

The Jolly Friar Brewpub

320 Bay Street, (in the Day's Inn),
Sault Ste. Marie, Ontario, P6A 1X1
705-945-8888

Rating: 🍺🍺 - 🍺🍺🍺

Owner: Dale Hammar

Operations: Brent Blair

Brewmaster: Dale Hammar

Founded: February 1988.

Production Capacity: 13,000 Imperial Gallons, Cask Brewing Malt Extract System.

(Logo courtesy, The Jolly Friar Brewpub.)

A pint of fresh bitter and a steak and kidney pie in the Canadian Shield. Ten years ago this was Dale Hammar's ultimate dream. Today Hammar the publican, 30 year homebrew veteran, teacher, part-time mineral prospector, and owner of the Wine Barrel, a homebrewing store, has made it possible to quaff "real" beer between Thunder Bay and Ottawa.

Offering 250 gallons of fresh, natural beer every week, along with a fair selection of imported drafts, the Jolly Friar, Northern Ontario's first brewpub, provides a reasonable alternative to the thirsty traveller in an otherwise sterile market.

Priced competitively, sales of the brew accounted for 90% of the pub's beer sales during its first month of business.

Located in the Day's Inn, this 170 seat facility may be larger than the average English pub it claims to emulate - but it does try with English fare and darts, and a view of the completely glassed in brewery.

Independently owned and operated by Hammar and several silent partners, they believe that they can make a go of it with a mere 1.5% of the local beer drinking market.

Aimed at the 20 to 50 year old audience, the Jolly Friar provides good beer along with wholesome food for reasonable cost in unaffected surroundings. Sault Ste. Marie, once known as the "Siberia of Canada" to British troops, can now claim to be a bastion for "real" beer with this British style pub.

Vital Statistics - The Brew

    Pilsner Lager, 5.2%
A medium bodied, light coloured lager with a distinct European hopping.
    Dale's Bitter, 4.3%
Full bodied with a medium brown colour, similar to a Northumbrian bitter, with
    a touch of sweetness in the aftertaste.
    Ale, 5.1%
Full bodied, amber in colour with domestic characteristics.
    Note: the above descriptions were provided by the brewmaster.
Menu - beer: Imported draft and bottled beer including Newcastle Brown Ale
    and Beamish Stout. All beers are reasonably priced. There is also a
    limited wine list and a full selection of liquors and cocktails.
Menu - food: English pub fare including Scotch eggs, Shepherd's Pie, fish and
    chips and ploughman's lunch. Desserts include sherry truffle and steamed
    lemon pudding. Salads, soups and sandwiches, milk and soft drinks are
    also available.
Dinner for two including beer, under $35.

Thunder Bay, Ontario,
The Port Arthur Brasserie and Brewpub

901 Red River Road,
Thunder Bay, Ontario, P7B 1K3
807-767-4415

Founded: February 1988.

Production Capacity: 18,000 Imperial gallons, Cask Brewing Malt Extract System.

Rating: I have not visited this brewpub, and they seem unwilling to divulge any information - let me know what you find if you go!

A former Kelsey's Restaurant converted into a brewpub.

Vital Statistics - The Brew

Two years ago the owner was thinking of introducing an English style ale, apparently he changed his mind as only Arthur's malt extract lager is available - yum??

Toronto, Ontario,
Allen's Bar - Restaurant - Backyard

143 Danforth Ave.,
Toronto, Ontario, M4K 1N2
416-463-3086

Rating: 🍺🍺🍺 - 🍺🍺🍺🍺 (An ideal alternative to the fried palaces, souvlaki shops, health food pits and instant ambience emporiums. A little more adventurous housebrew, or perhaps two housebrews and this would be a four.)

Publican: John W. Maxwell

Operated by the founding spirit of the Gambrinus Society "...dedicated to the appreciation of beer from all corners of the globe", John Maxwell; Allen's is a haven for beer aficionados who enjoy good food and some of the best of New York City's 1950s tavern culture.

Sporting a vintage jukebox that works, and a sense of comfortable purpose, restaurateur and advanced beer enthusiast John Maxwell said "...Allen's is a restaurant with a very good bar, not a bar serving food. I see it as the development of the Irish - American saloon, which in my native city New York, started as a front room with a bar and a very few booths or tables and a back room or

143 DANFORTH AVE · TORONTO · ONT · M4K 1N2

(Logo courtesy, Allen's.)

snug with table service. In the bar, opposite to it, a food bar was usually found, which provided all the establishment's kitchen facilities. As time passed and habits changed, the back room became a dining room, the food bars disappeared and full kitchens were added, usually in the basement. Allen's catches this evolution at about 1950, it still has the food bar, at which express items are offered, but the kitchen exists elsewhere and offers a very complete menu. The look, feel and organization of the place are true to what still existed...in the early '60s (by 1970, most of the pre and post-War places had turned into fern bars)."

Commenting about the menu which changes weekly John said, "The food is decidedly American...Everything, even the bread from which we make our melba toast, is from scratch. Allen's has no micro-wave and the hideous pre-packaged bar food and pub grub found in so many establishments will never appear there."

And if this is not enough to convince you that Allen's has something different to offer, John's philosophy towards beer is "...to serve interesting beer, with only a cursory nod to the commercial. If Blue is wanted, there are a 1,000 premises at which it is available; if Sierra Nevada Porter is desired, one must come to Allen's. The draft beer changes frequently, but is always Ontario micro-brewed."

Had enough? Wait until I get to the beer, single malt, scotch and food menus!

Vital Statistics - The Brew

Allen's Special Lager
Made by Brick, I didn't try it, there were too many other delights to test my palate, and capacity with.

Menu - beer: Befitting the birthplace of the Gambrinus Society, Allen's has a truly impressive beer list presented properly by knowledgeable servers. On tap Hart Amber Ale, and a special treat Niagara Falls Eisbock etc.; Belgian - Chimay, Grimbergen, La Chouffe, McChouffe, Morte Subite, Duvel; and a full range of Ontario micros as well as Fuller's London Pride, Beck's Dos Equis, Samuel Adams, Tucher etc.

And we can't forget the liquor. With over 30 single malt Scotches and six Irish whiskies to choose from, there is more than enough for the most discriminating drinker. And if you must after all of this - there is a limited wine selection.

Menu - food: While the menu changes weekly it includes on various occasions such items as black bean soup, potato and leek soup, deep-fried calamari with curried mayonnaise, chicken liver and apple tart with mustard sauce, deep-fried dill pickle with mustard sour cream, asparagus and feta cheese omelette with cornbread stuffing and celery sauce and it goes on...

In the summer there is a daily bar-b-que held in the bricked in backyard.

Lunch for two with beer around $35.

Dinner for two with beer around $55.

Credit cards: All major credit cards.

Atmosphere: Uptown New York City, circa 1950. Intimate, yet not cloying, a jukebox, booths and lots of polished wood.

Special Events: Celtic Night the second Tuesday of each month with a special menu and entertainment, and numerous other special events and menus.

Parking: Take the subway, on the south side of Danforth Ave.

Hours: Seven days a week.

Toronto, Ontario,
Amsterdam Brasserie And Brewpub

133 John Street,

Toronto, Ontario, M5V 2E4

416-595-8201; FAX 416-977-5214

Also the "Little Amsterdam" at 135 John St.

Rating: 🍺🍺🍺 - 🍺🍺🍺🍺

(this time I took my mother instead of my mother-in-law, and found everything much improved, it has lost that yuppie edge and is now more comfortable.)

President: Roel Bramer

Brewmaster: Harley Smith under the direction of Joel Manning.
Founded: Sept. 9, 1986.

Production Capacity: 36,000 Imperial gallons (2,787 kegs). Converted full grain Malt Extract System from Cask Brewing.

Public support for Toronto's first brewpub has enabled the Amsterdam to expand and improve its beer to the point that its products and production rivals some small microbreweries. Situated in a renovated warehouse, just south of trendy Queen Street West, the brasserie has been broken-up to include a long and glorious standup bar, a high ceiling restaurant with an international menu, an airy smoke-free dining room, a very pleasant, tree-lined outdoor patio, and most important of all, a dream-like cellar brewery poolroom and bar.

Visiting this time with my mother, she was immediately impressed by the fact that they brought her a coffee before even mentioning beer, unlike so many restaurants. With coffee and menus in hand before the fireplace, my dad and I ventured valiantly forth. An Englishman, Dad ordered a Nut Brown Ale. After one sniff his eyes brightened, and he waxed eloquently about how the beer reminded him of home. As for the food, it was as good as the beer. Attractively served in generous portions, I enjoyed a lightly spiced satay with succulent chicken bits, but sadly tired greens. All was forgiven, however, with the pappadon, a hugh Indian spiced "potato chip". Dad had succulent medium lamb curry, which was only missing some chutney to make it perfect. And Mom had the Grilled Swiss Cheese Sandwich, which was nothing less than a salad in between some bread. The desserts were equally adventurous and appealing. The apple pizza, made with apple pie, cheddar cheese and ice cream with a side order of strawberries was to quote Dad "...really very good". And the cassis ice cream, had real raspberries down to the pips.

Certainly worth a visit and head and shoulders above the plethora of pseudo "English" pubs, "new wave" eateries, and chain restaurants that have invaded downtown Toronto.

Vital Statistics - The Brew

Seasonal varieties along with the regulars. The beers are mercifully not over carbonated.

Stout, 6.5% (seasonal)
A lightly bittered nose, with a creamy but not over dense foam. More a porter than a stout, it was a pleasing drink even if not overly complex.

Lager, 5%
Reddish golden beer with a light head and balanced, flowery nose. Rich, lively fruity taste - like a liquid fruitcup, light pleasing finish.

Ale, 5% Nut Brown

A light head, and malty nose, with chocolaty overtones in the mouth, accompanied by light bittering, and a sweetish aftertaste. A convincing English style ale.

Menu - food: International cuisine. See introduction

The menu changes at least twice a year.

Lunch for two with beer under $30. Fixed price menu lunch and dinner $10.

Dinner for two with beer could easily be under $40.

The Amsterdam like so many places is reducing its prices to meet the contingencies of the times. Prices, however, for the beer do go up after 8 p.m. Sunday buffet brunch.

Tours of the brewery may be arranged.

Credit cards accepted.

Atmosphere: Airy, spacious converted factory, that manages to have some cosy corners. A nice change to the "British" look alikes. Outdoor tree-lined boulevard patio in the summer, and cellar/brewery bar.

Parking: On street, and parking lot behind the brewpub. Close to the Queen Street West streetcar line.

Hours: Seven days a week from 11:30 a.m. to 1 a.m.

Toronto, Ontario,

The Bow and Arrow Pub And Restaurant

1954 Yonge St.,

(Davisville subway, walk north along Yonge St., on the west side.)

Toronto, Ontario,

416-487-2036

Rating: 🍺🍺🍺 - 🍺🍺🍺🍺

President: Bob Desautels, part of the Neighborhood Pubs Group, see Guelph, Woolwich Arms.

Managers: Tim Smith, Frank Smyslo.

Assistant Manager: Scott Jarrett.

Founded: November 1992.

(Logo courtesy, Neighborhood Pubs Group - The Bow and Arrow.)

Housed in a "Tudor" style two floor pub and Restaurant, The Bow and Arrow fits the Yonge streetscape with its 1920s and '30s revival styles.

Inside a spacious lobby the first floor is divided into a large bar area with traditional pub style entertainment, and English snug in the front.

A comfortable pub, unlike some of the more contrived efforts at British tastes, they serve the Group's fine selection of Ontario brews and local wine, and foods. As fellow taster Gord Holder quipped, "If you can sell quality, why not?"

Why not indeed, especially if it is Ontario made!

Vital Statistics - The Brew

Menu - Beer: Ontario classics such as Wellington County, Conners, Creemore and many more.

Menu - Food: The portions are generous, as I didn't get here until 10 p.m., I was just ready for the "Cravings". We shared the chicken wings, properly done in their hot sauce, rather than served with a side order of sauce, and nachos supreme - salsa, cheese, sweet peppers and black olives. Additional menu items include steak and kidney pie, shepherd's pie, a cheese corner, and cheesecake with maple syrup. "The menu...includes...foods which were originally native to the Americas...tomatoes, potatoes, bell peppers, corn bread, maple syrup and chocolate." Along with regional specialties such as cheese.

Lunch for two with beer around $25.

Dinner for two with beer around $40.

Credit cards: All major credit cards.

Atmosphere: Comfortable, friendly, a perfect place to take the mother-in-law, especially if she is from the U.K.

P.S. Don't call the waitresses "honey" even in jest!

Parking: Take the subway to Davisville. Off Yonge Street parking.

Hours: Seven days a week.

Toronto, Ontario,
C'Est What? pub/Cafe

67 Front Street at 19 Church (there are two entrances).
Toronto, Ontario
M5E 1T8
416-867-9499

Rating: 🍺🍺🍺🍺 At last Toronto the Good has a brewpub that you can say "Forget your mother-in-law and take her daughter instead."

Owners: Timothy Broughton, George Milbrandt.

Brewmaster: Through a loophole in the law, Jay Turner of Select Brewing Services Inc., is allowed to prepare the mash and deliver the wort (unfermented beer) to the pub where the yeast is pitched (added). It is the act of pitching the yeast which starts fermentation, which creates alcohol, which defines the art of brewing in the bureaucratic mind. After delivering the wort, Timothy and George take over.

Founded: Pub opened February 13, 1988; started pitching wort (brewing) October 1, 1992.

Production Capacity: Because Select Brewing Services does the mashing, boiling and cooling the pubs "brewhouse" which essentially includes fermenting and storage tanks were installed for under $2,000, a far cry from the $100,000 plus usually spent on the average brewpub brewhouse. C'est What? is capable of fermenting a minimum of 110 litres twice a week.

(Logo courtesy, C'est What? Inc.)

Already the perfect reinforcer after a long train ride, and essential stop before you visit your relatives, the C'est What? has just got better. Already boasting the largest selection of Ontario micro draft, Timothy and partner George decided to start producing their own beer once they had hit the full range of available products from the small brewers "...to fill the gap and try as yet unbrewed beer styles."

In order to achieve their objective, the C'est What? was expanded through the basement west to Church St. Featuring Saturday afternoon Dixieland, the restaurant is now divided into two distinct bars. The old section is more for conversation, while the new part has entertainment and yet more beer.

Planning to expand with various specialty brews, plans call for a rotating selection of eight regulars, plus the efforts of a guest brewer.

Overall, while I found the styles adventurous, they were presented in a non challenging manner, acting as gentle introductions into the wide world of exotic brews. An excellent way to wean yourself off of the Big Brews. This is not a criticism, as any bar that serves Wellington County's Arkell with a handpump, knows their beer.

While I have not eaten here in sometime, I remember the food to be noteworthy, a glance at the menu should be enough to wet your appetite.

....

That's it for tonight, I am going for a beer.

Vital Statistics - The Brew

Some brews are full grain, while others are extract combinations. If you are lucky, a few cask conditioned and hand-pumped. The brews change on a regular basis, you would, however, be unlucky indeed, not to find one to your liking. And not to worry, with a vast selection of Ontario's best micro beers, you will never be disappointed.

Coffee Porter, 5%

Made with coffee beans, this winter warmer had a bitter espresso nose, a lightly roasted body, and a very warm and inviting aftertaste. Or put another way - a double espresso with a kick, -try it with a liqueur and you won't need to worry about sleeping. Eminently potable.

Stout, 5.5%

A light start, but the full roast flavour comes out in the aftertaste. A weak foam, not too sweet.

Menu - beer: 21 taps featuring the best products from Ontario's micros plus an impressive array of imports. They also plan to bottle their own wine, and have an interesting wine list.

Menu - food: Like so many restaurants, the menu is constantly changing.

One edition included: tabouleh, Greek salad, falafel, copi, souvlaki, vegetarian lasagna, shepherd's pie, curry, pasta, apple pie, mud pie, and "sex in a pan" chocolate mousse layered with cream cheese and whipped cream on a graham crumb base.

For the more adventurous there were spring rolls, yam frites, calarmari dip, brie fritters, Dijon chicken, etc. etc.

Lunch for two with beer around $30. You could do it for less, but then you would have to miss something.

Dinner for two with beer around $60.

Credit cards accepted.

Atmosphere:Basement bistro, Toronto's version of Montreal's La Cervoise. Great beer, food, and jazz with lots of little private nooks, gamestables (I mean scrabble, not pool), and people eating sofas. The living room I always wanted. There is a minimum table charge after 8 p.m.

Parking: Take the TTC, there is street parking if you are bringing a designated driver.

Hours: Weekdays from 11:30, weekends 2 p.m.

Toronto, Ontario,

DENISONS' BREWING Company Restaurant + Conchy Joe's Oyster Bar + Growlers'

75 Victoria St., (take the Yonge Street subway and get off at Queen Street, go east one block to Victoria and then south).

Toronto, Ontario, M5C 2B1

Denisons: 416-360-5877;
Conchy Joe's:416-360-0774;
Growlers':
416-360-5836;

Rating: 🍺🍺🍺🍺 (A brewery that serves "great food" rather than "restaurant that makes beer".)

Manager: Len Little/Ed Kusins.

Brewmaster: Michael Hancock, formerly with Molsons, trained Siebel Institute of Technology, Chicago (Brewing School).

Founded: Fall 1989.

Production Capacity: A traditional tower, full grain brewhouse, built in Hungary and designed specially for a brewpub. Capacity - 2,000 hectolitres a year.

(Logos courtesy, Michael Hancock.)

Boasting Canada's most impressive brewpub brewhouse, the gleaming copper, three storey Hungarian built facility is front and centre at this restaurant brewing complex. Located in two retrofitted historic buildings, the brewery serves as the heart of the establishment with its shinning copper fittings, carrying fresh brew directly from the aging tanks to the various bars and eager mugs. And all of this effort is worthwhile, not only is the food very good, the beer is little short of perfection. You will simply have to go to Europe to enjoy anything more authentic. If you visit during the summer be sure to order the Wheat Beer, at other times go no further than the unfiltered, dark "Royal Dunkel" lager. And if you can't decide what to choose from the menu, try the Conch Chowder at Conchy Joe's.

As nosy as always, I asked the often times outspoken Michael Hancock, where the idea for this brewpub came from? He said that all of the partners were business people and brewers, not restaurateurs, with a bias towards brewing.

This meant they wanted to create a brewery that served "great food", rather than a "restaurant that happened to make beer."

How more European can you get?

It sounds as if Toronto's brewpubs have come of age.

Vital Statistics - The Brew

Depending on the season 80 - 95% of sales housebrew.

Brewmaster Michael Hancock told me when I asked him what his brewing philosophy was that he was "Trying to make beer in the traditional manner; a Continental style lager, with a well defined taste, that above all else was balanced and hence drinkable." Unlike some brewpub brewers he is less interested in experimenting with wild recipes, such as raspberry beers, in favour of brewing consistently palatable brews.

Once again Michael tells his employees that "All our beers are lagers (bottom fermented), except wheat beer which is top fermented. Made with a selection of Canadian, British, American and Belgian malts; top quality whole flower German hops and carbon purified water. Our yeasts come directly from a Bavarian brewery. No other ingredients are used." He continues all the beers are "naturally carbonated". "An unusual feature is that all our beers are served unfiltered, the exception being Growlers' Lager and Spezial (seasonal), which have filtered versions available. This is quite normal in Germany where small craft breweries often do all of their on-premises business as unfiltered beer. The yeast and proteins remaining naturally in suspension provide great taste and help maintain the freshness of the beer."

Royal Dunkel, lager, 4.9% unfiltered
This beer redefines the taste of lager. A dark beer, it has a smooth, "mild/chocolaty" taste. The "flagship" brand adapted from the recipe of partner Prinz Luitpold's "Konig Ludwig Dunkel".

Growler's Lager, 4.7%, "cold-filtered" and always has been.
According to Michael this is "A Pilsner style lager, a little less heavily hopped than central European styles. Pale, clean delicate, with a very pleasant aftertaste (as opposed to NO aftertaste).

Growler's, Lager, 4.7%, unfiltered.

The beer foam leads the way to a fruity, well balanced chewable-malty palate, and lightly tart aftertaste.

Seasonal brews include a 6.5% unfiltered bock, a 5.7% unfiltered wheat, a 5.4% Spezial Oktoberfest lager, and a reddish copper, 5.4% Marzen lager from October to January.

Menu - beer: With all of these finely crafted products the selection of other brews is restricted to the "also rans".

Menu - food: With three restaurants I could spend the next several pages describing the food. Generally speaking, Growler's is the most affordable with Happy Hour and after eight, prices - it includes "a mound of baby fried calamari", squid stuffed with hot Italian sausage and onions, satay, chili and nachos, bratwurst, chicken wings, salads, pizzas, and pasta.

Conchy Joe's Raw & Nude Oyster Bar is a little more expensive and serves wonderful tiger shrimps, clams, terrific spicy conch chowder with sherry, grilled Caribbean Grouper, jerk chicken sandwich, burgers and of course oysters and clams.

Denison's is more formal and accordingly more costly, offering such appetizers as braised oxtails in old Italian manner, bamboo steamed escargot purses, pasta - spinach gnocchi, roasted boar round steak, grilled Yellow Fin Tuna, you get the idea. (I have to stop now and make supper).

Daily evening specials ranging from Roast Bromelake Duck on Thursday to Mixed Grill for two including Quail, chicken, filet of beef pancetta etc. etc. on Saturday.

Lunch for two with beer (Conchy Joe's as it is the median) under $30.

Dinner for two with beer at Growler's Happy Hour 3 p.m. to 8 p.m. under $25 to over $50 at Denison's. As for Conchy Joe's, oyster bars are my downfall - half dozen $8.99, clams half dozen $4.29 to $5.99.

Credit cards accepted.

Atmosphere: A brewhouse pub, in the basement and airy, contemporary, comfortable restaurant at street level. From casual to more formal, with the shinning brewing copper front and centre.

Parking: Metered street and parking lots or take the subway.

Open every day but Sundays.

Toronto, Ontario,
The Feathers

962 Kingston Road,
Toronto, Ontario, M4E 1S7
416-694-0443

Rating: 🍺🍺🍺 - Even Kingston Road's streetscape suggests that this is the local "high street pub" in the British tradition.

Proprietor: Ian Innes
Founded: 1981.

(Logo courtesy, Ian Innes.)

The first pub in Ontario, to pull cask-conditioned ale when Wellington County first introduced it, The Feathers was Toronto's first authentic pub. While they no longer carry Wellington County, they are proud that they don't stock Labatt's or Molsons and only dispense imports and a selection of Ontario's micros from their 14 draft taps.

Opened in the spring of 1981, in Toronto's Eastend Beach District, inundated with transplanted Brits, Scots, Welsh and Irish - you will hear as much of the Queen's English spoken here, as in any pub in Britain.

The dream of Edinburgh Scotsman, Ian Innes, the pub takes its name from The Feathers Hotel in Ludlow, Shropshire. A 17th century luxury hotel, which I had the pleasure of dining at several years ago. While Ian's Feathers does not offer wild boar, or schooners of Sherry (double-rations), the LLBO probably wouldn't allow it; I can only second Terry Culbert's comments, "The Feathers is a neighborhood pub where conversation and friendship is important and where entertainment and music definitely aren't the focal point".

A Victorian style pub, the interior is broken by a 17' mahogany standup bar, with the drinking mainly carried out in the front and the dining in the rear. In true British pub form, however, if you wanted to do the opposite, you could.

While I had already eaten rather well the Sunday I visited, I couldn't resist the thick, delicious chicken and leek soup, and ploughman's lunch, served the way it is supposed to be with real chutney and without meat. Designated as "Lighter Fare" the combination was enough to hold me until Monday at noon.

And when the inevitable comes, and nature calls, your trip back to the necessary is highlighted by a rotating collection of photographs by photo-journalist Terry Culbert, offering his "unique view" of "the British way of life". You might know Terry for his features on Global News. Intrigued with the unusual and noteworthy, Terry, you won't be surprised to learn is also a silent partner in the pub.

If you can't afford to fly to England, are homesick, or just want to see and feel what a real British pub is like, you need go no further than The Feathers.

Vital Statistics - The Brew

Feather's Lager, 5% Contract brewed by Algonquin.
A lightly hopped, well balanced, slightly fruity lager. Insiders tell me it is Algonquin's Bruce County Lager recipe. Whatever it is, if you can resist the other products, it is a tolerable lager.

Menu - Beer: They might have bottled beer, I don't know, but the micros are -Creemore, Conners' Special Draft, Publican's Best Bitter, Algonquin Ale, Lager and Formosa; also Guinness, Smithwicks, Tartan, Double Diamond...

Menu - Food: Peameal on a Kaiser, Cornish Pastie, Scotch Egg and Salad, Toad in the Hole, Steak and Kidney Pie, Bangers and Mash, Steak and Mushroom Pie, Welsh Trout and of course Roast Beef and Yorkshire Pudding. And who said Anglo-Canadians don't have any ethnic foods?

Lunch for two with beer under $25.

Dinner for two with beer around $40.

Credit cards accepted.

Atmosphere: "the high street pub".

Parking: You could take the streetcar, or there is ample on street parking.

Open seven days a week.

Toronto, Ontario,
Granite Brewery,

245 Eglinton Ave. E.,
Toronto, Ontario, M4P 3B7
416-322-0723

Rating: 🍺🍺🍺🍺 (The brewpub where the brewer's drink.)

Owners: Ron and Kevin Keefe.

Brewmaster: Ron Keefe trained by Alan Pugsley at the Wildgoose Brewery in
    Maryland and by brother Kevin who learned his art at the Ringwood
    Brewery in England.

Founded: 1991.

Production Capacity: 1,400 hectolitres (three brews a week). Half a million
    dollars was spent to convert a six month old Yuppie bar into a perfect
    brewpub. Purchasing a $100,000 brewery from Moncton's Fat Tuesday's,
    this is a traditional full grain English brewery with open top, copper clad
    fermenters, that give the wort plenty of oxygen to grow into some of
    Ontario's best ales.

*(Logo courtesy, Ron Keefe,
Granite Brewery.)*

When the Keefe brothers open a brewpub they suffer no compromises. Opening the first Granite in 1985 in Halifax, Kevin Keefe gained world attention when beer guru Michael Jackson gave their Peculiar and Bitter the nod.

Opening in Toronto's trendy Englinton East brewpub strip, they have turned a former "meat market" into the pub the brewer's drink at.

Maintaining their Maritime connections, Moosehead was launched in Ontario from their taps. And on occasion they host special events, but promise never to stage a karaoke night.

With a bar, "library lounge" and back dining room overlooking the brewery and centred around a fireplace, I placed myself squarely before the hearth with appetite and thirst on call to do this review. I was not disappointed. While I enjoyed an extremely flavourful Ratatouille, my companion ate his way through a pound of fresh steamed garlic mussels, accompanied by a quantity of incredibly well made beer. Call it age if you like, but neither of us got around to dessert or even to the entrées being well satisfied with the so called appetizers.

Dessert for me at least was a non issue anyways after one sip of the liquid "chocolate mousse" or cask conditioned Stout.

If you can only go to one brewpub in Toronto - visit the Granite.

Vital Statistics - The Brew

Ingredients. Using a 100 year old yeast strain from the Ringwood Brewery in England the Keefes describe their ales.

"The Granite Brewery uses wholly natural ingredients in its brewing process. These ingredients include Canadian two row barley malt from Western Canada, caramel malt which provides flavour and colour and black malt (from England) which yields additional colour. Crushed Canadian wheat flour is used for head retention. (Not all traditional beers adhere to the Reinheitsgebot). Our beers are all grain brews, without adjuncts such as rice or corn. Hops are added during the brewing process to add bittering and aroma characteristics. We use hops in a concentrated pellet form from Washington State. The two hop varieties we use are called Fuggles and Cascade hops. The Granite's ales are REAL ALE, meaning all natural ingredients are used as described above. It is not run through a mechanical filter. Isinglass finings are added during the conditioning state to clear the beer. A centuries old method of filtering, Isinglass finings are obtained from the Sturgeon fish. Positively charged they react with the negatively charged yeast cells to form "flocs" which settle to the bottom of the vessel.

Since REAL ALE requires hard water, gypsum is added during the mashing process to achieve this."

Best Bitter, 4.5%

With a creamy head, full hop nose from the Yakima finishing hops, yeasty - apple flavoured mouth, fresh and full balanced body, this well finished beer with a pleasing aftertaste is so refreshing it demands another.

Peculiar, 5.6%

Modelled from North Yorkshire's Old Peculiar known affectionately as "lunatic broth" this beer is nothing less than a liquid Cadbury bar. Smooth and chocolaty, with a long lingering caramel malt aftertaste and finish.

Dessert in a bottle.

Keefe's Irish Stout, 4%

Stout should have a good firm foam, this Cask conditioned brew not only has a terrific froth, but delivers a delightfully complex mouth starting with chocolate malt, followed by roasted malt and cut with a light bitterness. Superb.

Dry Hopped Best, Bitter

I missed this elixir, but "Toronto Star" beer writer Steve Beaumont considers it to be the Brewpub Beer of 1992.

Menu - Beer: If you insist they also offer various domestic drafts and Canadian and imported bottled products along with lesser potables such as spirits and wine.

If you are adventurous you might like to try the beer blends; Amber and Tan: Best Bitter and Peculiar: Black and Tan: Best Bitter and Stout, etc.

Menu - Food: Reasonably priced, carefully prepared food which ranges from fish and chips in beer batter to Raspberry curry chicken, to steak and kidney pastie. Soups include beef and beer stew, seafood chowder and soup of the day; salads, and of course desserts such as cheesecake of the day.

Lunch for two with beer around $25.

Dinner for two with beer under $45.

Credit cards: All major credit cards.

Atmosphere: Comfortable home-like setting, ideal for long dinners and conversation. The music is not too loud, a summer outdoor patio.

Parking: You can easily take the subway to Eglinton and then walk, or take advantage of the free parking lot next to the pub.

Souvenirs are available.

Hours: Seven days a week.

Toronto, Ontario,
Jame's Gate Pub

1661 Bloor St. West, (exit Kipling Subway Station)

Toronto, Ontario,

416-530-4034

Rating: I didn't have time to rate, but they weren't the slightest bit interested in assisting, and probably don't need it, as they are already serving a capacity house.

Owner: Robert Costello

Brewmaster: Robert Costello

Founded: Opened October 1989; brewing November 1990.

Production Capacity: Custom-made malt extract brewery located "somewhere in Mississauga". Produced 2,000 hectolitres of Chestnut Ale in 1992; Brick make their light lager. With demand exceeding capacity, plans for expansion are in the works.

Secretive about the whole operation, or perhaps bemused, publican Robert Costello started brewing when provincial regulations were altered to permit brewpubs to brew off premises. A self-trained brewer, from a family of Irish brewers, distillers and pub owners Costello has taken part of the name of the famous Dublin Guinness Brewery, to create an Irish pub complete down to the Saturday night string band.

Just seating 22, the Jame's Gate is only open in the evening when the seats are quickly filled with regulars. Next door Costello operates Whelan's Gate, a full service restaurant.

Vital Statistics - The Brew

> *Light Lager*
> Brewed by Brick
> *Chestnut Ale*
> British style malt extract.

Beer - menu: No domestic brands, but Beamish, Guinness, Murphy's and Harp on tap. It would be worth a visit just to drink these three stouts side by side.

Atmosphere: Irish pub.
Hours: Evenings only, call ahead.

Toronto, Ontario,
Quinn's Brewpub

949 Danforth Ave., (on the subway line)
Toronto, Ontario, M4J 1L9
416-466-2007

Rating: 🍺🍺 (Not uptown, and proud of it!)
Owner: Mike Quinn
Brewmaster: "Mr. Brew" trained publican Mike Quinn.
Founded: Started brewing December 1991, open since 1981.
Production capacity: "Mr. Brew" (see Setting Up) furnishes the wort, Mike pitches the yeast. Only needing refrigeration fermenting and conditioning tanks, the brewpub opened with approximately $20,000 worth of equipment. Mike can brew 700 litres every two weeks.
Full grain capabilities, German yeasts.

FINE ALES · CASUAL DINING

(Logo courtesy, Quinns Brewpub)

Occupying the old Stafford Hotel and Tavern opened in 1938, when Mike Quinn, a former newspaper distributor and his brothers tookover they wanted to create a "Canadian Pub", reflecting both English and American influences. Divided into two floors, Quinn's is a community pub attracting younger people with Country and Western and pool tables downstairs and the more sedate crowd upstairs with good food, a fireplace, an old rocker for entertainment and 16 taps perched on a long 1865 bar populated with 10 carved wooden faces made for a retired merchant sailor from Buffalo. Best described as a "Cheers" style bar boasting bartenders with over 9 years experience, the second floor has a warm atmosphere which is suitable for families along with just about everyone else from the neighbourhood. Definitely not "downtown" the price for a pint may be amongst the lowest in Metro.

Always favouring draft over bottled beer because the additives bothered him, Mike started out in 1981 with six taps, four more than most taverns bothered with then.

Eventually expanding his beer selection Toby became on of his most popular brands. Mike then decided to start "pitching" his wort to provide a competitively priced alternative to domestic beer. It was also a novelty. Enjoying beer himself, Mike wanted to produce a natural beer that the majority of customers would enjoy. Willing to experiment and accept the verdict of his clientele, Mike hit upon his dark lager by accident, when he asked for a recipe with a little more character. The result was a product his customers enjoyed to the detriment of Toby.

For the less adventurous he developed a regular European style lager.

For the future he is planning to produce small batches of such products as wheat beer, which he describes as "fabulous", on a rotational basis.

Overall Mike is looking to the afterhours Country market with non-alcoholic brews.

Vital Statistics - The Brew

Dry lager, 5%

A reddish amber brew made without chemical additives.

(40 - 45% rice in the recipe.)

Dark lager, 5%

A rocky head, with a malty, chewable palate.

Menu - beer: Draft - Wellington County Ale, Algonquin Amber, Creemore, Conners' Best Bitter, Sleeman's lager, Moosehead, Toby, Guinness etc. The regular bottles and limited imports. Liquor, and special coffees.

Menu - food: Lunch specials, large plates of bar style Italian, Mexican and Canadian foods. Perhaps the most awe inspiring item on the menu is the "All Star Team" featuring wings, garlic bread, cheese fingers, shrimp, onion rings, potato skins and veggies. Weekend breakfast special - omelettes.

Lunch for two with beer around $20.

Dinner for two with beer around $30.

Atmosphere: If you remember the old television show the "Pig and Whistle" you know the upstairs lounge and restaurant. Comfortable.

Parking: Off the Danforth, but take the subway.

Hours: Seven days a week from 11 a.m.

Toronto, Ontario,

Rotterdam Brewing Company

600 King St. West, (east of Bathurst)

Toronto, Ontario, M5V 1M3

416-868-6882; FAX: 416-977-5214

Rating: You let me know what you think of the world's largest brewpub! (Forget your car, and take the subway to the King Street West streetcar line.)

President: Roel Bramer

Brewmaster: Joel Manning

Founded: 1988

Production Capacity: Continental full grain mash system, the world's biggest brewpub.

Proudly displaying 21 copper kettles, brewing full grain beer, offering over 200 different bottled beers from around the world, plus 28 different drafts, the

Rotterdam, housed in a century-old warehouse, is the world's biggest brewpub, and an obvious destination.

Providing Sunday brewery tours with a buffet lunch, the emphasis is on beer. Similar to its prototype, the Amsterdam, this brewpub has its own bakery and offers meals cooked with beer, along with other continental cuisine.

Rather than spoil the surprise that awaits you, I am going to let you judge the Rotterdam for yourself, and invite you to write to me at the address at the back of the book with your opinions about the world's largest brewpub.

Vital Statistics - The Brew

Scotch Ale

Lager

Pilsener

Various specialty beers such as Kriek, Bock, Oktoberfest and strong winter ale.
Lunch for two with beer under $30.

Dinner for two with beer around $45.

Sunday buffet brunch and tours. Beer tastings. (Daily samplings in common with many brewpubs.)

Credit cards accepted.
Atmosphere: Fieldstone cellar and long bar. Tree lined outdoor patio for the summer.

Parking: Metred on the street, take the streetcar.

See Toronto's Amsterdam for the pub's sister.

Toronto, Ontario,
Rodney's Oyster House

209 Adelaide St. East,   *Mailing:*

Toronto, Ontario,   Box 73, Toronto's First Post Office,
416-363-8105   260 Adelaide St. East,

FAX: 416-363-6638   Toronto, Ontario, M5A 1N1

Rating: 🍺🍺🍺
Owner: Rodney Clark
Manager: Jan Kis
Founded: 1988.

Oysters and beer go together like champagne and strawberries.

(Logo courtesy, Rodney Clark.)

Before prohibition huge barrels of chilled raw oysters graced most fashionable drinking emporiums. Either eaten straight off the half shell, or marinated in a *mug of beer* to allow little bubbles to form on the soft skin of the oyster, as a prelude to its final destination at the bottom of a willing gullet, fresh oysters are a far more agreeable appetizer than the deep fried "legally acceptable" snacks offered at most pubs.

Rodney's oysters, however, go beyond the mere snack, and become meals in the image of a traditional oyster house.

Offering chowder, oyster, salmon, scallops, chicken paté, salads, quahaugs, periwinkles, Jamaican spiced shrimp and coconut in curry rice, to list a few of the delicacies on the menu the afternoon I visited, the emphasis is obviously on freshness. To accompany each order Rodney's has a tray of eight hot spices on each table, with fifteen additional ones behind the bar as backup.

For the brave, or perhaps the foolish, the most impressive is Grace Noel's grenadine pepper mixture aptly named "Back From Hell". The hottest sauce I have ever tangled with, a pinhead full is enough for most. Made on the premises, this and other sauces can be purchased at the bar.

To douse the flames in your throat, Rodney's sells both Hart Amber Ale, and Conner's Best Bitter. Two effective extinguishers. Contrary to common North American lore, the sweet syrup beers don't quench your thirst after a flamethrowing exercise, half as well as the English style bitters. Just look at what the Indians serve in any of the many curry houses springing up across Ontario to reinforce this point. While the micro list was small it included Upper Canada Light, Niagara's Gritstone Ale, and Eisbock, and Sleeman's. (And wine if you must.)

To my mind the mark of a good restaurant is one that knows what it does well, as well as one that knows what it doesn't do well.

When we asked for coffee, the waiter said their's was fine, but if we wanted something really special to go up the street to a fine coffee bar. Now that's class.

Lunch for two with beer around $30. (Half orders welcome.)

Dinner for two with beer around $50.

Credit cards accepted.

Atmosphere: Fresh fish! Similar to a fish market cafe without some of the unpleasant odours.

Hours: Monday to Saturday. Closed Sundays.

Toronto, Ontario,

Spruce Goose Brewing Company

130 Eglinton Ave. E.,
Toronto, Ontario, M4P 2X9
416-485-4121

Rating: Their slogan says it all 'Have you been Goosed today?''
Brewmaster: Charles MacLean
Founded: 1991.
Production Capacity: Malt extract.

With a model of billionaire Howard Hughes' aviation dinosaur, the Spruce Goose hovering over the basement dance floor, from the ceiling of a first floor observation deck - the Spruce Goose is an untamed hormone haven. Beating out nondescript contemporary music to patrons more interested in ogling each other than anything else, a visit is a living statement that the generation gap is alive and well.

Served a 5.5% concoction of Goose Joose by a walking steroid, I thought I might enjoy the place more if it had remained Mother's Pizza.

Sorry I didn't obtain more details, but after two visits I lost heart. I suppose I am getting old!

Vital Statistics - The Brew
   Goose Joose Dry, 5.5%
Tastes like Molson Dry, and that's being polite.
   Goose Joose Ale
Brown with the cloying aroma of malt extract. I never got beyond smelling it
      before I gave up.
Atmosphere: Sophomore, meat market - fine if you are a loose hormone.
   Parking: Get off the Eglinton subway and walk east, on the north side.

Toronto, Ontario,
The Upper Canada Brewing Company

2 Atlantic Avenue,

Toronto, Ontario, M6K 1X8

416-534-9281; FAX: 416-534-6998

(downtown Toronto off King Street West, across from
the CNE, Dufferin Gate entrance, call for directions.)

President: Frank N. Heaps

Brewmaster: Dr. Richard Rench (Masterbrewer), Institute of Brewing
(Burton-on-Trent, 13 years), Ph.D. Birmingham. Doug Brewster, formerly
with Molson's, is the assistant.

Founded: June, 1984.

Production Capacity: Custom made brewhouse.
1984 - 7,000 hectolitres
1989   45,000 hectolitres
1991 - 75,000 hectolitres, making the brewery the third largest microbrewery in Canada, and Ontario, in the same year with 9.4% of the small
brewer's market.

*Upper Canada's new "designer"
labels. Almost all you ever wanted to
know about the brew is printed on a
back panel.*

*(Label courtesy, The Upper Canada
Brewing Company.)*

Europe's favourite Canadian beer, Upper Canada's products were the first
North American beers to win acceptance in West Germany, the Netherlands,
Belgium, and Luxembourg.

Tackling the image conscious, fizzy quaffing heart of the Canadian market head on with a distinct, flavourful, all natural, premium beer, brewed according to the strictures of the Bavarian Purity Act of 1516 - the brewery was the brainchild of former Toronto consultant Frank Heaps. Inspired by the success of Vancouver's Granville Island Brewery, and the growing demand for imported beers, Frank raised $3.5 million to convert an early 1900s Toronto warehouse into this brewery, retail/fashion boutique and reception centre.

Once the home of more than a dozen breweries, Upper Canada is now the city's only surviving brewery.

Believing "naively" that everybody would beat a path to his door once they discovered his beer and still hoping for 1% of the Ontario market, increased sales through strong marketing and the firm's connection with Corby Distillers has opened up international possibilities. Despite his success, Heaps often relates that he wouldn't ever want to relive that first year and a half. Quipping to a Toronto "Globe and Mail" reporter that "we probably bottle less (beer) than the big guys spill on their bottling floor,"the company's mission "...to produce all natural lagers and ales, without chemicals or other compromises, as good as the best in the world," is now paying off. "We are now in the black, the investors are happy, the bankers are more comfortable, and I can sleep at night. Things are looking up," related Heaps to the "Globe's" Barbara Aarsteinsen. To provide necessary capital and an international distribution network, Corby Distillers acquired 40% minority interest in the brewery in 1991.

The secret to Upper Canada's continuing success has been finely crafted beer made with spring water, Canadian barley, European and Canadian hops, and superbly trained brewers - coupled with a dedicated, persuasive, and innovative sales team. Through their efforts Upper Canada can now be found in its rightful home, in the licensed dining areas at historic Upper Canada Village near Morrisburg, Ontario.

Packaging his products in cases and with labels full of information about the beer, these essays sometimes take as long to read, as it does to enjoy a pint of the beer they are describing.

Upper Canada Brewing Co., deserves a special place in Ontario's micro-brewery industry because it led the way by breaking the ground for others to follow and return to the brewing traditions brought to Ontario by the German immigrants, and the beers enjoyed by United Empire Loyalists, the English and the Irish.

Upper Canada demonstrated that there is a market for honest premium beer, pure beer, beer brewed plain and simple with water, malt, yeast and hops.

Vital Statistics - The Brew

A Reinheitsgebot brewery, they proudly state that "All of our beers are made in strict conformance with the world's highest brewing standards - the Bavarian Purity Law of 1516. That is to say, they are made in small batches with only, water, malt, hops and yeast. As is common practice with the vast majority of beers, we will not use adjuncts, additives, chemicals or preservatives."

Adhering to the strict brewing laws followed in Germany, Upper Canada became the first North American brewer to be permitted to retail its beers in Germany. It should be pointed out, however, that most microbrewers avoid adjuncts and chemicals, and that the German brewing tradition is fine as it is, excludes the possibility of producing the very fine ales the Irish, English and Belgians are famous for. In other words, there is more than one way to brew a great beer.

Upper Canada also brews with untreated spring water from the Caledon Hills.

Various brews available in bottle and on tap.

Colonial Stout, 4.8%
Dedicated to Lieutenant-Governor John Graves Simcoe, who pleaded for the Loyalists to open a brewery in Upper Canada, to provide a wholesome alternative to American "drams", Simcoe as an officer would have favoured dark, full porters and stouts. Too light in the mouth for me, while pleasant it is more like a porter. Maybe its a summer stout!

Dark Ale, 5%
Once the most distinctive beer brewed in Ontario, the taste has been somewhat refined. It does, however, still retain its clean, traditional brown complexion, sweet, and thick blackstrap molasses - healthy - aroma, and assertive bittersweet taste. With a fruity, sweet, warm aftertaste, it is a brew you either like or don't like, and I enjoy it a lot.

Lager, 5%
As soon as you open this brilliant amber orange brew you are enveloped by the flowery nose from the Hallertau, Northern Brewer and Hersbrucker hops balanced with a hint of fruit. A tingly full round mouth, the "honey like sweetness" is concentrated with an assertive bitterness, leaving you with a warm, sweet, "burnt-orange" lingering aftertaste, that begs a second sip.

One of Ontario's leading micro lagers, it is the brewery's number one seller and was awarded a gold at the 1992 International Food, Wine and Beer Show in Toronto.

Light Lager, 4%
Reddish amber in colour, this beer looks right, is refreshing, and isn't unpleasant. And if you know what I generally think about Light beers, you will know that this means it is just fine.

Pale Ale, 4.8%
While I didn't have the opportunity to properly evaluate this brew before publication the executive of the CABA had this to say about it: "The aroma of Upper Canada Pale Ale...is malty, bready, fresh, and floral - definitely inviting. A pleasant flavour of Cascade hops comes through in the taste well balanced by a malt base, with a clean smack of bitterness in the finish. Although full of flavour, this ale was also dry and light bodied enough to enjoy through the evening."

Unlike other Upper Canada products which use only English hops, this brew uses North American Cluster for the boil, and Cascade in the finish. Fermentation is also done in traditional British flat-bottomed fermentors rather than the conical ones usually employed.

Point Nine, 0.9%

Brewed as a beer, Point Nine has an orange amber complexion, lightly hopped nose, well balanced body and does not possess that cloying malty taste associated with non-alcoholic brews.

Publican's Best Bitter, 4.8%

Too lightly hopped to be a typical best bitter, this orange ale, has a gentle aroma, foamy head, balanced body and slightly malty - bitter aftertaste.

Rebellion, 6% (malt liquor)

A brilliant gold body releases a long lasting whipped cream like head, that covers a rich fruity, apricot, malty, dusky slight vinous aroma, and leads to a complex chewy, malty bittersweet astringent mouth and warm puckering aftertaste.

A vibrant, young, rambunctious brew, this beer is not for the timid. A most ideal summer strong beer, it puts the lie to the notion that all malt liquors need to be malty and somewhat noxious to be "high alcohol".

True Bock, 6.5%

An exceptional beer by anyone's standards, this lager has a red mahogany body with a dense, thick, foamy, well laced head. The chocolaty, malty aroma, leads to an enticing candy-like toffee mouth, that can best be described as "adult candy". The sweet, fresh aftertaste grows to a pleasing bitterness, that makes you smack your lips with pleasure as the taste permeates every corner of your mouth.

Wheat, 4.3%

A German style summer "Weizen" lager, this beer is made with malted barley and wheat, rather than just barley alone. A bit too heavy for my tastes, it may be served with a slice of lemon, like Corona. Fortunately for Wheat, the lemon enhances the beer, while with Corona it replaces the beer!

They also produce private label lagers for Canadian Pacific Hotels in Ontario, the "R.M.S. Segwun", and brew Tsingchuen Lager under license.

Tours available by appointment.

Hospitality lounge.

Beer sold at the brewery along with a gift, sportswear and collectibles boutique.

Open on Sunday.

Available throughout most of Ontario.

Toronto, Ontario,
Vinefera Bar and Grill

150 Eglinton Ave. East,
Toronto, Ontario, M4P 1E8
416-487-9281

Rating: Undergoing a dramatic personality change, it is too early to comment on
it.

Owner: Shou Teng Lin

Brewmaster: Unknown at time of printing

Founded: 1992

Production Capacity: $100,000 Continental Malt Extract 5 Vessel, single brew
system, supplemented by an additional $50,000, the brew is now full
grain.

Vital Statistics - The Brew
German Style lager

(another may be added later)
In describing his lager Alan says,"The recipe
I have introduced falls somewhere
between the lighter Munich Helles and
the slightly darker Vienna Lager. The
malt is a blend of 160 kg of 2-row and
40 kg of darker Munich malt. A two
step infusion mash is used". Hops are
Northern Brewer and the rarer Spalt.
"The fermentation is carried out at
fairly cold temperatures, since the
abundant tank space in the brewery
allows both the fermentation and cold

(Logo courtesy, Vinefera Bar and Grill.)

aging to be done slowly for a smoother flavour. The finished product is a
light copper colour, with a rich perfumy aroma and full palate. The
aftertaste is a lingering hoppiness with spicy notes."

While I have tried the brew, it was served too cold, and Alan had not been
here long enough for me to provide an honest evaluation. I understand though,
that it is well hopped and has lots of aftertaste! Sounds promising.

Menu - food: Salads, appetizers - deep fried calamari, Martinique shrimps,
    spring rolls, grilled shrimp satays; burgers, pasta, entrées - sole Florentine,
    Oriental Chicken stirfry, veal Marsala.

Lunch for two with beer around $25.

Dinner for two with beer around $40.Credit cards: All major credit cards.

Atmosphere: Undergoing renovations at time of writing. Rotating specials
    throughout the week.

Parking: On Eglinton Ave. East, it is best to leave the car at home and take the
subway.

Open seven days a week.

Waterloo, Ontario
Brick Brewing Company Limited

181 King Street South,
Waterloo, Ontario, N2J 1P7
519-576-9100; FAX: 576-0470

President: Jim Brickman

Director of Marketing: Bill May

Brewmaster: Stephen Smith arrived after over 15 years in Quality Control at
    Labatt's to takeover the brewing operations with two others, in 1988.

Founded: First brew produced December, 1984. Ontario's first active micro-
    brewery, plans for this operation started in 1978. Costing $2.5 million
    dollars to brew that initial keg, Brick was the first Canadian micro to win
    a gold medal at the Monde Selection, in 1990. The brewery became a
    Public Corporation on December 12, 1986.

Production Capacity: Located in a renovated warehouse constructed in 1827, the
    brewhouse was purchased from Richard Morton DG of Burton-on-Trent,
    England, and now includes a chemical analysis lab.
Starting with 4,500 hl, the brewery topped 42,000 hl in 1991 placing it second
in the Canadian micro industry with 15.8% of the market.

Opened as Ontario's first microbrewery in the shadow of the Labatt's plant in
Waterloo, Brick is now the only brewery left in this brewing town. Growing
rapidly, the brewery now employs 47, but stands to expand again as a result of
the closure of Pacific Brewing Co. of St. Catharines, and a new deal to brew
Pacific Real Draft for British Columbia's International Potter Distilling the
owners of Granville Island Brewing, here in Ontario. As part of the agreement

(Logo courtesy, Brick Brewing Co. Ltd.)

Granville Island will brew under license one of Brick's products giving it exposure on the west coast.

To quote an obviously pleased Marie Peacock, assistant to Brick president Jim Brickman, "We were the first microbrewery in the east and they were the first in the west, which makes it kind of interesting that we are going to team up." Interesting indeed, it just shows that there is more than one way to skin the "interprovincial" barriers.

It was Jim Brickman's willingness to experiment that started the brewery in the first place. This winter I asked him why? He responded that he believed "...there was a market for a small specialty brewer, that produced something other than the "benchmark" products by Labatts and Molsons." He felt "not all beer should be the same." Originally believing that one brand would be enough he found that to be a successful local brewer and attain the necessary volume of sales that he had to start producing several beers.

Not competing with the major breweries, Jim believes that micros should remain small and regional, otherwise be prepared to merge. While he was not advocating this, he does feel that the trend is towards specialty beers that are "handcrafted" and aged naturally. Unwilling to be critical though, Jim was then quick to point out that "Overall Canada's large brewers have a terrific reputation." Still the "microbreweries as a group took more of the market share than the large brewers expected. While the large brewers' sales have fallen off nearly 10%, the small brewers have grown by 33%. The microbreweries have made an impact; now available across Ontario they are a distinct 'category'. They offer variety above and beyond the imports." Again reluctant to lampoon the majors, Jim continued "...brewing is a learning process," and he retains his "admiration for the quality of work done by the big brewers."

When asked about the way beer was sold in Ontario, Jim stated something most small brewers know. "The system needs changes, but has made growth possible because of its size and the fact that it is everywhere. All in all a good system." In other words while some beer enthusiasts may be critical of the Brewers Retail, it is a rare small brewer who wouldn't admit that they would not have survived without it.

Now that the brewery has been showing a profit for the last several years, it was probably not necessary to ask Jim if he would do it all over again , but I did anyways. He responded "Yes." That he was going "...to continue to make good beer with an eye for opportunities, while looking for reasonable growth without mistakes. I don't want to be the biggest microbrewery in Canada, but I do want to be the most profitable."

Vital Statistics - The Brew

All lagers, with the exception of Amber Dry and Red Baron, are made according to the strictures of the Reinheitsgebot. Brick was one of the first brewers in North America to use cold sterile filtration, and two years before Miller, using Millipore Filters. According to Jim Brickman who would ever "Hot filter beer?"

With all of the principal beer writers in Canada avowed ale men, the accomplishments of the lager brewers are sometimes overlooked. This is too bad because they make some truly outstanding beers as the following letter dated Brussels, 7.7.1992 from the "Monde Selection Institut International Pour Les Selections De La Qualite International Institute for Quality Selections' indicates:

Ladies and Gentlemen,

Our Standing Organizing Committee is pleased to inform you that your Company has been awarded the

Trophy of International High Quality

for having obtained a gold medal in 3 consecutive years.

We congratulate you and your Company and remain, Ladies and Gentlemen.

Very Sincerely yours,

George Debruyn,

Chairman.

The products were Brick Premium Lager Beer

A Gold Medal

Brick Red Baron Beer

A Grand Gold Medal

Amber Dry Beer

A Grand Gold Medal

Winning 10 Gold Medals in three years at this International Competition led Jim Brickman to say "This recognition is really what it's all about and that is to produce world class quality beers at International Standards. It also confirms our continual commitment to high quality standards and gives tremendous accreditation to our employees for their efforts. We are all very pleased with this confirmation".

And rightly so, the 1992 awards meant that "Brick Amber Dry and Red Baron both won a Grand Medal with a perfect score".

"The announcement received from the Organizing Committee stated that the awards were made according to the results of analysis and tests carried out by the Laboratory, and deliberation by the Selection Board panel of Judges."

Amber Dry, 5.5% also known as Rathskeller Dry at McMaster's Student Union, Fed Beer U. of Waterloo Student Federation.
Originally an experimental brew, it is now the brewery's leading brand.

> Brewed with carastan malt to give it the colour of "cognac", the brew includes some cornflakes. An anomaly, this dry has taste and sin of sins aftertaste!

Anniversary Bock, 6.5%
Seasonal, aged three months, buy it and hoard it when you see it.

> A testament to great beer, this tawny, full bodied bock gives off an enticing raspberry nose, covered by a tasty foam that leads to a full molasses mouth with an underlining taste of chocolate. The warm aftertaste and feeling of satisfaction this brew produces is exceptional.

Like most great bocks, every year is slightly different. It is made from a blend two row and roasted malt, and includes Hallertau and Yakima Cluster hops.

The Lagers
Just to see if there was an appreciable difference in the three lagers, I conducted a blind tasting and found that there was!

While all displayed good balance, the difference showed up in the nose where the Premium Lager had the most pronounced aroma, Red Baron some sweetness due to the corn, and Henninger a subtle flowery bouquet.

Premium Lager, 5%
A nicely balanced, all malt lager, typical of the best of the Canadian Premium lagers, and the one most people associate with what beer should be.

In short, a fine honey pine lager, with an assertive flowery aroma, derived from the Hallertau and Yakima Cluster hops, a cream foam, and a delicious malt start followed by a pleasant finishing bittering.

Red Baron, 5%
Flavoured with fewer hops than Premium, this is a well balanced, slightly sweet beer, that grows in enjoyment. A perfect hot summer's day beverage, especially for those that are less adventuresome, yet want a natural brew.

Henninger Kaiser Pilsner, 5%
Brewed under license for Henninger Brewery, Frankfurt.

> Acquired from the retreating Amstel facility in 1992, this brew increased the brewery's sales by 14%.

Containing a few more Hallertau and Yakima Cluster hops than Premium, this beer ranks with the best European, and makes it a waste of money to buy the fine, but often stale German imports from the LCBO. A light amber Reinheitsgebot lager, this pilsner has a whipped cream froth, a flowery nose with hints of malt that come through in the taste. Don't serve the beer too cold or in a frozen mug (in fact no beer should be served in a frozen mug, this abomination is only suitable for vodka) as the warm malty, nicely bittered taste grows in your stein to a pleasantly lingering aftertaste.

Waterloo Dark

On tap only in Waterloo Region. Not sampled.

Group tours may be arranged from Monday to Thursday with two month's notice. The hospitality lounge overlooks the brewkettles.

Brewery retail store and souvenir outlet.

Sold more or less throughout Ontario, and a participant in the Oktoberfest festivities, when they brew Premium Oktoberfest beer.

Ample free parking adjacent to the brewery.

Waterloo, Ontario
Huether Hotel - Lion Brewery and Museum

59 King St. North,
(use Princess Street entrance)

Waterloo, Ontario, N2L 2X2

519-886-3350

Rating: 🍺🍺🍺🍺

A must for all history fanatics. In the process of expansion they discovered the malt cellar lost for nearly a century. The building's Victorian facade and vaulted brewing cavern are designated under the Ontario Heritage Act.

Proprietors: Bernie and Sonia Adlys with sons Kelly and David.

Brewing: While everyone gives a hand, Kelly studied chemistry at Guelph University.

Founded: June 2, 1987 (the hotel has been dispensing and brewing beer on and off since 1842.)

Production Capacity: Starting out with a 33,000 Imperial gallons (2,555 kegs) Cask Brewing and Malt Extract System, they are planning to double the capacity in the near future to meet the demand; they have also started mixing English barley malt into their extract. They are hoping to bottle some of their beers for home consumption.

Evolving into a brewing complex the Adlys have also opened The Lion Beer Factory U-Brew next door.

(Logo courtesy, Huether Hotel - Lion Brewwry and Museum)

A museum that makes and sells its own beer and turns a profit. Heritage was never so rewarding! Seizing the opportunity to return a somewhat faded Victorian beauty to its former glory, the Adlys family have remodelled the old Kent Hotel, installed brewing coppers in the ancient brewing vaults, and restored the Huether Hotel to its rightful place as the home of good beer and food.

In 1842 William Rebscher established the first brewery and inn here. Fourteen years later Adam Huether (HEE-ter) took over and renamed it the Lion Brewery and Huether Hotel. Adam's son Christopher added a large single towered hotel complete with a Second Empire mansard roof and Victorian facade during the 1880s. At the turn of the century the property was sold to the Kuntz brewing family who used it for malt storage, and changed its name to Hotel Ewald. By 1930 restrictive government regulations closed down all brewing activity, and the building sold for $18,500. Five years later Albert Synder picked up the old hulk for $700, and renamed it the Kent.

John Adlys and Frank Dale acquired the business for $100,000 in 1953. Fire in 1969 destroyed part of the mansard roof and the tower. The erosion was not arrested until seven years later when John's son Bernie with his wife Sonia, along with their sons purchased the brewery and started restoration of the whole building, resulting in the Huether Hotel receiving Waterloo's 1984 Civic Improvement Award. This work finally led to the designation of the vaulted cavern and Victorian facade under the Ontario Heritage Act in 1988. In 1991, while expanding to the rear, they dug down into the ground to discover a lost 19th century malt cellar filled with bricks. It is now used for banquets.

In 1987, the Adlys started producing beer, and renamed the hotel the "Huether".

Exhibiting the most complete public collection of beer memorabilia, photographs, press clippings, and artifacts from the brewpub's storied past, the Huether is a must for all beer enthusiasts. Just the site of the working brewery in the old cavern is enough to send shivers of envy down every homebrewer's spine. The large beer hall adjoining the brewery, is also the closest you will get to Germany this side of the Atlantic. As for the all natural beer, you will not be disappointed. Neither will you go away hungry after sampling some of the food from the wide array of "deli" fare. The ideal location for a large special gathering, you can't go wrong in following the Adlys invitation to "tap into" the area's heritage and see what's "brewing" while enjoying their family oriented hospitality.

The Heuther Hotel is a large facility with seating for 700. To enter the brewpub, use the side door off Princess Street. Altogether the building includes a billiard hall, an old fashioned - Legion style bar on the first floor along with a karoake turned peeler bar on occasion. Don't worry this is all on the first floor, the cellar brewpub is worlds apart, as the numerous children and families attest.

And what about the future? With work underway to double the brewery's capacity, the successful U-Brew and plans to retail their products in bottles, the Huether might just become the first brewpub to become a microbrewery when and if the laws change.

Let's hope they do!

And for the curious, the second floor at the rear of the building is rented to an independent movie theatre - "The Princess".

Vital Statistics - The Brew

Beers aged two to three weeks.

Premium Lager, 5.6%

"The Globe and Mail's" Report on Business column for January 12, 1993 reported:

"Suds Watch In the Article 'My 101 Favourite Beers' from the latest issue of All About Beer magazine, James D. Robertson remembers 3,692 brews from around the world on which he has compiled notes -and the 1,000 or so others he has only tasted. The author explaining that he has 'a remarkable sensory memory' enabling him to remember exactly how a particular beer smells and tastes has three Canadian selections: 'One of my all-time favourites, O'Brunswick Malt Liquor from Bavarian Specialties of Dieppe, N.B., is no longer available sine the brewery closed. Still, there is Island Bock from Granville of Vancouver and Huether's Premium Lager from the Huether Hotel...'" Popular with critics and the general public alike the Adlys have a difficult time keeping this elixir in stock, and it was unfortunately not available when I arrived with my empty mug.

Adlys' Ale, 5%

A traditional 1950s, honey pine, Legion Hall style Canadian Ale. A creamy head, with a malty nose and a hint of hops.

English Ale, 5%

This dark almost walnut hued ale possesses a malty mouth. Hops are scarce, yet it is not too sweet, there is a dryish aftertaste.

Lion Lager, 5%

A mainstream, clean gold amber, lightly hopped beer with a creamy head, and a dryish mouth.

Lion Lite Lager

Did not taste.

Lion Dry
Did not taste.

Black and Tan, 5%
Half Adlys' and half English ale, the combination creates a drink with an incredibly fruity nose, reminiscent of black currants. With a sweetish almost cherry-like aftertaste, the combination tastes like a quality malt liquor, leaning towards a barley wine. Without trying the Premium Lager I would recommend going for this one alone.

Menu - beer: With such a wealth of local beer, they can be forgiven for only offering other Canadian brands. There is a full compliment of cocktails, liquors, liqueurs, coolers and even some wine.

Menu - food: Perogies, panzerottis, fried shrimp, wings, nachos, rolled ribs, schnitzel and potato skins, served the only way they know how to in Waterloo, in huge portions. If you must stick to something slimming, they even offer a "Dieter's Delight" salad. Also typical pub side orders of pickled eggs and pickles. A wide selection of sandwiches, and non-alcoholic beverages for the driver.

Free cake for your special party.

Lunch for two including beer under $20.

Dinner for two including beer under $25.

Credit cards accepted.

Atmosphere: A family filled pub, probably Canada's most authentic beer hall. The closest you will come to a Rathskeller this side of the Atlantic.

Group tours and collectibles are available.

Parking: Metred, ample street.

Open seven days a week.

Windsor, Ontario
Charly's Brewpub

(Timeout Brewing Co.)
4715 Tecumseh Road East,
Windsor, Ontario, N8T 1B6
519-945-5512

Rating: It's impossible to rate this place, if you took your mother-in-law here you would probably be looking for a new wife.

Owner: Dave Copper

Founded: December 1987.

Production Capacity: 500 barrels.

Continental Breweries Inc., Malt Extract System.

Billed as "The Best Lunch Bucket in Canada", the slogan says it all. The closest brewpub to a biker's bar in Canada.

Vital Statistics - The Brew
TimeOut Lager, 5.2%
You might be better to stick to the name brands.

Menu - food: Bar snacks.

Credit Cards: No.

Atmosphere: Basic Ontario country/western tavern.
Parking: Large free adjacent parking lot.

CHAPTER 5

Quebec

Chambly, Quebec
Unibroue Inc.

2032 Bourgogne,
Chambly, Quebec, J3L 1Z4
514-447-6650;
FAX 514-658-2838. (Quebec 418-831-4348)

President: André Dion

Vice-President: Robert Charlebois (yes he is the vocalist.)

Brewmaster: Gino Van Thiegem from Louvain University Belgium, trained at Riva Brewery Belgium (producers of white beer, wheat ales). There are two additional brewers.

Founded: June 1986 as Massawippi Brewing in Lennoxville, the firm became known for a short while as Broubec Inc. and then Unibroue, launching its first beer in February 1992. The brewery has now been moved to Chambly to be closer to the Montreal and Quebec City markets.

Production Capacity: 30,000 hl

(Label courtesy, Unibroue Inc.)

Quebec's first microbrewery has led the way again, this time in North America, brewing the first commercially produced Belgium white and abbey ales in living memory. Controlling interest of the old Massawippi plant was acquired by André Dion in January 1991. Former president of Rona-Dismat Inc., Dion retired in 1990 at age 49, to work for himself. Approached by the Association of Quebec microbrewers to organise their distribution system, Dion ended up running a brewery to be able to part of the day-to-day operation of his own business. He also believed that a microbrewery that made a distinct European style product, was a sound investment, after studying the 36% rise in the growth of imported beers in Quebec between 1987 and 1990, and the stagnation of the mainstream market. He renamed the firm Unibroue, to underline his desire to one day organise the microbreweries. Holding a 70% interest in the firm, Dion teamed up with 60s PQuiste performer Robert Charlebois through Radico, obtaining 20% of "the action" for $280,000. Well aware of Charlebois' fame, the duo even considered naming their first brew "La Charlebois", but better business sense prevailed, according to Robert who told "Montreal Gazette" reporter Alan Hustak that "...I didn't want that (his name). That might have been too risky." Planning to change people's tastes Charlebois continued, that one day they were "Gonna be bigger in Quebec then Molson." And still retaining his "revolutionary" charm, Charlebois coined the company's slogan "N'en prends pas quand tu conduis, même une Blanche de Chambly." Very roughly translated as, "Don't follow when you can find your own - Blanche de Chambly."

Rather than produce another British or German taste alike, in October of 1991, Dion signed a "technology agreement" with Belgium's Riva Brewery to learn the secrets, the appreciation and techniques of brewing a traditional white (wheat) beer. With an investment of $1.5 million, Blanche de Chambly was launched in February of 1992. In October of 1992 La Maudite, the first 8% beer to be legally brewed in Quebec since Maurice Duplessis' government restricted the sale of beer in corner stores to 6.2% was introduced. With plans to spread across Canada once interprovincial barriers come down, beer aficionados can only hope that this happens soon.

VITAL STATISTICS - THE BREW

While they initially produced the old Massawippi products, these will be phased out for the more distinctive bottle conditioned Belgium style brews.

Blanche de Chambly, 5% Bottle

You have to try it, if you are not familiar with Belgium style beers. Be prepared for something different, be prepared for taste, and yeast in the bottle. Bottle conditioned, the brew undergoes a secondary fermentation in the bottle allowing for a thick, rich head, and an extended shelf life. As the brewery explains "...you can determine the number of gulps taken to empty your glass by counting the number of white rings (Belgium lace) left by the fine bubbles of foam on the side of the glass. Any unwanted oxygen captured inside the bottle is quickly consumed by the action of the fermentation...in terms of life expectancy (the beer) can be kept for years rather than months." In fact it will probably improve if kept! Made over a two month period, the beer is brewed with barley malt, wheat and hops - along with "a few natural spices."

Draft

And if you liked it from the bottle, try it on tap-for something beer drinkers
might have enjoyed in Medieval Europe.

As for the taste, on tap, it was cider like, with an incredible vinous nose. I am
going to leave this one to you, except to say watch out for the yeast. If you
aren't used to drinking it, it might be best not to, as it can start to gurgle away in
your stomach.

White Beer

As you can tell from the above, not all good beers are brewed or were brewed
with barley malt, yeast, hops and water, as the Germans would have us
think. Hops for example are relatively new to the brewing world, only
gaining wide acceptance sometime around 1400. Before and after this,
beer could be seasoned with juniper berries, coriander and curaco to
mention some of the more common additives. As for white beer, it is an
ale made with raw wheat and oats, and barley malt, flavoured with curaco
orange peels, coriander and Michael Jackson speculates "cumin" seeds.
Pale and fruity, it is produced in Flanders. The ideal dessert beer!

La Maudite, 8%

Simply heavenly, or should I say devilish? A full tasting traditional strong beer.
This beer has a cherry cloak, unbelievable foam, and spicy, yeasty nose
underlined by cloves. Full bodied, warm, meaty, sweetish mouth and a
flavour that just doesn't let up. Watch out it goes down very fast. So good,
I compared it with Belgium's famous Duvel. I found it to be more
aggressive, and with a similar yeasty nose, but not as complex, or light in
colour. Modelled after Belgium's Lucifer, this is a high alcohol beer
"with an attitude." This "attitude" apparently starts with the label, that
has upset more than one Quebec traditionalist. According to the legend of
the "Chasse-galerie" (which varies), a party of voyageurs canoeing from
the Lake Athabaska area, were complaining that they would never reach
home before the fall freeze-up. The devil heard, and offered them this
challenge. If they could keep quiet until safely in their beds in Montreal,
he would fly them and their canoe home, and that would be the end of it.
But, if they uttered a sound, he would take their souls. Banking on the
voyageur's well-known inability to keep quiet, it looked as if the devil
would lose his bet, until the voyageurs suddenly saw the twin towers of
Montreal's Notre Dame. The excitement was too much, and they all
started cheering and pointing out their homes. In an instant they realized
their error and screamed "maudite", or damn-it.

Bottle conditioned, the beer takes eight weeks to brew. Like Blanche de
Chambly, it will age in the bottle.

Hudson, Quebec,
Restaurant Mon Village

2760 Cote St. Charles

Hudson, Quebec, PO Box 531, J0P 1H0

514-458-5331

(Trans Canada Highway, Hudson Exit 22)

Rating: 🍺🍺🍺 (An Anglo-Quebec Country Inn, a generation out of step.)

Owner: David Crockart

Partner: Spencer Whatley

Founded: March, 1987 (The date the brewery started.)

Production Capacity: 9,000 Imperial gallons, with kegging equipment. Cask Brewing and Malt Extract System.

If your thirst for fresh ale gets the better of you while you are travelling between Montreal and Quebec, Mon Village is your only hope. Situated off of the Trans Canada Highway at Hudson, Quebec (Exit 22), surrounded by lightly treed, rolling fields, a large parking lot, antique market, and summer theatre in a nineteenth century, wooden sided farmhouse, Mon Village offers several comfortable dining lounges, a large fireplace, and an inviting bar. Next door is an old bakery converted into a brewery containing a stainless steel boiler, several fermenting tanks, kegs and a plethora of gauges, rubber hoses, wrenches and equipment necessary to brew 850 litres of beer per week.

While I called Mon Village "the quintessential Canadian brewpub for the 1990's" in my last guide, I am afraid that neither its menu, nor ambience-distorted by annoying piped in "lifestyle music" has kept up with the times. Simply put, the two of us felt that the food, while attractively presented was cloyingly heavy and a generation out of step. Similarly the over finished antique decor was overdone, and would fit more aptly in a photograph in "Canadian Homes" magazine than in real life.

The proprietors of Restaurant Mon Village converted the old bakery on the right, into a brewery.

RESTAURANT MON VILLAGE

The news, however, is not all bad. The beer is good, and the restaurant still occupies Thomas Parson's 1860 farmhouse. And pub expansion did not obliterate the original structure. Rather if you are a nostalgia buff you will probably think it enhanced it, with emphasis on lots of wood, the stone fireplace, antique farm implements, antique tables, press back chairs, and modern stained glass windows.

First toying with the idea of operating a brewpub in Ottawa, the would-be brewers returned to Quebec where they were more familiar with the market. Converting an adjacent, abandoned bakery they started brewing their own. Focusing on creating a country inn atmosphere, Mon Village reflects the personality of the Anglo-Quebec enclave around Hudson. And while I may have been disappointed with the menu and the music, to my mind it is still the best and most accessible, restaurant found off the 417 between Montreal and Ottawa, a stop you are sure to enjoy, even if you don't like beer!

VITAL STATISTICS - THE BREW

Dark Ale

With a creamy head, my wife said it was as "tasty as a Guinness without the excessive bitterness." Perhaps not how a beer taster would phrase it, but it gives you the idea. One of the best brewpub ales I have tried on this tour, the malty nose becomes fruity as the glass warms up. The same complexity followed by gentle bittering occurs in the taste.

Light, Lager

I was so pleased with the Ale, I didn't risk the lager.

Menu-beer: Only products from the Big Two. A full assortment of wines and liquors.

Menu-food: When I went to Mon Village last time, I had the pig's knuckles. Finding them as good as anything I had had in Waterloo, County, I wanted to try them again. They didn't meet my expectations and the sauerkraut was so drowned in caraway seeds that it was inedible. As for the potatoes, they should have been saved for vodka. Lor ordered mussel linguini, and while the mussels were fresh, the sauce was just too creamy. Now I have that off my chest, I should note that the gazpacho and vichyssoise were both very good.

A traditional menu based on meat, sauces and potatoes.

Desserts - cheesecake, pecan pie, Charlotte's cup (brandied fruit and ice cream), and specialty coffees.

Lunch for two including beer, around $40.

Dinner for two including beer around $65

Fall and winter Sunday brunch.

The Mon Village complex includes an antique boutique and summer theatre. Easy access to cross country ski trails.

Credit cards accepted.

Atmosphere: Anglo-Quebec kitsch.

Parking: Ample, close, free.

Lennoxville, Quebec,

GOLDEN LION BREWING CO.

La Brasserie Lion D'or

6 College Street, Box 474,

Lennoxville, Quebec, J1M 1Z6

819-565-1015 (pub)

819-562-4589 (brewery)

Rating: 🍺🍺

University pub, a chance to relive your youth.

The Bishop's Best Bitter makes a visit a must.

President: W. Stan Groves

Brewmaster: Stan Groves, trained 6 weeks at the Ringwood Brewery, England. Brewmaster Groves has a passion for hops.

Founded: July 1, 1986 (open as a brasserie only before.)

Production Capacity: Free standing, custom designed brewery after the Ringwood system. Brew 48 weeks of the year producing 768 hectolitres of beer. They plan to expand and open in Ottawa's Byward Market.

(Logo courtesy, Golden Lion Brewing Co.)

The Golden Lion, Canada's first brewpub/ micro- brewery was opened because publican W. Stan Groves with brewmaster son Stan "wanted to go back to the roots of the pub business." This decision came about after Stan, a business and economics major from nearby Bishop's University, took a Eurail tour of Europe's famous brewing regions. Believing Lennoxville was the perfect place to open a brewpub because of the well travelled and cultured population and the young and adventurous tastes of the University crowd, Stan took a brewing course at the highly regarded Ringwood Brewery in England in 1985. Upon his return to Canada, he lobbied the provincial government to create quality-control, and health and sanitation bylaws to allow pub owners to brew.

With locally made equipment and second hand dairy vessels for fermenters, this full grain brewery now boasts English conditioning tanks, holding distinctively hoppy brew.

VITAL STATISTICS - THE BREW

With the exception of the Pale Ale, which has a few cornflakes, the other brews are all malt. A hop lover's paradise; the beers are a little light on malt, but wonderful anyways. This might be called the home of the ad man's dilemma "aftertaste".

Bishop's Best, Bitter 4.5%

You can almost eat the hops in this amber, mouth puckering ale. Well worth a try for novelty alone, and an excellent antidote to the "soo-i-cide" wings. Discovered when one of the Groves accidentally added double the amount of the hops called for in the recipe, the brew is a pub staple.

Township's Pale Ale/La Blonde des Cantons, 4.5%

A hint of fruit in the palate, designed to replace lager. (The Quebec market demands some carbonation be injected into this brew.)

Lion's Pride, Real Ale 4.5%,

Served too cold, this well hopped English ale was modelled after Fuller's London Pride.

Stout 5%

A creamy head leads to a warm, roasted malt nutty brew, with a hint of yeast in the aftertaste.

Stout aficionado Gord Holder said "nice job, give it a nod" and with that, three of us spent the next four hours nodding.

On occasion they brew specialty beers such as their aphrodisiac laden Valentine's Bière d'Amour.

Menu- Beer: Guinness and Black Label on tap, along with bottled beer from the Big Two. No other alcoholic beverages, this is a Quebec brasserie.

Menu-Food: BBQ or "soo-i-cide" wings, pizza, nachos, tacos, burgers and assorted pies.

Take-out, Wednesday is wing night.

Lunch and dinner for two with beer under $20.

A small selection of souvenirs available.

Atmosphere: A University pub decorated with beer memorabilia and Sherbrooke's Silver Spring Brewery in particular. Tied to the rhythms of the school year, the pub boasts two rooms centred around a horseshoe bar. Pool tables. The men's washroom is decorated with cartoons by Larson.

Parking: There is a small parking lot and ample street space.

Closed Sundays.

Lennoxville, Quebec,
LA BRASSERIE MASSAWIPPI

see Chambly

UNIBROUE INC.

Montreal - Microbreweries.

Montreal, Quebec,
BRASAL GERMAN BREWERY INC.

Brasal-Brasserie Allemande Inc.

8477 Cordner St.,

(south bank of the old Lachine Canal)

La Salle,(Montreal,) H8N 2X2

514-365-5050; FAX: 514-365-2954.

President: Marcel Jagermann (a family operation)

Managing Director: Etan Jagermann

Distribution Manager: Daniel Boileau

Brewmaster: Harald D. Sowade, 32 years brewing experience, trained at the Weihenstephan, brewed for Dortmunder Union, 17 years Technical Director at the 6,000 hl Haberckl Brewery in Mannheim.

Founded: September 1, 1989 official opening. The name is taken from the "Bras" for beer and "al" for German.

Production Capacity: 20,000 hectolitres, or six million bottles. The brewhouse is from Austria along with the fermenting kettle, the filtration and bottling system are German, and the storage and aging tanks are Canadian. In 1990 Brasal ranked 6, selling 8,000 hl of beer for 7.3% of the Canadian microbrewery market, giving it second place in Quebec.

BIÈRE • BEER

(Logo courtesy, Brasal-Brasserie Allemande Inc.)

When the trend with most microbreweries has been towards English style ales, I asked Etan Jagermann why his family decided to add yet another lager to the sea of lagers already available? Etan responded, "Arriving from Austria, the family saw that while the major breweries offered 35 different brands, that they were all essentially the same. And that if the consumer wanted something different they had to purchase overpriced, usually stale imports."

"They asked themselves what could they bring new to the Quebec market?" The micro end was already full of English beer, so taking their heritage into consideration they decided to "...produce quality German lagers, to compete with the imports. They believed the market needed a German beer made according to the strictures of the Reinheitsgebot, made with quality and consistency in mind."

Having found the second place in the Quebec micro market, they apparently met consumer needs. For the future, Etan plans to "strengthen and increase his position in the Quebec micro market, and to export his products across Canada and internationally."

VITAL STATISTICS - THE BREW

Made with imported hops, malt and yeasts, the brewery uses specially filtered water. Apart from this, Dr. S. Donhauser, a professor at the famed German Brewing Institute at Weinhenstephan gave this "Technical Opinion"

"The beer Hopps Bräu, from the Brasal-Brasserie, Allemande Inc., Montreal, has been analyzed using chemical and immunochemical methods for additives not permitted by the German REINHEITSGEBOT (beer purity law). The examination covered antioxidants, foam stabilizers, preservatives as well as raw-fruit and enzyme additives. The beer contains none of these additives. The beer complies with the German REINHEITSGEBOT (beer purity law) and as of the date of the analysis also to paragraphs 9 and 10 of the German Tax Laws."

Real Light, 3.1%, Vrai Légère

Usually I avoid "light" beers like the plague but I must admit, that this is a good beer. Brasal has shown that Light beers need not be thin, mean and tasteless but can possess character. A perfect breakfast brew. Well hopped, it was made darker than Hopps Bräu to show that Light's can be full bodied. The lightest low alcohol beer in Canada, it only has 89 calories.

Bock, 7.8%

A rich tawny, warmer, with a silky foam, enticing apricot nose, and sherry like body, underlining its 7.8% alcohol. A sweet, warm, nutty aftertaste. Try it as an after dinner drink. Brewed between November and March, the beer is aged three months. Slightly more expensive, it is sold in four packs to be more affordable. Brewed according to a German recipe that Brewmaster Sowade used for 17 years before coming to Canada, he confirmed that in Europe, Bock was a Lent Brew, originating in the Middle Ages when people were obliged to fast. Traditionally the brew started one week after Ash Wednesday.

Hopps Bräu Lager, 4.5%. Winner of the 1991 Certificate of Excellence for new products, (Quebec)

The brewery's flagship beer, Brasal was the only Quebec micro to start with a Blonde Beer.

A European style lager, it has a flowery nose with a hint of roundness and an aerated foam. Once again this is a brew to be enjoyed fresh. Now available at the LCBO.

Spécial, 6.1%, aged 6 weeks (lager)

A refined, subtle lager, with a warm copper cloak, rocky laced foam, rich sherry like nose, and extremely well balanced palate that produces just enough of a mouth watering aftertaste to lead to another...

Brasal also imports Clausthaler, 0.5% near beer.

An interview with Brewmaster Harald D. Sowade

Trained in Germany, Brewmaster Sowade brings over three decades of European and North American brewing experience to Brasal.

Rather than ask him about his brewing philosophy, which is obvious as he adheres to the Reinheitsgebot, I asked him about some modern trends and received the following direct answers, to what I think he thought were "silly" questions.

Perhaps he was right, who really does care about "Dry" when surrounded by vats of fresh bock?

When asked about Dry beers, Harald said it was "...a Japanese invention and he didn't know what to make of it." As for the Canadian examples they "...are sweet and not dry, done to fool the consumer, really just the same old brew under a different name. A marketing man's beer. Dry has a nice ring to it, and might make some think of champagne."

Fine, but I then asked would you brew it?

Harald smiled, and said "No. Beer is not beer without aftertaste."

On bottled draft, Harald said that the "...microbreweries were making bottled draft from the very beginning. The only difference is now the marketing people had discovered it as a sales tool. Micros had always made bottled draft simply because pasteurization equipment was too expensive." He went on, "kegged draft is better than bottled because in the keg it is not exposed to oxygen, or the sun, and the larger quantity prevents quick temperature variations - it is fresher. Whereas in the bottle there is a risk of oxidation." He recommended that we all do as he does "and always drink draft keg beer, poured with CO_2 and not oxygen."

And with that we retired to the hospitality lounge and turned to the serious business of drinking our beer!

Montreal, Quebec,

LA BRASSERIE MCAUSLAN BREWING INC.

4850 St. Ambroise St. (corner of Remi)

Bureau 100, Montreal, Quebec, H4C 3N8

514-939-3060

President: Peter McAuslan

Brewster: Ellen Bounsall, BSc Ottawa U., now oversees a brewing staff of three. Ellen was originally trained by Peter Pugsley of Ringwood fame.

P.R.: Cynthia Montgomery

Founded: May 30, 1989, Official opening. Started producing draft Feb. 1989.

Production Capacity: From 13,000 hl to 20,000. In 1990 McAuslan's was Canada's fifth largest micro, and first in Quebec. Selling 13,000 hl in 1992 it is still number one in Quebec.

Custom made English style system, full grain, brick and copper gas fired brewkettle.

Note the best before date on the label, a necessary precaution in Quebec, where despite the best efforts of the brewers, you have no idea how long your favourite brew may have wasted away in the corner store.

(Label courtesy, Peter McAuslan)

As the first new brewery to open a bottling line in Montreal since the 1930s, and producing top quality, flavourful ales, McAuslan Brewing has maintained its position as the province's number one microbrewery. Now available throughout Quebec, released through the LCBO's vintages and sold in New England, the brewery continues to expand.

Founded by Peter McAuslan, who has been brewing his own since he was 18, the brewery's flagship brand, St. Ambroise Pale Ale, is considered by many to be Canada's best all round beer.

Taking two years and $800,000 to put the project together, the brewery now employs 25 people, well up from the eight it started with. Covering 7,500 square feet, the brewery was styled after Ringwood in England. Here McAuslan and brewster Ellen Bounsall both formerly of Dawson College, produce their unpasteurized brews according to traditional British recipes. Their four beers have proven to be so popular that several restaurants and one chain now have McAuslan produce their house beer.

VITAL STATISTICS - THE BREW

St. Ambroise Pale Ale, 5%, draft-bottle

A perfect crystal clear copper cloak, sits over a well balanced, assertive nose, leading to a whole - full mouth aftertaste leaving an exceptionally enticing invitation to another sip. Or if you prefer a hearty ale covered by a creamy head with a body so well hopped you can almost see the hops while simply savouring the bouquet.

Made with three types of barley malt, water, yeast and milled wheat flour - for head retention - according to a traditional recipe from the North of England.

Griffon Extra Pale Ale, 5%

An assertive well balanced, hop and warm malt nose, with the hops front and centre in the mouth, backed up by malt. I have found it is a great antidote for a writer's block.

Oatmeal Stout, 5.5%

Tremendous character and complexity in this beer is provided by the crystal, chocolate and pale malts, along with the precooked rolled oats (the oatmeal), the 40% roasted barley, wheat, and the cornflakes. The result is a brew with a pronounced almost edible roasted nose followed through in the taste and aftertaste. Oddly popular in the United States, on tap its smooth, creamy head leads to a simply wonderful elixir.

This beer may not adhere to the dreaded Reinheitsgebot, but who cares?

Griffon Brown Ale, 5%

A crystal tawny brown ale, with a rocky but short foam, subtle chocolate nose, and nicely balanced taste that starts with fruit - apricot? and goes to chocolate. Light in the mouth, the aftertaste is chewy, fruity - followed by a pleasant puckering and a second sip.

Brewery tours by appointment.

Beer cannot be sold at the brewery, but is available throughout Quebec. Be careful where you buy it though, in some trendy locations you can pay up to $36. for 24. This is gouging pure and simple, and underlines the weakness of the corner store system. In Quebec, also try not to buy singles as they will often charge almost $2. a pint!

Montreal, Quebec,

LES BRASSEURS GMT INC.

5710 Garnier Street,

(in an industrial area near the Rosemount Métro.)

Montreal, Quebec, H2G 2Z7

514-274-4941

President: Daniel Trepanier

Founded: March 1988. The name is taken from the first initial of each of the original partner's surnames.

Brewmaster: Andre Lafreniere

Consultant: Georges Van Gheluwe.

Production Capacity: In 1990 they sold 5,600 hectolitres, ranking them no. 8 with 5.1% of the microbrewery market across Canada, and no. 4 in Quebec. Capacity, 1993 - 13,000 hectolitres.

Located in a functional industrial building, the brewhouse was made by Falco Ltd., a Montreal stainless steel manufacturer.

Original brewhouse: one 20 hl brewkettle, three 40 hl fermentation/ maturation tanks.

A full grain lager brewery. The thirsty may not purchase any samples at the brewery, but the products are available in brasseries throughout Montreal.

VITAL STATISTICS - THE BREW
La Belle Gueule, 5.2%, Bottle and draft
When it is fresh, it is the equal of the best pilsners. When it isn't, well?
Tremblay, lager, 5%
Too early to rate. I have been told though that this is a lighter tasting, more mainstream beer.

Montreal - Brewpubs.

Montreal, Quebec,
BAR LA CERVOISE

4457 Boulevard St. Laurent

(corner of Mont Royal),

Montreal, Quebec, H2W 1Z8

514-843-6586

Rating: 🍺🍺🍺

Forget your mother-in-law; take her daughter instead.

Owner: Jean-Pierre Trépanier

Brewmaster:

Founding: James Gordon. Today: Shawn Tordon, Senior Brewer, former homebrewer, BA Science Biology, MBA; Tom Robson, brewer, former homebrewer, BJCP Judge, Food and Beverage Consultant.

Production Capacity: 24,000 Imperial Gallons (1840 kegs) Cask Brewing and Malt Extract System. A five vessel system expanded to seven and modified with equipment from Unitank, Quebec

Founded: Started brewing September 1, 1988.

(Logo courtesy, Bar La Cervoise)

Comparable to a Paris bistro, the Cervoise has a garage door front that rolls open to provide a barside view of the street. To my mind it is the best beer bar in Montreal. Serving the products of most of Quebec's micros and a wide selection of beers from around the world this pub is an ideal place to drink and watch the world pass by on "La Main". Decorated with local art, the emphasis is on relaxation.

Neither the pool table, the television, or the background music overwhelm good conversation, or the beer.

I wouldn't bring my mother-in-law here, but I would take her daughter. This oasis was started by the late Guy Lavallee and J.P. Trépanier. The brewery located at the back was installed to give this 150 seat brasserie a competitive edge. To brew the beer, James Gordon, a beer enthusiast who literally risked his personal freedom to learn homebrewing in Saudia Arabia, was hired. Gordon related to "Gazette" reporter James Quig, "...it was the only way to get a drink in that country." Since 1989 the brewery has been under the supervision of Shawn Tordon. Assisted by Tom Robson, their philosophy is to brew unique, balanced beers that are a cut above the taste of the lowest common denominator, that meets acceptance with their clientele, while giving them self satisfaction as brewers.

VITAL STATISTICS - THE BREW

La Main, Ale
The most adventurous of the two house brews, this amber brown bitter has a spicy hop aroma underlined by fruitiness. A balanced brew, it has a smooth clean finish with a lingering mild bitterness.

La Futée, Lager (pilsner)
Aged four to five weeks, this European style lager, features more hops in the nose than malt. Light and balanced in the mouth, with the malt coming through in the aftertaste. (Yes aftertaste, as I have said before is important!)

Also look for the seasonal brews such as the Meade Spring Ale, Oktoberfest beer, Christmas Cranberry beer and others brewed when the "inspiration arises."

Menu - beer: Boréale, la Belle Gueule on tap along with a large selection of Belgium, European and Canadian beers.

Menu - food: French style bistro snacks.

Credit cards accepted.

Atmosphere: The best beer bar in Montreal, a good place to drink and solve the problems of the world, without courting personal poverty. Not meant for children.

Parking: On the street, near the Mont/Royal subway stop.

Hours: Seven days a week, 3 p.m. to 3 a.m.

Montreal, Quebec,
LE CHEVAL BLANC

809 Ontario Street,

(Northeast corner of St. Hubert, behind the Voyageur Bus Terminal)

Montreal, Quebec, H2L 1P1

514-522-9205 (-0211)

Rating: 🍺🍺 (in a class on its own, the mother-in-law rating has very little to do
with this trendy French Canadian tavern, now a combination brewpub/
microbrewing.)

Proprietor/Brewmaster: Jerome C. Denys.

Founded: 1987, started brewing (The business has been in the family since
1924.)

Production Capacity: 1,000 litres of beer per week.

Evolved from a Continental system to a custom made brewery, Denys grows his
own yeast, and mashes his own malt.

Striving "to make 'Le Cheval Blanc' beer what Schwartz is to smoked meat,"
brewmaster and brasserie owner Jerome Denys has turned this family tavern
into a must stop for beer enthusiasts.

With all of the brews dominated by the taste of cloves, Denys brews his
Blonde (pale), Blé (wheat) and Brun (brown) beers each week from scratch.
Denys, in charge of the family business, was inspired to brew his own brew after
visiting a brewpub in New York City. In the process he restored the family's
long, narrow traditional countertop arborite tavern, and placed two fermenters
into the countertop to proclaim the pub's new life. Located behind the bus
terminal near St. Denis Street, there is just a hint of the illicit, making it the
Montreal you have dreamed of if you are an Anglo and in love.

VITAL STATISTICS - THE BREW
Always experimenting to find the perfect recipe 'Deny's Belgium style beers
have an unmistakable "housetaste" of cloves.

Blonde
The taste of cloves is unmistakable.

Blé - wheat
A wonderful fruity, tart beer underlined by cloves. Compare this beer with
Blanche de Chambly.

Brun - brown ale
More like a porter than a brown ale. Great on a cold winter's day.

Menu - beer: Limited.

No credit cards.

Atmosphere: An upscale tavern, and a good place to practice your French. Not meant for children.

Parking: On the street in lots.

Hours: Closed Sundays.

Montreal, Quebec,
CROCODILE CLUBS

5414 Gatineau St.
(and Lacombe).

Métro stop: Côtes-des-Neiges,

Montreal, Quebec, H3G 1Z5

514- 733-2125

4238 St. Lawrence Blvd.
(Boul. St-Laurent).

Métro stop: Mont/Royal

Montreal, Qubec,

514-848-0044

Rating: 🍺🍺 - for the decor alone.

Owner: Andre Remillard, L'Hotel de la Montagne, 1430 de la Montagne, Montreal, Quebec, H3G 1Z5.

Founded: February 1988 (Gatineau St.)

Production Capacity: Continental Breweries Inc. Malt Extract System, and Croco Bière Blonde - Pale Ale brewed under licence by McAuslan. Yes there is hope for some good beer here along with the decor.

CROCODILE - RESTAURANTS - BARS - DANCING

The brass Crocodile awaits your pleasure at the St. Lawrence Blvd. club.

Part of the Thursday's Group of Montreal restaurants, the homebrew may not be memorable, but everything else is. If you are in Montreal and want to try something different, you will find it here. In the words of one of the marketing people "The Crocodile has a great many things going for it. It combines bar,restaurant, brasserie and discothèque all under the same roof, 'but fortunately on different levels.

The Gatineau location is a chrome palace designed to be reminiscent of the 50's. The Boul. St-Laurent facility is in an old textile building that has been turned into a brass crocodile heaven. With lights, escalators, and glitz you need a beer just to relax and get your bearings.

Brunch is served every Sunday and is highlighted by a visit from Mr. Crocodile handing out crayons and colouring books.

Need I say more?

VITAL STATISTICS - THE BREW

I have tried the housebrew several times, and always find myself going to the Croco Pale Ale made by McAuslan. Perhaps the Clubs' clients do appreciate more than glitter, or maybe they just think a bottled product is better. Whatever the case may be, the brew has a flowery nose, creamy foam, and is not bad at all. At least if you are at the St-Laurent location, it will hold you until you get to a La Cervoise, just a short stroll north of here.

On the menu I saw they had "bock" and naively ordered it. In French "bock" can mean large.

Menu - beer: Standard imports, and Canadians, also alcohol.

Menu - food: Fish soup, pâtés, palm hearts, crab cake, salads, sandwiches, burgers, quiches, grilled chicken and steak, pancakes stuffed with seafood and spinach, rabbit basted with cream and mustard seeds, lamb and duck, chocolate mousse, cheesecake, caramel custard, espresso and cappuccino, you get the idea...this listing simply does not do the menu justice.

Lunch for two including beer under $30.

Dinner for two including beer around $55.

Credit cards accepted.

Atmosphere: Chrome and glitz; brass crocodiles and glitz.

Parking: Street.

Open seven days a week.

North Hatley, Quebec,
PILSEN RESTAURANT AND PUB

55 rue Principale,
North Hatley, Quebec, J0B 2C0
819-842-2971

Rating: 🍺🍺🍺 - 🍺🍺🍺🍺
Proprietors: Gail and Gilles Péloquin

(Logo, courtesy, Pilsen Restaurant and Pub.)

The Pilsen is not a brewpub, but it is a perfect village inn, perched alongside the Massawippi River, offering huge "country" servings, and some of the best Quebec micro beers on tap.

The pub on the first floor is furnished with antiques and is reminiscent of a "colonial" tavern, a more formal dining area is on the second level. Quite apart from a visit to the Pub, a trip to North Hatley, with its antique and gift boutiques gives you an opportunity to see how Montreal's Westmount Anglophones relax.

Menu - beer: On tap: Blanche de Chambly, a must; Massawippi Pale Ale, Boreale Stout - (if you are not careful you will be here for the night.) Also bottled beers - Duvel, Maredsous, La Chouffe, Grolsch, Mort Subite, etc. (Wines are available if you insist.)

Menu - food: Ensconced under a mounted boar's head, I enjoyed a seafood chowder teaming with shrimp and pollock, that when combined with freshly baked buns was almost a meal in itself. Duty, however, called and I completed my lunch with a tame order of suicide wings. The lunch menu includes smoked salmon on a bagel, Ploughman's lunch with pâté of boar and potato skins. The dinner menu ranges from lamb brochette to breast of chicken with strawberry sauce, to rabbit with mustard sauce, pheasant, boar and buffalo steak. If you still have room, the desserts are worthwhile. Specialty coffees.

Lunch for two including beer, around $30.

Dinner for two including beer, around $60.

Credit cards accepted. Reservations appreciated.

Atmosphere: The dining room overlooks the Massawippi River and Lake. It is a traditional Quebec country village inn. While you will be able to practice your French if you wish, North Hatley is one of the few English enclaves left in Quebec.

Closed Mondays during the winter.

Parking: Behind the restaurant, free.

Quebec City, Quebec,
L'INOX MAITRES BRASSEURS

(an inexact translation for L'Inox would be chrome or stainless steel)
37 St. André St. *(37 rue St-André)*
Quebec City (*old Lower Town along the waterfront, Vieux-Port de Quebec*).
Quebec, G1K 8T3
418-692-2877

Rating: While I haven't been here, fellow imbibers tell me it is worth a visit for
  the stainless steel motif alone, described as "urbain-contemporain."

Owner: Nouveaux Brasseurs Associés Inc.

Manager/Brewmaster: Pierre Turgeon

Founded: November 11, 1987

Production Capacity: 600 hectolitres from a custom made Montreal malt extract
  brewhouse.

*(Logo courtesy,)Nouveaux Brasseurs
Associés Inc.)*

When three veteran homebrewer friends André
Jean, Roger Roy and Pierre Turgeon learned
that Provincial regulations permitted brewpubs
they decided to realize a long time ambition and
planned to open a pub of their own. Investigating
the various facets of the business and looking for a
good location they pooled their resources to locate
in Quebec City's rapidly evolving historic Lower
Town. Like most modern small brewers the
major hurdle to success was obtaining sufficient
finances as the bank deemed the project too
risky. Eventually they were able to secure the necessary funds from the
Mouvement Desjardins credit union. Brewer Pierre Turgeon notes when they
opened their beer was far from "perfect." He reports now, however, that they
have three regular taps, vying for five products along with various other
specialty brews.

VITAL STATISTICS - THE BREW
  La Trouble-fête
Belgium style white or wheat beer.
  La Transat
European lager.

La Trois-de-pique
A 7% bock, I have translated this as the "Triple sting".
La Scottish
Light brown.
La Bitter
English bitter.

Menu -food: French Canadian bar food "European hotdogs", baguettes, Austrian, Hungarian and Alsatian sausages.

Lunch for two with beer under $20.

Dinner for two with beer not more than $20., unless you are there for a night of drinking.

Atmosphere: With the brewery on the first floor, the second floor houses the bar and billiard tables; 200 seats plus 90 additional seats on the terrace during the summer. Described as "contemporay-urban."

Parking: Probably difficult, but this historic area is made for walking.

Hours: May be closed on Sundays, call.

St. Casimir, Quebec,
BRASSERIE PORTNEUVOISE LTEE.

225 Hardy St.,
St. Casimir, Quebec, G0A 3L0
418-339-3242

President: S. Haydock

Founded: First opened in 1989, and known for its distinctive brews, it closed in 1992. A year later Hercule Trotter is reported to have acquired it, and after spending some million dollars on restoration, plans to reopen.

While it is too early to rate the products of the new owners, I hope that they try to recreate interesting brews like the vinous strong ale, and maple syrup L'Erabiere.

St. Jerome, Quebec,

LES BRASSEURS DU NORD INC.

18 J.F. Kennedy Boul., St. Jerome, Quebec, J7Y 4B4

(Laurentian Autoroute exit 44, J.F. Kennedy is the first left after the overpass, the brewery is about one km down on the right side.)

514-438-9060; (Montreal 514-434-2392): FAX 514-438-3179

President: Laura Urtnowski

Brewster: Laura Urtnowski supervises and trained brewer René Massé.

General Manager: Bernard Morin

Sales: Jean Morin

Founded: June 1988

Production Capacity: From a mere 2,860 hl when they opened the brewery is now capable of brewing 20,000 hl per annum. Tied for sixth place in the Canadian microbrewing industry in 1990 with Brasal, it shared second place with Brasal again in Quebec in the same year. The brewery is now reporting sales of 14,000 hl placing it neck and neck with McAuslan's.

The stainless steel equipped brewhouse was fabricated by Inox-tech of Montreal (Ste. Catherine). Brewed in an all-grain infusion mash system.

(Logo courtesy, Les Brasseurs du Nord Inc.)

Beer was probably first brewed in Europe by women. As a drink made for everyday consumption, alewives in Medieval England would include brewing as part of their domestic activities. As the demand for beer grew, alewives or brewsters started brewing commercially. As early as 1267 the English court stipulated fines and punishments for brewers and bakers who retailed unsatisfactory products. One law stated that:

If the offence be grievous and often and will not be corrected, then he or she shall suffer corporal punishment, to wit the baker to the Pillory, the brewster to the Tumbril or Flogging. (R. Protz "The Great British Beer Book", Impact Book, 1987 pg. 15.)

The female brewing tradition, if not the fines came to Canada. Until the middle of the 19th century, specially trained domestic servants would, for an extra few pennies a week more, brew beer for their employers. In Ontario, particularly in German speaking communities, women took over their deceased husband's brewery. And in Nova Scotia, it was Susannah Oland's brown ale recipe that launched the famous Oland Army and Navy Brewery at the time of Confederation.

...When homebrew enthusiast Laura Urtnowski teamed up with former university classmates Bernard and Jean Morin, she was just reinstating tradition. The three trained in history, geography, philosophy and economics were unemployed. The only constant was their interest in making a better beer. In March 1987, they decided to go commercial. After investigating the provincial draft import market, which had grown from sales of 639,000 litres a year to 1.4 million litres per annum in two years, the trio decided to build a brewery in St. Jerome to serve the Montreal and Laurentian markets with fresh, pure, all natural premium beer with a European flavour at a lower price. In order to create their niche in this expanding market, they built a 2,000 square foot brewery, that has grown in capacity from 2,860 hl to 20,000 hl a year.

To learn her art more thoroughly, Laura apprenticed for two weeks, at the highly acclaimed Wellington County microbrewery in Guelph, Ontario, under English brewmaster Alan Griffiths.

"There she learned how to make the transition from the kitchen stove and five gallon pail to a 650 gallon stainless steel industrial brewery. This doesn't entail only a difference in scale, but also a gain in expertise in everything from yeast taxonomy to boiler design."

Now Laura has passed on her secrets to a man, apprentice brewer René Massé.

VITAL STATISTICS - THE BREW

Like most micro beers, the products are "cold-filtered and unpasteurized."

Boréale Rousse ale, 5% (northern red)
I am sorry to report that this once very distinctive, fruity superb ale, does not quite have the character it once had. Still very good though, you can look forward to enjoying the hue of the rich tawny complexion, capped off with a rocky dense foam, that tastes like whipped cream. While the nose hints at raisins, the taste is Belgium in complexity - light vinous and nutty, well balanced. As for aftertaste - it is prevailingly refreshing, underlined by a warm dryness, capped off with the pleasing taste of dried fruit.

Noire (stout) 5.5%
A full bodied stout, lots of malt and a spicy nose, compare it with McAuslan's oatmeal stout if you want to have an interesting conversation with someone about beer.

Blonde (pale ale), 4.5%
In the Boréale tradition, this is unlike any Canadian micro pale ale, with its light amber complexion. In good form it has a long lasting lacy foam, and a flowery, apricot fresh aroma. The balanced round, tingly taste, is underscored by hops, leaving an aftertaste full of malt, malt and more gentle sweet malt. Almost cream ale in style.

Provincial legislation doe not permit direct sale of the products or encourage tours.

CHAPTER 6

CIDER

Since the start of prohibition 77 years ago, Ontario has been without a fullfledged Cidery; now we have two.

To obtain the raw ingredients to ferment 'essence of lockjaw', a particularly potent and rough applejack cider, was a leading cause for the widespread planting of apple orchards in pioneer times. Pressed into cider and enjoyed during haying and threshing season, our forefathers primarily prized the apple for its ability to slake their gargantuan thirst for this rack or hard cider. Around 1900 temperance forces made all alcoholic beverages socially unacceptable and cider consumption began to drop off.

The apple's versatility though, insured its continued popularity as a food, while cider's adaptability allowed it to be used as the base for many apple related dishes. In "Pen Pictures of Early Pioneers Life in Upper Canada" written in 1905 by a 'Canuck' cider was made from windfall apples, with the poorer grades being converted to sauce popularly known as apple butter and vinegar.

J. MacFarlane in Canada's first cookbook "The Cook Not Mad or Rational Cookery" wrote in 1831 that to make 'apple sass' "Take to three gallons of cider, five pounds of white sugar; 1-1/2 bushels of apples. First boil and skim your cider. Let it boil 1/2 an hour. Stew your apples in a portion of the cider. When your sauce is thick and glossy, add the cider and sugar. Season with cloves etc."

An 1863 recipe for 'apple water' said "Take one tart apple of ordinary size, well baked, let it be well mashed, pour on it one pint of boiling water, beat them well together, let it stand to cool, and strain it off for use. It may be sweetened with sugar if desired."

Cider jelly could be made by boiling cider to the consistency of syrup and then cooled.

Recipes abound for poached, baked, fried and dried apples, puddings, stuffings and pies. And today it is impossible to pass a fall bake table without being tempted by apple cake, bread, squares and butter.

Modern recipes describe apple cocktail appetizers, apple chicken melt, apple shortcake, gingered apple squash soup, apple beef stir-fry and even apple coleslaw with sweet and sour dressing.

Apples are not only good for eating and drinking. Devonshire England is the birthplace of the saying "Ate an apfel avore gwain to bed. Makes the doctor beg his hand." Which translated from Medieval English means "an apple a day keeps the doctor away."

In ancient times apples played a role in matchmaking. In Greece shy young men would toss an apple to the girl of their fancy, if she caught the apple the date was on, if not he had to look elsewhere. In 600 B.C. Athens a single apple was served to a bride and groom to eat, in favour of an expensive wedding.

Apples have also played a role in mythology. The Celts believed in the Kingdom of the sun, and Isle of Apple where there was no old age, sickness or sorrow. And in an early version of Snow White, it was claimed that the Trojan War started after Eris threw an apple into the middle of a wedding reception with "For the Fairest" inscribed on it.

Apples not only appeal to humans, but to horses. According to the highly popular late 19th century home economist Dr. Chase in his "New Recipe Book or Information for Everybody", sour apples, due to the pectin in them were good for horse digestion. Chase quoted an expert who claimed "I have occasionally fed sour apples to my horses, with an excellent result. They are a certain cure for worms. I feed half of a whole pailful a week...I find (the horse) derive much benefit from them, and gain flesh more rapidly than others which did not receive an apple feed."

Fortunately today we do not need to go to such lengths to obtain a glass of hard cider. And at no more than 6.5% alcohol we are not likely to suffer from 'lockjaw' from imbibing in too much cider, but may enjoy it as "a pleasant beverage."

Like grape growing, apple orchards depend on the right geography.

The southern slopes of Northumberland County, overlooking Lake Ontario are ideal for apples.

Ideally hard (alcoholic) cider should be made without the addition of water or sugar, wet seasons may force some producers to add sugar.

Production.

1. First select a blend of small acidic apples. Cider apples, may not be suitable for eating. Or produce a cider from a mix of Russets, Red Delicious and McIntosh. The varieties are as endless as the apples and producers available, and the exact blends are well kept secrets.

2. Crush and press the apples to produce a sweet cider or unclarified and unsterilized apple juice. At Northumberland Brewers they squeeze 200 litres per press.

3. Ferment or "brew" the juice by pitching (introducing) the yeast and let it work for six to eight weeks at 70 degrees F until it reaches the terminal or dry condition.

4. Filter three times.

5. Mix.

6. Store.

7. Bottle or Keg.

Brighton, Ontario,
NORTHUMBERLAND BREWERS INC.

Cidery

Pine Springs Farm

R.R. 4, Brighton, Ontario, K0K 1H0

613-475-2143

(Hwy 401 exit 509, on Hwy 2,
2 kms west of Brighton.)

Head Office:

Joe Howieson, Chairman,

230 Perry St.

Cobourg, Ontario,

K9A 1P3

416-372-4159

Chairman: Joe Howieson

Production Manager (Brewer): Paul Chatten

Founded: February, 1993 (the farm has been in the family since 1929.)

Production Capacity: 180 hectolitres with capacity to expand to 540 hectolitres.
An adapted Continental Brewing System with Micron filters, housed in a
40-year-old apple storage shed.

Essentially a two-man operation, seven partners invested $40,000 to get
going. The single most expensive cost, was the $10,000 spent on Sankey draft
kegs.

Called a brewery, the facility falls under the regulations as a winery, though it
makes cider. This means the products may be found at some LCBO outlets
rather than the Beer Store.

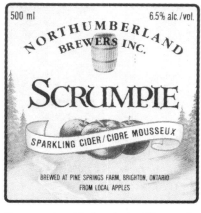

(Logo courtesy, Northumberland Brewers Inc.)

The fact Northumberland Brewers received
the first cider manufacturing licence issued
by the LCBO, is a satisfying irony.

Domestic hard cider production, like all
alcoholic beverage manufacturing, was terminated by prohibition legislation between
1916 and 1919. Under the supervision of
Ontario Attorney-General William E. Raney,
the regulations were rigorously enforced. As
fate would have it, Raney's son Norman
married a Brighton lass named Gladys
Soloman. In 1929 the couple moved to Pine
Springs Farm. Their daughter Elizabeth
according to the family tree "...stayed on the
farm and married Earle Chatten. Their son,
Paul Chatten" co-founded Northumberland

"Gladys the storage tank. Traditionally named after a woman, this one was named in honour of Gladys Soloman, wife of Norman Raney, the son of William E. Raney, the Ontario Attorney-General who put teeth into Ontario's temperance laws.

As a market garden and juice farm complex, Pine Springs actually embraces three farms, covering 225 acres, with 55 acres devoted to over 20 varieties of apples. With 40 acres of orchards devoted to juice, Pine Springs not only sells to juice companies, but produces sweet, natural, unsterilized and unclarified apple juice.

With years of experience in cider production and excess capacity, all it took was for Paul Chatten to meet veteran home wine and cider maker Joe Howieson. Originally from Edinburgh, Howieson worked in nuclear power research and development. Always wanting to be in business for himself, he teamed up with Chatten upon retirement "...to reintroduce the people of Ontario to the joy of cider drinking." With Ontario's liquor laws now more amenable to experimentation, Howieson took advantage of the situation to create a cider modelled after those found in Somerset England, where cider competes with draft beer as a beverage of choice.

Confident in their product Chatten said he "expects to be mimicked, but not equalled."

VITAL STATISTICS - THE CIDER

Scrumpie

As a style this is the subtle knee-bending elixir my mother always warned me about. Described as the "natural essence of apples", Scrumpie is made from fermented apple juice. While water is never added, refined sugar may be if the season has been too wet.

An old English word meaning "small apples", in Somerset England, where cider has a large following, the term refers to the strongest or roughest ciders.

At the best of times ratings are mildly subjective; and I am afraid that I must admit when confronted with kegs of fresh cider at an official opening, my objectivity went down in direct proportion to the quantity of cider quaffed.

Brighton Mayor Bill Pettingill enjoys the first glass of LLBO approved cider in Ontario in 77 years, on Wednesday February 24, 1993 while Joe Howieson looks on approvingly.

Without much prompting, I engaged in a little taste comparing with a number of other guests at which Scrumpie was pitted against Bulmer's "Strongbow", 5.3%, Taunton's "Diamond White", 8.2%, New Zealand's "Normandie", 6%, and Vermont's "Woodchuck", 5%. Needless to say Scrumpie's draft sparkling cider came out number one, not because we were all being polite, but I ask you how can you beat an absolutely orchard fresh product?

With my handicap in mind, here are my impressions. Unfortunately, when I tried the bottled cider a few days later, the bloom had somehow faded. Oh well - I will simply have to try again, and until then take the taster's traditional out "Too early to rate!"

Fermented with their own yeast culture, Joe Howieson said "Alcoholic cider is an acquired taste" and "... it will be necessary to educate the palates of the people of Ontario to fully appreciate it." I think he is being a little too pessimistic. The cider he is talking about is not the sweet, fizzy product sold through the LCBO and in Quebec several years ago, but a true dry English hard cider.

Serve slightly below room temperature.

Scrumpie Sparkling Cider, Bottle, 6.5%
Lightly carbonated with a fresh apple nose, refreshing and dry. Well worth a try, not at all like the traditional sweet North American cider.
Scrumpie Draft Cider, Bottle, 6.5%, On Tap
Too early to rate.
Scrumpie Sparkling, carbonated, 6.5%
You might as well have been sitting in Somerset - this cider is just like the beverage you find in British pubs. A full apple fresh aroma, medium dry, not too tart. I could have stayed all day.

Scrumpie draft, "Still", uncarbonated, 6.5%
As fresh as a newly picked apple, this cider was not as dry as its English
counterparts, but still wonderful.

The Cidery and its products are available at Pine Springs Farm -Roadside
Market, where you can also purchase apple foods, sweet cider, natural local
spring water, and pick your own apples in mid September.

Open daily except Tuesdays, Christmas and New Year's Day.

Sold only at Pine Springs Farm in bottles, but available on tap in pubs
between Oshawa, Peterborough and Kingston.

Collingwood, Ontario,
BROTHER JOHN'S CELLARS LIMITED

Mail c/o John Denbok,

R.R. 1,

Collingwood, Ontario, L9Y 3Y9

Telephone: John Wiggins, 705-466-2531; FAX: 705-466-3306.

Partners: John Denbok, John Wiggins (Creemore Springs Brewery)

Production Manager: John Denbok

Production Capacity: Initially the plant was located in an industrial mall unit in
Collingwood. Plans are to build a permanent cidery in an apple orchard
just south of Collingwood.

With John Wiggins of Creemore Springs Brewery fame teamed up with apple
grower John Denbok, cider lovers can look forward to some quality products
and interesting target market promotion, that will appeal to appreciation rather
than vast consumption.

The Denboks, a well known apple family around Collingwood manage
Georgian Triangle Apples, known widely for their Apple Valley and President's
Choice Cider, to name a few of their products.

With Ontario essentially without any hard cider production before this winter,
and with an overabundance of apples provincially, John Denbok and John Wiggins
saw a chance to produce European style ciders at Ontario's first estate "Cidery".

With most of Ontario's apple crop given over to sweet tasting apples it was
necessary to find a small bittersweet European apple that would provide the
requisite puckering power caused by its acidic astringency.

Following his usual methodic pattern Wiggins used research done at the
University of Guelph's Department of Food Services to find the ideal apple
varieties and procedures.

The result is a cider made of a blend of apples including an historic Ontario fruit.

The "Brothers", John and John recommend that their cider be served chilled in wine glasses, in the British tradition. The two Johns point out that as well as being an alternative to wine, with only 55 calories, it is a beverage for the weight conscious.

VITAL STATISTICS - THE CIDER

Bottles only, no sugar or water is added to these products.

Olde Traditional, Sparkling, Cider, 6%

Described as having a dry, tart, bittersweet taste, with a "clear, crisp finish", I found the several examples of the product I sampled to be reminiscent of apple pie filling with a puckering finish. While it did not remind me of English cider at all, it would be good with Stilton or Brie.

"Prise de Mouse", Sparkling Cider, 6%

A champagne style cider made with a six month secondary bottle fermentation, giving it a natural bottom of sediment, this product will be released before Christmas 1993.

Not possible to describe before publication.

Available at the LCBO throughout Ontario, no details about plant tours, or souvenirs yet.

CHAPTER 7

THE BEER STORE

- the history of Brewers Retail Incorporated.

Peter Flach , President, Brewers Retail Inc.

"As I write this, in the hot, beer–drinking summer of 1993, Brewers Retail is entering the most exciting and challenging period in its 66– year history.

While the government has reconfirmed Brewers Retail's mandate to remain the principle retailer and distributor of beer in Ontario, the breakdown of Interprovincial and International Trade barriers is creating tremendous new business opportunities for us. Our plans and preparations to sell a wide variety of beer and related products from across the country, the U.S., and indeed from around the world, has been comprehensive. Some of these changes have literally changed the landscape of our 431 Beer Stores, with new, bold and creative color- schemes, and expanded floor space allocated to wider prouduct display to give our stores a unique ambience that creats a customer-friendly atmosphere. Some of our new stylish, self-serve stores in places like Scarborough, Peterborough, St. Catharines and Newmarket, are being called Beer Stores of the Future.

But it's all just window dressing if the number one ingredient is missing, and that's Service – with a capital "S"! Brewers Retail, its owners and employees are committed to being a customer-driven organization. You might say we are obsessed with the desire to offer excellent customer service and operating standards at all levels of the organization.

That commitment starts with me. I have made a long-term commitment to this organization and I don't take my responsibility lightly. I want to reinforce our company's continuing goal to be the preferred system for beer distribution and retailing in Ontario.

There are challenges ahead but there are also good times ahead for Brewers' Retail and Ontario's beer consumer."

Peter Flach, President

Mississauga, Ontario,
BREWERS RETAIL INC.

1 City Centre Drive, ste 1700,
Mississauga, Ontario, L5B 4A6
416-949-0429; FAX 416-949-1847.

On June 1st 1927, the Liquor Control Act of Ontario became law ending eleven years of prohibition, placing the distribution of all alcohol under the authority of the Liquor Control Board. To meet the public's demand for beer the Brewer's Warehousing Company Limited was formed on October 26th of that year. Becoming the Brewers Retail Inc., it is the only government chartered, multiple brewery owned retail outlet chain in the world. To understand how this system evolved it is necessary to appreciate the Provincial government's need to regulate the sale of beer to the thirsty, to the satisfaction of the brewers and drinkers alike without offending the still very powerful temperance lobby. It is also necessary to go back to World War 1.

On September 17, 1916, the Ontario Temperance Act prohibited the sale of alcoholic beverages except native wine, for purposes other than medicinal, scientific and sacramental. Legislated as a patriotic wartime measure while the lads were away in the trenches, the law meant that Ontario's 44 breweries either had to diversify, close down, sell their products by mail order, or produce "near beer". In November, two months later, a Federal Order-in-Council went one step further and closed all breweries and distilleries for the duration of the war. This action finished off all but the most enterprising operators, and in 1927, there were only 15 survivors left. Of these hangers-on, only Labatt's made it through the dry years with the same management..

On June 1st 1927, the Liquor Control Board Act of Ontario became law and breweries could once again begin brewing full strength beer for home consumption. Unfortunately, hotels were restricted to retailing 2.5% near beer, known derisively as "Fergie's Foam" after a "dry" Conservative Ontario Premier, until 1934.

Immediately upon repeal, the government issued licenses to local contractors to operate Brewers' Warehouses to carry the products of all breweries. In operation by the end of June, provincial inspectors were appointed to each store to endorse every sales slip and enforce the law.

The system as B.R. Thomson noted in "The Distributor", a monthly in house magazine published by the Brewers' Warehousing Co. Ltd. was extremely inefficient. Thomson wrote:

"As I was the only employee engaged by the contractors, it necessarily followed that I had to receive shipments from the brewers, carry out the purchases, clean the premises, do the banking, and endeavour to keep records for the brewers and books for the contractors...For the first month, my normal working hours were from 7 a.m. to at least 10 p.m; often it was past midnight when I completed the necessary records...in the beginning, furniture was at a premium. For a desk I had one packing case and another to sit on. The cash register consisted of my two side pockets ...Approximately one month after the opening date we received a visit from a gentleman wearing a bowler hat. He was an inspector from the Liquor Control Board. His comments regarding our, premises left us with the unmistakable impression that he did not like the place in which we were doing business. Other than the fact that it was an old garage without any windows and with only part of the floor boarded, it could be classed as a 'warehouse', as the stores were then known. Compared with present day standards it was somewhat lacking in facilities - no water - no plumbing -no heating." (A. Shea, "Vision in Action," 1955, pg. 104.)

(Photo courtesy, Brewers Retail Inc.)

Brewers Retail Store No.32, Hamilton, circa 1942.

Encumbered with numerous regulations, before World War II all stores ' windows were painted to prevent the public, particularly children from seeing the "demon beer".

Realizing that the private contractors would be difficult to supervise, the government called the brewers to meet to restructure the industry before it had gone too far. These consultations resulted in the provincial government and Liquor Control Board requesting "...that the breweries set up an organization which would assume responsibility for distributing brewery products according to the provisions of the Liquor Control Act." Under the subsequent charter, Brewers Warehousing Co. Ltd., a private non-profit company was charged with the provincial distribution of beer "...for the breweries which supplied the product and were also the shareholders of the company." (Shea, pg. 104.)

Not closing the independent contractors immediately, there were 70 contractors with 86 outlets selling the products of 35 breweries including five out of the province by year's end.

Initially acting in an administrative capacity, Brewers' Warehousing Co. Ltd., renewed each Contractor's agreement on an annual basis. "The Beer Sellar" relates "As beer was shipped on a consignment basis, Company auditors visited each operation in the province at regular intervals to carry out financial and stock audit ensuring that the policies of the Company and Liquor Board were being followed by the Contractors."

With sales up by 50%, the 100th store opened in Palmerston in 1928, retailing the products of 42 brewers. Regulations, however, continued to plague the beer drinker and in 1930 the L.C.B.O. added a $2.00 wine and beer consumer permit to the one already required for the purchase of alcoholic beverages. Tourists got off cheaply with a 25¢ single purchase permit.

Always concerned about the negative aspects of over consumption, the L.C.B.O. cancelled one out of every 24 permits for such reasons as "over-purchasing" to "lack of necessary means." In Toronto during the "Dirty 30s", municipal authorities requested that all applicants for relief (the dole), obtain a certificate from the L.C.B.O. stating that they did not have a valid liquor permit.

Prohibition may have been lifted, but the public's perception about beer as a beverage coupled with the Great Depression prevented the taste for malt returning at once. In 1933 there were 102 retail outlets with the breweries only operating at 16% capacity. These statistics told all. In 1913 the average Ontario drinker consumed 9.4 gallons of suds, in 1932 he only quaffed 2.6 gallons. (A. Shea, pg. 9.)

(Photo courtesy, Brewers Retail Inc.)

Brewers' Retail Storage, 2149 Danforth Ave., circa 1942.
(Brands: Silver Spire, Labatt's IPA, Dow Old Stock, O'Keefe Old York Ale.)
Frontenac White Cap Ale - all long gone friends

"In stores, beer was piled behind the counter in full view of the customer. At times, there was a great deal of 'jockeying' for position and most brewers would be anxious that their products be displayed in full view of customers. In 1929 this was changed when curtains were put across the store between the customer and the storage area." ("The Beer Sellar," pg. 14.)

The low consumption rates were due to numerous factors, not the least being the fact beer was only available for home consumption. To improve beer's image and to lobby for political action, the brewers formed the Moderation League to work for licensed lounges and stop "speakeasies". Before 1934 beer was sold by salesmen who earned between 25¢ and 40¢ for each case sold. Often the sales representatives would fill out sales permits illegally and deliver the beer to unauthorized locations. Known as B agents, these bootleggers often carried business cards that hinted at their true occupation with mottos such as "Bondy the Plasterer". (A Shea, pg. 10)

The young E.P. Taylor tackled this cumbersome distribution problem head-on by negotiating with both the provincial Liberal and Conservatives for change. After talking to the politicians Taylor discovered that prohibition was politically dead. The Conservatives informed Taylor that "If we thought the Liberal party would meet us on this thing, no issue would be made at the election." Armed with this statement, Taylor next approached the up and coming Mitch Hepburn who commented that "...the whole thing is ridiculous. We'll throw that dry plank out of the Liberal party, and if (the Conservatives think they are) going to make capital out of it in the next election...(they) can't do it."(A. Shea, pg 29.)

And sure enough, by the 1934 election, each party was committed to revising the Liquor Control Act. After the vote, an amendment was duly passed on July 23, 1934, to reduce the amount of red tape to purchase a case of beer and legalize the sale of beer and wine in beverage rooms an hotels, along with other locations for the first time since 1916.

Almost immediately sales increased and illegal activities all but ceased. For those who enjoyed draft it was now available for home consumption along with the licensed trade. Before World War 11 you could purchase a quarter or a half-barrel of beer to enjoy around the radio with friends.

(Photo courtesy, Brewers Retail Inc.)

Brewers' Retail at 440 Danforth Ave., Toronto, after 1942.

Acting upon an employee's suggestion the company's name was changed from 'Brewers' Warehouse 'to 'Brewers' Retail Store', in 1941.

War time rationing, however, ended this happy phase of our history, when a Federal Order-in-Council issued in December 1942 decreed, that the annual volume of beer sold by any one brewery should not exceed 90% of its previous year's production.

(Photo courtesy, Brewers Retail Inc.)

Brewers' Retail Store No. 47, Stratford, World War II.

By a Federal Order-In-Council issued in December 1942 beer production was limited to 90% of the previous twelve months before November 1st of that year. This led to rationing.

A series of government regulations followed that restricted beer purchases and controlled beverage room operations forcing them to close by 10:30 p.m. daily except Saturdays and holidays. Beer rationing was finally lifted in February 1946.

(Photo courtesy, Brewers Retail Inc.)

Brewers' Retail Store, 2160 Dundas St. W., Toronto World War II.

Wartime rationing line. The man to the left is probably smiling because he purchased his beer before the store's daily quota ran out.

In 1944 the Liquor Authority Act became law giving the Liquor Authority Control Board (now the Liquor Licence Board of Ontario), the responsibility for issuing, cancelling and transferring of licences.

In May 1943 beer ration books were introduced. "In May, four coupons were declared valid while for each succeeding month six coupons were valid. One coupon would buy six pints, two would buy 12 pints or six quarts, and four coupons could buy 24." Limit 36 pints per person a month. ("The Beer Sellar", pg. 16.)

For those interested in the origins of modern packaging, the introduction of upright standard weight and size cartons for a dozen large or two dozen small bottles in 1942, marks the arrival of the adman.

Before this, packages varied tremendously. In some places beer was packaged in wooden cases, while in a few locations it was sold in "apple barrels", which were wooden barrels holding ten one dozen pints, or six one dozen quart bottles. The familiar cardboard carton was available in a variety of shapes and sizes. The author of "The Beer Sellar" relates: "The majority of brewers' products were laid in reverse rows, i.e. in a 24 pint carton with three rows of eight pints laid flat, one on top of the other. All bottles, or every other bottle had protective sleeves wrapped around it. Very few cases were the stand-up carton" found today.

In 1958 the stainless steel "golden gate" barrel replaced oak barrels. Starting around 1987 the more portable Sankey keg replaced the early stainless steel barrels.

Bottles were converted to the famous brown stubby in 1962, ten years later draft home beer consumption was re-introduced, and in 1980 brand advertising was permitted in stores for the first time. In 1983 much to the joy of the bottle collector and showing the influence of the marketing man, private mold bottles once again appeared, regulating the stubby to history.

(Photo courtesy, Brewers Retail Inc.)

Gravenhurst Store No. 90, World War II.

Brewers Retail did not acquire the last remaining 38 contract warehouses until 1948.

With retailing now consolidated, the war and rationing over, the Company began entering communities previously not serviced, opening twenty new stores by the end of 1949, bringing the total to 147.

The firm now began studying ways to efficiently handle the "product". With large scale expansion on the horizon, Brewers' Warehousing Realty Limited was created in October 1953 to finance the construction program of specialized stores capable of handling palletized stock.

(Photo courtesy, Brewers Retail Inc.)

The store at Eglinton and Brimly Road, Toronto 1955.

Between 1953 and 1958 the Company underwent its most intense period of expansion and modernizatioin, completing 118 stores and depots and relocating 36 others. According to Company officials "Emphasis was placed on customer parking ... store exteriors as well as serviceability of facilites."

(Photo courtesy, Brewers Retail Inc.)

The streamlined layout of one of the new Brewers' Retail Stores reflects fashionable post war interior design

Brands available: Blue Top, Bradings, British American, Carlings, Dow.

(Photo courtesy, Brewers Retail Inc.)

Madoc, Type "A" store, 1956.
On July 20, 1956, the Company opened this store in Madoc and a second in Hastings bringing the total to 200.

(Photo courtesy, Brewers Retail Inc.)

Norm Ciceri waters the lawn at Guelph store. At least I hope it was water! 1959.
By 1960 the Company had 289 stores.

(Photo courtesy, Brewers Retail Inc.)

Marathon, 1962.
During the 1950s the Company started to reconstruct truck bodies to create their own fleet of trucks.

In 1964 the familiar logo of three arrows signifying the distribution of beer to all points of Ontario with the centre dot representing the top of a keg or bottle was designed and appeared on the firms' 350 trucks a year later.

By 1965, Ontario beer could be obtained at the beer store or delivered to a private residence. It could be consumed in beverage rooms, taverns, restaurants, dining rooms, bars, cocktail lounges, cabarets, private clubs, military messes, on trains and in hotel rooms. You could not, however, enjoy your favourite pint outside of the confines of your own home or military messes on Sundays, until the potential loss of tourism revenue during Centennial year led the government to permit the sale of beer in 1967. And even then you had to eat some food in case you drank too much.

Regulations have relaxed somewhat since 1967. The drinking age was dropped and then raised again. The first self-serve beer store opened in 1971 and the Company celebrated 50 years of operation with 400 stores in 1977.

For beer lovers, the arrival of Brick Brewing Company of Waterloo, followed soon afterwards by Upper Canada Brewing Company in 1984, and the subsequent appearance of their products on the shelves at the Brewers Retail soon put the lie to the old adage that "all beers taste the same."

A year later the firm employed approximately 2,000 regular staff, had 445 outlets and did over $1 billion in sales, making it one of Canada's largest companies.

This size drew criticism from the new "cottage" or microbreweries (under 75,000 hectolitres a year) who often found difficulty raising the funds to buy into the Brewers Retail, but now generally admit that they would not have survived without the Company's distribution system; and a campaign to sell beer in corner stores which was finally defeated in 1987.

While some ardent beer drinkers still call for the sale of beer in corner stores, citing Quebec and New York State as working examples, I wonder if they have really ever tried to find a variety of drinkable, reasonably priced specialty beers in these stores? Yes they may have some luck, but $12. for a six pack of extremely stale dated micro product is not unheard of in Quebec. And in New York, you might be able to buy Utica Club for less than $3. a six pack, but do you want to? I know that others will counter that not all micro beer is expensive and old in Quebec, especially if you know where to go - but if you don't, good luck! Just a comparison of the number of micro breweries in operation in Ontario over Quebec should demonstrate that we are not that hard done by.

In the last several years the recession has cut into beer sales as with everything else, in the Brewers Retail case it was made worse by the competition of cheap American suds sold at the L.C.B.O. In response the Brewers Retail closed 39 outlets in 1991, reducing the total to 43. Further changes are inevitable as interprovincial barriers to the sale of beer and the GATT talks take effect.

All, however, is not doom and gloom, the microbreweries are still showing healthy growth rates, and we can still get a pint of world class beers made here in Ontario, at the Beer Store.

CHAPTER 8

Gone But Not Forgotten

- Historic Ontario Breweries

With more than 725 breweries in Ontario and 70 plus in Quebec over the last three centuries, this photographic survey barely scratches the surface of brewing heritage and memorabilia. It will, I hope, make you aware of the role brewing has played in our history and will reacquaint you with some famous brands and names.

Unfortunately, no matter how enticing the Nut Brown Ales, Tonic Stouts, and various Lagers and Porters may sound, we can only use our imaginations to taste them with. And maybe that's fortunate because I tried to replicate some historic brews, and either my brewing skills were deficient, or tastes have altered dramatically because the final product was awful. If you are interested in pursuing our rich brewing heritage further, (recipes included), I would suggest my "Art and Mystery of Brewing in Ontario". While new research has uncovered far more information than is included in this book, and while the book was designed only to be an overview introduction to the topic, at the present time it is only study of the Ontario brewing industry. Even worse there is nothing dealing with Quebec province-wide.

The "Holy grail". The remains of Canada's first Commerical Brewery. One of the original vaults in Jean Talon's Brewery (1671-75) located under the old Boswell, come Dow Brewery: Quebec City, circa 1903.

From "One Hundred Years of Brewing", 1903.

Brantford

(Photo courtesy, Lee Byerlay.)

Label Westbrook and Hacker Brewing Company, Brantford, 1903 - 08.

Destroyed by fire.

Before prohibition most labels do not list a brew's alcoholic content. This admission of our "sins" was something both teetotallers and revenue men seemed to want us to know. An Extra Stout would be a stronger beer around 7% alcohol by volume.

Carlsruhe

(Photo courtesy, Bruce County History.)

The Lion Brewery, Carlsruhe around 1910 built circa 1865 by Jacob Kuntz. Willed to Kuntz's grandson Charles Schwan, the brewery was also known as the Schwan Brewery from the middle of the 1870s.

Various family members including Veronica Schwan operated the business, which did not completely close until 1932.

I have heard rumours that this old brewery is still standing.

Cornwall

Poster for the St. Lawrence Brewery Cornwall, circa 1916.

As Cornwall's first municipally subsidized industry, the prospects for the brewery in a town with a large industrial workforce, ready water supply, good transportation, and compliant Town Fathers should have been good..

Unfortunately nothing could reverse temperance, and while op[ened in 1908 by inverstors from Sherbrooke, the brewery is largely remembered for making near beer or as they politely state "Mild table Beer."

It closed in 1920. The building was then converted to an ice factory, and is now gone.

The poster was found during a bout of household renovations as wall backing, and was torn off with a hammer as the clawmarks show.

Fort William
(Thunder Bay)

(Photo courtesy, Gordon Holder.)

Old Country Style Stout, circa 1935.

Kakabeka Falls Brewing Company operated from 1909 to 1913 when it was acquired by J.J. Doran, from 1960 to 1962 it was known as Doran's Northern Breweries Ltd.

Hamilton

(Photo courtesy, Gordon Holder.)

Peller Brewing Limited , 1945 formed, operated 1946–1953.

Opened by Hungarian born Andrew Peller, this was the first independently operated brewery started in Ontario since the end of prohibition.

Unable to directly advertise his beer because of archaic laws, Peller purchased ice plant equipment. With ice to sell the company produced ads that read "Don't forget the Peller's Ice", letting the public figure out the rest.

Sorry Molson's and Labatt's your new "Ice" beer campaigns are far from new! Canadian Breweries purchased the brewery in 1953.

La Salle

(Photo courtesy, Gordon Holder.)

Hofer Brewing Company, La Salle, 1928 to 1939 when acquired and closed by Canadian Breweries.

Located south of Windsor on the St. Clair River facing Detroit, the brewery was one of several established to cater to the mob during American prohibition. Built by La Salle's entrepreneurial first mayor Vital Benoit, Hofer supplied suds to Detroit's Purple Gang along with others.

Orilla

The Orilla Brewing Company, XXX Porter, 1896-1904, likely under another name until 1915.

In 1908 humourist Stephen Leacock started building his new summer estate on the shores of Lake Couchiching, on an inlet he christened Old Brewery Bay, in honour of the Jackson Brewery ruins, still located as part of the present occupant's hot tub compound, across from Leacock's home.

Leacock, a devotee of the hop remarked that he evaluated visitors by the way they reacted to the name. He said:

"I have known that name, the Old Brewery Bay, to make people feel thirsty by correspondence as far away as Nevada."

While this bottle was not produced at Jackson's old brewery, Orillia's brewery was not closed until 1915.

Sault Ste. Marie.

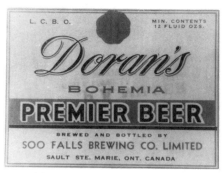

(Photo courtesy, Gordon Holder.)

Label, 1940's. Soo Falls Brewing was first formed in 1902, in 1911 J.J. Doran took it over operating it under the same name until 1961 when it was changed to Doran's Northern Breweries Ltd., in 1979 it was changed again to Northern Breweries Ltd., but was now employee owned.

Northern Breweries Ltd.

Northern Breweries started when J.J. Doran a hotelkeeper from North Bay, teamed up with J.J. MacKey and George Fee to found the Sudbury Brewing and Malting Co. in 1907. From this base the group started acquiring breweries across the north, with the acquisition of the Soo Falls Brewing Co. Ltd. in 1911, the Kakabeka Falls Brewing Co. in 1913, Timmins' Gold Belt Brewery in 1929 and finally the Port Arthur Brewing Co. Ltd. in 1948. In1961 with the KaKabeka facility now closed, the name of the four remaining breweries were changed to Doran's Northern Ontario Breweries Ltd. A decade later Doran's came under the control of Canadian Breweries Ltd., losing 40% of its value after the takeover, the business was offered to the workers in 1977, making it the first employee-owned brewery in North America.

Today plants are located in Sudbury, Thunder Bay with the head office in Sault Ste. Marie. Their brews are available in Southern Ontario.

Toronto

The name Davies Brewing and Malting Co. may have only been in use from 1883 until 1901, but the Davies started brewing as early as 1830. In 1849 Thomas Davies opened theDon (Bridge) Brewery, which became Davies Brewing Co., a fire in 1907 effectively terminated production, and the Company closed in 1910.

Toronto's premier brewing family in 1885, the city boasted 13 breweries, the Davies had interests in five of them along with numerous taverns.

Labatt's History
Thumbnail sketch -1847-

"I fancy I should like brewing better than anything else."
John Kinder Labatt's letter to his wife, 1846.

(Photo courtesy, Labatt Brewing Co. Ltd., Central Research Library and Archives.)

Letterhead detail, 1865.

This woodcut engraving depicts Labatt's house as being much larger than the brewery, when the brewery was probably larger than the house.

"x", "xx", and "xxx" are not brands of beer as some writers have suggested, but indicate the amount of malt used and consequently the amount of alcohol made. As malt was taxed, these designations told the revenue man how much he could collect.

"x would be a light table beer, "xx" a regular 5% and "xxx" a stronger ale or stout.

Labatt Brewing Company Limited was founded in 1847 on the site of its present Simcoe Street location, in London, Ontario, by John Kinder Labatt and partner brewmaster Samuel Eccles from St. Thomas. Labatt and Eccles acquired the London Brewery from innkeeper John Balkwell who started the brewery in 1828.

Originally out from Ireland in 1830, Labatt's first dealings with the brewery involved the sale of barley from his farm.

Not satisfied with farming, Labatt went to England to study business and it was here that he decided to become a brewer. Returning to London he formed a partnership with Eccles, and purchased the stone Simcoe Street brewery. Within six years, John Kinder became sole proprietor of Labatt's Brewery, with its six employees and 4,000 barrel capacity.

Sensing the need to expand the market for ale to the rural area, Labatt along with brewer John Carling, started work on the Proof Line Road (Highway 4 and Richmond Street). The real transportation breakthrough came in 1853 when the Great Western Railway steamed into London.

As an active businessman, Labatt founded the London Permanent Building and Savings Society and Western Permanent Building Society, became a member of the London Board of Trade, and held shares in the London and Port Stanley Railroad.

In spite of the growing prosperity, it was evident that the London Brewery could not support all three of Labatt's sons and young John Labatt was sent to learn the trade from John Smith, a family friend in Wheeling, Virginia in 1859.

INDIA PALE ALE 1864-1993

The temperance label depicts the gold medal awarded to John Labatt for his India Pale Ale at the Paris International Exposition of 1878. In good old fashioned bureaucratic manner the original medal sites "J.L. Labatt" in the banner; responding in kind the company replaced it with John Labatt on the labal, after the beer's father.

IPA went on to win numerous awards, and until the end in 1993, remained Labatt's most well hopped all malt product.

Developed as John Labatt's master apprentice brew upon completion of his training in "The Art and Mastery of Brewing", India Pale Ale successfully competed with lager as a clear, well hopped, moderate strength beverage.

(Photo courtesy, Gordon Holder.)

After completing his apprenticeship in 1864, and with his new recipe in hand, John was placed in charge of Smith's Prescott Brewery. When Smith's fortunes declined as a result of being on the wrong side in the American Civil War, he offered the brewery to his former protegé. Unable to raise the necessary funds to purchase the enterprise, John's brothers Robert and Ephraim stepped in and bought the brewery out from under him. The two older Labatt boys now left London, leaving their elderly father without a brewmaster. It was now only a matter of time before John Junior returned to London to brew his IPA.

Upon his father's death in 1866, John Labatt, 28, and his mother Eliza directed the brewery's fortunes. In half a dozen years John became sole owner, and in 1876 won the first of a string of awards for his IPA and Stout. A year later he finally purchased the Prescott Brewery operating it until 1906. In 1878 IPA won a gold at the International Exposition in Paris.

Following this success Labatt opened an agency in Monteral. Employing 70 hands in 1887, Labatt was now one of Canada's largest domestic brewers.

At the turn of the century John's sons John S., armed with a degree in chemistry from McGill and a brewmaster's certificate from the Brewing Academy of New York, with Hugh F. joined the firm.

(Photo courtesy, Labatt Brewing Co. Ltd., Central Research Library and Archives.)

John Labatt in his Simcoe Street office around 1900. That fine pair of mutton chops often graced Labatt's posters and advertising. Was this an early version of President's Choice?

Essentially a British style brewery, Labatt's brewed its first lager in 1911. In the same year, the firm was incorporated becoming John Labatt Limited. In 1915 John Labatt, aged 77 died. A year later Labatt's stops malting its own barley, and then prohibition becomes law.

TEMPERANCE

To endure the "dry years" Hugh and John Labatt The Third brewed beer containing more than 2.5% proof spirits for export to the U.S. for private consumption.

Through careful management, Labatt was the only one of the 15 surviving breweries of the 44 that entered prohibition, to emerge in 1927 with the same management.

(Photo courtesy, Labatt Brewing Co. Ltd., Central Research Library and Archives.)

The fact Extra Stock Ale was guaranteed to keep 21 years indicates that there was some yeast still in the bottle.

XXX Stout, circa 1930.

While brewers could legally brew full strength beer after 1927, hotels were restricted to retailing beer 2.5% alcohol by volume, known derisively as "Fergie's Foam", until 1934, when hotels could once again stock regular beer.

Labatt's along with the rest of Ontario's brewers probably used the proof spirits rating to make the beer appear stronger than it was. The arrowhead trademark is said to be a sign of quality. When pressed though, the Company doesn't really know its origins. I believe it bears a likeness to the broadarrow the British Army's ordnance department stamped onto all its equipment. As the London based Carling family were the brewers to the local 19th century garrison, the utilization of this mark would have been a marketing ploy by Labatt, indicating that his beer was also Army approved.

(Photo courtesy, Labatt Brewing Co. Ltd., Central Research Library and Archives.)

Crystal Lager Beer, 1930s

The neck label indicates that the beer was "Union Made". Labatt's employees joined the International Union of Brewery Workers in 1907. In 1936, Labatt's employees joined the National Brewery Workers Union as Local No. 1.

(Photo courtesy, Labatt Brewing Co. Ltd., Central Research Library and Archives.)

Copland's Budweiser, circa 1908.

In 1945 John Labatt Limited became a public company with 2,327 shareholders and 180,000 shares issued. A year later Labatts made its first foray into acquisitions and purchased Copland Brewing Co. Ltd. of Toronto, effectively doubling its capacity after renovations.

Founded in 1832 by William Copland, the firm amalgamated with the Ontario Brewing and Malting Co. of Toronto in 1901.

(Photo courtesy, Gordon Holder.)

Introducing Budweiser around 1908, the brand disappeared with the arrival of temperance; re-emerged as "Canada Bud Beer" with a lookalike American style label under Canada Bud Breweries from 1926-1943 until the brewery was converted to the production of O'Keefe by Canadian Breweries; it was re-introduced to the Canadian palate by Labatt's in 1981.

Copland's Tonic Stout.

Probably a sweet stout, this brew likely contained lactose and as such may very well have been "of special nutritive importance to mothers, convalescents, aged" and infirm.

Don't be shocked into believing that this was an overstrength beer, 9% proof spirits is approximately 5% alcohol by volume.

Other memorable Copland brands included Simon Pure Old Ale, Finest Ale, Nut Brown Ale, Pale Ale, Pat's Stock Ale, Red Ribbon Ale, Stock Ale, Stout and Triple Stout.

(Photo courtesy, Gordon Holder.)

Labatt's new "family" of matching labels (in the centre), 1954. While the marketing man's word gained ground rapidly after World War II, Labatt's first magazine advertisement appeared in "Canadian Home and Gardens" in 1937.

(Photo courtesy, Labatt Brewing Co. Ltd., Central Research Library and Archives.)

Labatt's Metro Brewery, 1992.

Work began on this $13.5 million dollar, 520,000 barrel brewery covering 33 acres of land in 1969.

After the Copland purchase, Labatt did not expand again until acquiring Shea's Winnipeg Brewery in 1953. Before entering the national market, they had to comply with Federal regulations that insisted each province they did business in had a brewery. Accordingly La Brasserie Labatt Limitée opened in La Salle (Montreal) in 1956; Lucky Lager Breweries Ltd. of Vancouver was acquired in 1958 subse- quently becoming Labatt Breweries of British Columbia; Labatt's Saskatchewan Brewery Ltd. was purchased in 1960; they added Bavarian Brewing Ltd. of St. John's Newfoundland in 1964; opened Labatt's Alberta Brewery Ltd. in 1964 and acquired Oland and Son Ltd. of Halifax, Nova Scotia and New Brunswick in 1971.

After the national, furore over the proposed sale of Labatt's to Milwaukee based Joseph Schiltz Brewing Co. in 1964, the Company reacted to this outburst of Canadian patriotism by restricting foreign ownership to a maximum of 20% of the voting shares. This debacle led to the reorganization of the firm the same year turning John Labatt Limited into a management holding company under Labatt Brewing Company Limited.

Growing internationally with the formation of SKOL International Limited as the starting point, Labatt's now has worldwide brewing interests.

In February 1993, Brascan (the Bronfmans through Hees-Edper), sold their controlling 38.5% stake in John Labatt Limited for $993 million to a dealer's syndicate. While speculation was sparked whether or not Anheuser-Busch would buy into the firm, Labatt President George Taylor told "Toronto Star" reporter Tony Van Alphen that:

"While we might speculate on (the takeover of another company), I think I can safely say that the shares are broadly held and I have no reason to believe that the company will be pursued by a predator."

When sold, John Labatt Ltd. had interests in brewing, dairy (Ault) foods, and entertainment. Owned 90% of the Toronto Blue Jays, TSN, the cable sports channel, and various event production companies. With its Head Office in London, it had 12,000 employees, $2.7 billion in revenue and a profit on $104 million for the first six months of 1993.

For beer lovers, 1993 also saw the demise of IPA, first brewed by John Labatt as his Masterbrewer's beer in 1864. In the name of efficiency, Labatt also closed their century old Waterloo plant. Originally known as the L. Kuntz Park Brewery, the foundations for this facility were laid in 1864 by David Kuntz.

Whoever ends up controlling the Company, Labatt's Ontario currently produces over twenty beers, including Blue and Blue Lite, which sold 2,992,000 hectolitres in 1991 accounting for 16% of the national market, making this duo Canada's number one selling brews.

P.S. Sorry sports fans, no Blue Jays history here!

(For a first hand account of the history of "Blue" see the "Interview with Al Brash" at the end of Sleeman's entry.)

Molson's History

Thumbnail sketch - 1786 -

On July 28, 1786 John Molson wrote in his diary:

"This day bought 8 bu(shels) of barley. MY COMMENCEMENT ON THE GRAND STAGE OF THE WORLD."

With the brewery located at the foot of the St. Mary's rapids, just east of walled Montreal, humourist and noted admirer of malt beverages, Stephen Leacock wrote in "Montreal, Seaport and City":

"Molson built his brewery a little way down stream from the town, close beside the river. Archaeologists can easily locate the spot as the brewery is still there."

Growing steadily, the Molsons became distillers, railway promoters, boat builders, bankers, philanthropists - in a word, influential.

By Confederation brewery production peaked, placing Molson's firmly in 4th place in the Quebec market. This position altered when National Breweries was formed in 1909, turning Molson's into the province's single largest brewery.

John H.R. Molson & Bros. operated between 1861 and 1911.
(Photo courtesy, Gordon Holder.)

In 1945 Molson's became a public corporation allowing for the implementation of expansion plans. Two years later, the brewery's production capacity was tripled. By 1953 Molson's with only one brewery, was Canada's largest brewer. Already well known in Ontario where they had been retailing Export and Stock ales since 1928, they were now ready to go national.

The Molson family first entered Ontario when Thomas moved to Kingston in 1824 to circumvent Lower Canada's Civil Code. In Quebec if he predeceased his wife the bulk of his estate would go to his spouse, in Upper Canada he could will his holdings to his children. Apparently prospering Molson remained here until 1835. Now casting his eyes on the growing Toronto market, Toronto City Council in 1850 refused to grant the Molson's a building permit to protect the local brewing industry. Not satisfied with this unfavourable turn of events, Thomas Molson took his money and moved to Port Hope, while the rest of the clan returned to Montreal, to prosper as bankers, soldiers and brewers.

Molson started brewing Stock Ale in Toronto in October, 1956.
(Photo courtesy, Gordon Holder.)

Finally in 1953 Molson's was able to purchase nine and a half acres of reclaimed property along Toronto's lakeshore, ironically six acres of it from E.P. Taylor of O'Keefe Brewing. Work immediately started on the new $11,000,000 facility that would employ 300 people.

Officially opened on August 17, 1955, the 300,000 barrel brewery's front door was located on land that had been under 12 feet of water in 1912.

Now with two breweries in two provinces Molson began its careful expansion that led it to become Canada's largest brewing organization.

In 1958, in their next phase the firm purchased Sicks' Breweries Ltd. with facilities in Vancouver, Edmonton, Lethbridge, Regina and Prince Albert. Two years later they acquired Fort Garry Brewery Ltd. In 1962 they purchased Newfoundland Brewery Ltd. of St. John's. To reflect the fact that they had breweries from coast to coast and in every province except the three maritime provinces, the corporate name was changed to Molson Breweries of Canada Ltd. Reinforcing its national position, Molson's began to co-sponsor Hockey Night in Canada in 1965 - by 1966 they claimed 20% of the Ontario market. In 1968 the Ontario brewery had a 1,000,000 barrel capacity. The next year the brewhouse building was finished making it the largest single complete brewing facility in Canada. Major expansion next occurred with the purchase of Formosa Spring Brewery in 1974.

Six years later the Company held 40% of the Ontario beer market. The next decade saw Molson Breweries as one part of The Molson Companies Limited, with interests in retail merchandising through Beaver Lumber, chemical products through the Diversey Corporation, sports, entertainment, and venture capital.

With the merger between Molson and Elders in 1989, Molson produced 12.6 million hectolitres of beer annually, available in 24 brands to more than 100 countries.

While Canadian and Canadian Light Lager ranked second in 1990 and 1991 with the Canadian consumer drinking 2,244,000 hectolitres giving it 12% of the market.

For historians Export Ale, developed during the first decade of the 20th century by brewmaster John Hyde and Herbert Molson, is still number 3 with 7% of the market.

Formosa Springs Brewery

Formed in 1870, a century later the brewery was purchased by Benson and Hedges. In a twist of corporate logic Benson and Hedges then closed the Formosa Brewery to open a new Formosa Brewery in Barrie. Molson's in its first Ontario acquisition, now purchased the enlarged Formosa Barrie Brewery in 1974.

Label circa 1940
(Photo courtesy, Gordon Holder.)

In the meantime the brewery in Formosa remained dormant until Northern Algonquin Brewing Company reopened its doors in 1989, as part of the microbrewery movement.

Molson Ontario, Rexdale, 1993.

Originally constructed in 1961 for Canadian Breweries, after the 1989 merger with Carling O'Keefe (Elders IXL), the Toronto Fleet Street Brewery was closed, and prepared for demolition, while brewing operations were moved to this facility near Pearson International Airport. Ideally situated at the junction

of Highways 427 and 401, the brewery's location provides tremendous visibility and accessibility.

The merger not only reduced Ontario's major brewers to two, it also freed up a number of men, some of whom started working for microbreweries such as Algonquin. Excess equipment from the Fleet Street brewery for example, has also been dispersed, with some of the storage tanks now lined up in front of Great Lakes Brewing.

MOLSON

CANADIAN BREWERIES LIMITED

Created on March 8, 1930 as the Brewing Corporation of Ontario, the future Canadian Breweries acquired 23 companies with 150 brands in its first 23 years. Over the same time frame it closed 12 of the breweries and reduced the brands to nine. In August 1989, Carling O'Keefe as it was now known, was controlled by Elders IXL, who merged with the Molson Companies Limited to create Molson Breweries, making it the largest brewer in Canada.

In 1992 this new mega brewery produced 26 beers, and 5 durangos. The famous names that survived the merger from Carling O'Keefe were: O'Keefe Ale, Toby Black Label, and Old Vienna.

This capsule chronology traces the rise and fall of Canadian Breweries.

1930, March 8

The Brewing Corporation of Ontario was formed.

October 9

The name is changed to the Brewing Corporation of Canada Ltd.

1937, April 21

The name becomes Canadian Breweries Ltd.

1968

Rothman's of Pall Mall buys the enterprise.

1975

The name is changed to Carling O'Keefe Limited-Carling O'Keefe Limitée.

1987

Carling O'Keefe becomes part of Elders IXL, Australia's largest corporate conglomerate and the seventh-largest brewery in the world.

1989, August

The Molson Companies Limited and Elder IXL combine their North American brewing organizations to become the new Molson Breweries.

Detailed Chronology

1930

The Brewing Corp. of Ontario was created when the Brading Breweries Ltd. of Ottawa, British American Brewing Co. Ltd. of Windsor, The Kuntz Brewery Ltd. of Waterloo and Taylor and Bate Ltd. of St. Catharine's joined.

1930, October 1

The new business acquires 51% of Canadian Brewing Corp. Ltd. of Montreal. With this they obtained Dominion Brewing Co. Ltd. of Toronto, Regal Brewing Co. and its subsidiary Grant Springs of Hamilton, Empire Brewing Co. Ltd. of Brandon, and Kiewel Brewing Co. Ltd. of St. Boniface, Manitoba.

In the same year the firm acquired Carling Breweries Ltd. of London.

1931

Acquired Budweiser Brewing Co. of Canada Ltd., in Belleville and closed it in 1936.

1934

Purchased and closed the Welland Brewery Ltd. Acquired Cosgrave's and O'Keefe Brewing Co. Ltd., both of Toronto.

1935

Purchased Riverside Brewing Corp. Ltd. of Windsor and closed it.

1937 to 1943

Acquired complete control of Toronto's Canada Bud Ltd. and then closed it.

1939

Acquired Hofer Brewing Co. Ltd. of La Salle, near Windsor and closed it.

1940

Took full control of Reinhardt's in Toronto, and amalgamated it with Cosgrave's discontinuing the Reinhardt labels in 1949.

1943

Acquired Bixel Brewing and Malting Co. Ltd. of Brantford in 1943 for $100,000 and closed it a year later.

1944

Acquired Capital Brewing Co. Ltd. of Ottawa and Walkerville Brewery Ltd.

1946

Acquired Dominion Malting Co. Ltd.

1952

Negotiated the purchase of Old Comrades Brewery Ltd. in Tecumseh. Acquired control of National Breweries Ltd. of Quebec, the makers of Dow and Kingsbeer.

1953

Acquired Ranger Brewery in Waterloo, and began producing Dow here in 1955.

Acquired the Peller Brewing Co. Ltd. of Hamilton.

1954

Carling Brewing Co. of Cleveland acquired plants in St. Louis, and Belleville, Illinois, and becomes on of the ten largest brewers in the United States. The concern sells Victory Mills Ltd. to Proctor and Gamble. The malting division is renamed Dominion Malting (Ont.) Ltd.

1955

Acquired Griesedieck Western Brewery Co.

1956

Bradings is now totally subsumed by Carling Breweries. The Carling plant at Tecumseh, and the O'Keefe plants in Ottawa and Walkerville were closed.

1959

Acquired Heidleberg Brewery Co. Inc., of Tacoma Washington.

1961

Acquired Calgary Brewing and Malting Co. Ltd., along with it Bohemian Maid Brewing Co.

1962

Acquired Western Canada Breweries, Beamish and Crawford brewing in Cork Ireland, and Bennett Brewing Co. Ltd. of Newfoundland

1964

Acquired Arizona Brewing Co.

1968

Argus Corp. Ltd. sold Canadian Breweries Ltd. to Rothman's of Pall Mall, Canada.

1971

Acquired Doran's Northern Breweries Ltd.

1975

Acquired Jordan Valley Wines. Canadian Breweries changes its name to Carling O'Keefe Breweries of Canada Ltd.

1977

Sold Doran's Northern Ontario Breweries back to the employees. Sold the American Carling National Breweries Inc., and its subsidiary Century Importers.

1982

Acquired Century Importers Inc. to distribute Carling O'Keefe in the U.S.A.

1987

Elders IXL Ltd. of Australia purchases Carling O'Keefe.

1989

The Molson Companies Ltd. and Elders IXL combine to become Molson Breweries of Canada Ltd., making it the largest brewer in Canada and fifth largest in North America.

(Photo courtesy, Gordon Holder)

The famous stag head on a label of Brading's Old Stock Ale, Brading Breweries Ltd., 1950 to 1957.

In 1865, 33 year old English brewmaster from the town of Brading on the Isle of Wight, Harry Fisher Brading, along with partners Israel and Attwood opened the brewery that was destined to become the cornerstone of Canadian Breweries.

Originally known as the Union Brewery, Brading became the sole owner in 1880.

Undergoing the usual management and corporate changes, Bradings as it came to be known, benefited from prohibition as it was able to sell 'mail order" beer. Under the rules:

"An Ontario customer could write to a Quebec merchant, place an order for beer and enclose payment. The Quebec merchant could then transmit this order to the Brading plant in Ottawa, which would ship the beer direct to the consumer. Thanks to this Brading's was able to sell enough to pay off a $90,000 mortgage before the law was amended." (A.A. Shea, 1955, pg. 114.)

In 1924, E.P. Taylor joined the board of director's.

Events now moved quickly. The company was renovated, and E.P. started to formulate plans that led to the creation of Canadian Breweries. To further these designs E.P. prompted Brading's to purchase controlling interest in the Kuntz Brewery in Waterloo. Within a year Taylor had created the Brewing Corporation of Ontario, and was ready to launch a new era in Ontario's brewing story.

(Photo courtesy, Gordon Holder.)
British American's famous "Handsome Waiter" label, circa 1925.

The Company was formed in 1883, and the Handsome Waiter label introduced in 1921. The story as related by A. Shea as to the origin of the Handsome Waiter follows this outline.

Hoping to open a brewery in Canada, 26 year-old Detroit native Louis Griesinger brewed several sample kegs of beer. He now contracted a sales agent to market this as yet unnamed brew in Chatham. After sampling a stein of this lager, an appreciative innkeeper asked for its name. The quick-thinking traveller, W.K. Sheldon, christened it Cincinnati Cream to underline the fact that it was produced by a "secret formula" brought to Canada from the North American home of good beer, by young brewmaster Griesinger.

In 1930 British American became one of the four founding breweries of Canadian Breweries.
the product continued to be produced. Undergoing several corporate name changes and extensive renovations, the brewery was closed in 1969, and now houses the Art Gallery of Windsor.

INSIST UPON

The
**Real
Kuntz's**

Seek
the
Star
on
Label

PROGRAMME—Continued
"The Fairy Ring," a novelty of marvellous
beauty.
Exhibition balloons, avenues of royal palms,
streamers of poppies, eight mammoth special mines,
flight of 24 golden turbillions and explosion of eight
mammoth star mines.

Seek the star on the label and the word "WATERLOO."
Only then can you be sure of getting the superfine lager that
is so much imitated in all but exquisite quality. You would
not knowingly buy an imitation once you'd tasted the real
thing. Its flavor surpasses—and has for sixty years.

Kuntz's
ORIGINAL LAGER

Sold by cafes, hotels and liquor dealers.
Bottled only at the brewery in Waterloo by
KUNTZ BREWERY Limited

Hamilton Agency—Corner West Avenue and Young Street.
GUS KUNTZ, AGENT   PHONE 2983

(Photo courtesy, Hamilton Public Library, Special Collections.)
Kuntz advertisement, 1911.

The Kuntz Brewery in Waterloo was founded in 1844. Twenty years later work started on the L. Kuntz Park Brewery, used by Labatt's until 1993. Over the years family members took the Kuntz brewing secrets to Carlsruhe, Hamilton, and Ottawa. While prohibition legally closed the brewery, the Kuntzs' along with many Ontario Germans found the law peculiar to say the least, and continued to brew for the export market. Apparently some of this "export" beer was consumed at home, and as this was illegal, no taxes were paid. It was now just a matter of time before Revenue Canada noted this, and while brewing for the domestic market became legal again, these activities were cut short in September 1929 when the Attorney General of Canada was awarded $200,000 in tax arrears from Kuntz. Now cash strapped, E.P. Taylor busily creating Canadian Breweries, seized this chance to acquire the $1,000,000 facility for Brading's for $10,000, and assumption of all outstanding debts in 1930.

Forming a key element in Taylor's plans the firm's various holdings were streamlined. In 1934 Kuntz's soft drink division was amalgamated with O'Keefe to create Consolidated Beverages. Two years later Carling-Kuntz Breweries absorbed Carling of London and centralized the production of these units at the Waterloo plant.

Herb Kuntz returned in 1940 to manage the brewery. He witnessed the removal of the Kuntz name in 1944 when the company was reorganized as Carling Breweries Ltd. In 1977, the old factory was purchased by Labatt's who closed it in 1993 and prepared it for demolition.

(Photo courtesy, Gordon Holder.)

Carling's Red Cap Ale, circa 1940. Red Cap Ale was introduced in 1927, reflecting manager Charles Burn's love of horseracing.

Carling Breweries Ltd. of London was formed in 1840 by Thomas Carling to fill the mugs of the thirsty British garrison.

Growing steadily into Quebec and the Maritimes before World War 1, prohibition did not shut the brewery down until 1920. Within two years the business was in new hands - with a new charter and a new name - Carling Export Brewing and Malting. When prohibition ended, the company assumed its old name Carling Breweries Ltd. 80,000 square feet in size, with storage facilities covering 10 acres, Carling's was the largest brewing complex in Canada. In 1928 the firm opened a $400,000 bottling plant in Montreal.

The Depression found Carling overextended and the company became one of Canadian Breweries first major amalgamations in 1930.

Six years later the London facility closed when Carling moved into the old Kuntz plant in Waterloo.

By 1955 Carling could brew 500,000 barrels a year. The firm established in 1840 to satisfy the thirsts of willing British troopers, now had plants in Cleveland, St. Louis, Belleville (Illinois), Tecumseh (Ontario), Waterloo, Toronto and Montreal.

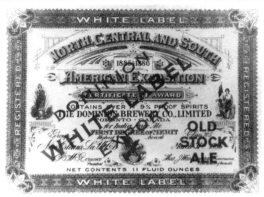

(Photo courtesy, Gordon Holder.)
Dominion Brewery Co. Ltd. label circa 1930.

The Brewery was founded when Robert Davies left the family controlled Don Brewery in 1878. Before prohibition it was legal for a brewery to own taverns. At one time Davies owned 144 Toronto taverns, the Don and Copland Breweries and had majority interests in the Dominion Brewery.

The Company re-emerged in 1926 after temperance, when Dominion and Regal of Hamilton amalgamated to create the Canadian Brewing Corp. Ltd., in 1930 it was taken-over by Canadian Breweries. (Brewing Corp. of Canada Ltd). The renovated Queen Street East brewery is still standing, along with the worker's row housing across the street, and you can even purchase a pint of brew at Gennaro's, housed in the original brewery pub.

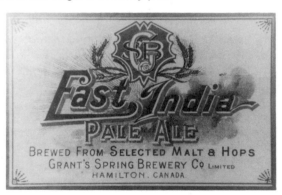

(Photo courtesy, Gordon Holder.)
East India Pale Ale, circa 1900. Labels for the popular IPA style often carried the additional word "East". Pre prohibition labels rarely mention alcoholic content.

Originally formed sometime around 1842, a copywriter taking aim at the teetotal medicinal "tonic" takers in 1899 wrote:"It is claimed when Grant's beer is drunk moderately it will invigorate and tone up the system much more efficiently than the majority of widely advertised tonics, whose only claim to excellence is the fact that the principal constituents of Grant's beer are used in small amounts in their make-up."Canadian Breweries acquired the plant in 1930 and closed it a year later.

(Photo courtesy, Metropolitan Toronto Library, Baldwin Room, 964-4-1)
The "Hands" at the O'Keefe Brewery Co., 1891 - 1923.

Formed in 1840 by Charles Hannath, Irishmen Eugene O'Keefe, with countryman Patrick Cosgrave and George M. Hawke purchased the brewery in 1862.

In 1879, O'Keefe's became one of Canada's first large scale brewers to produce lager; he followed this up by becoming one of the first to use motorized delivery trucks, and the first to install a mechanically refrigerated storehouse.

The tragic death of O'Keefe's son, however, changed Eugene's priorities and he turned to the Catholic Church. After a series of corporate changes E.P. Taylor was able to add O'Keefe's to his portfolio in 1934. Capitalizing on the downtown Toronto location at Victoria and Gould, Taylor turned this brewery into his head office.

While the brewery has been demolished, the Art Deco inspired office building at 297 Victoria Street, is now part of the communications centre of Ryerson Polytechnical Institute.
As for the O'Keefe name, it was revived in 1975 as Carling O'Keefe.

(Photo courtesy, Gordon Holder).

Cosgrave's Half ale and Half porter, circa 1925.

When Patrick Cosgrave arrived in Canada West. in 1849 from Ireland he claimed Canada "needed a real porter." Trying his luck at Pucky Huddle (Mississauga near Square One), he returned to Toronto to join forces with Eugene O'Keefe. He struck out on his own in 1863, when he acquired the old West Toronto Brewery on Niagara Street. Growing steadily the firm was taken over by son James F. Lawrence, who acquired the Toronto Brewing and Malting Co. on Simcoe St. in 1915.

The timing was bad and prohibition forced the introduction of near beer, sales collapsed and the breweries were closed. After a number of changes, the firm emerged from prohibition as the Cosgrave Export Brewing and MaltingCo. The Queen Street brewery was sold to Canadian Breweries in 1934. The old Cosgrave plant was converted to the production of O'Keefe ale in 1945, to be

(Photo courtesy, Gordon Holder.)

Salvador Lager Beer, circa 1935. According to the brewery's copywriter this was the "National Beverage", "Life Saver" that "...made Toronto famous."

Known as the East End Brewery from 1862, Lothar Reinhardt acquired the brewery in 1889. In 1900 Reinhardt opened the Salvador Brewery in Montreal, *brewing ale, porter and lager. The Toronto brewery was closed during Ontario's dry years, but reopened as the Reinhardt Brewery Co. Ltd. as soon as prohibition was lifted. It was acquired by Canadian Breweries in 1936, the old brands were replaced by the Cosgrave label, and then Carling's products, before it was closed in 1949.*

(Photo courtesy, Lee Byerlay.)

   Crown cap for Bixel's near beer circa 1918.

Originally established under the name The Spring Bank Brewery, the operation was turned into a tannery in 1863, ravaged by a fire, and then rebuilt. In 1888 the business became known as the Bixel Brewing and Malting Company. Canadian Breweries acquired the facility in 1943 and closed it in 1944. The brewery stood until 1979, when it was once again levelled by fire.

(Photo courtesy, Gordon Holder.)

   Walkerville Brewery Ltd., circa 1930.

Formed in 1890 to produce lager beer only, the brewery suffered the usual indignities associated with the dry years, even being acquired by Herman Radner of Detroit in 1924.

The firm was subsequently acquired by Canadian Breweries in 1944 and renamed Carling Breweries (Walkerville) Ltd., it then became the O'Keefe Brewery and was finally closed in 1956.

CHAPTER 9

The Tastings

It is a curious fact that all of Canada's beer writers prefer ale. Accordingly lagers, light beers and almost anything else are given sometimes rather shoddy treatment. I believe that this is more than a little bit presumptuous, as the vast majority of the beer made and consumed by Canadians is the type most writers delight in making fun of. To try to correct this imbalance, and to make this guide of some use to you lager lovers, and non Anglophobes I have tried a new approach to "tasting".

Here the various styles have been evaluated by trained and untrained, but enthusiastic panels of beer lovers of all persuasions, according to each brew's characteristics, rather by my preferences. To counteract any bias, the leanings of the panel have been boldly stated with each category.

Because the "tastings" were not conducted by beer tasters alone, the answers may not fit into the standard descriptive phrases, but do offer very clear opinions of the products sampled. One of the most noteworthy by products of any tasting conducted by untutored drinkers is in fact - their harshness to products they find offensive, and their high regard for those they favour. Feel free to disagree and write in your opinions!

Cheers!

Beer Appreciation Scale

Brewpub-Brewery: _____

Brand: _____

Date tasted: _____

Assign a numerical value to the characteristics listed below and enter into 'total" column.

Look-Complexion	*Total*
Clarity -amber and light beers- hazy to brilliant	0 - 10
-dark beers- hazy to brilliant	0 - 10
Head -for beers from large modern breweries,	
no head to most desirable.	0 - 10
Or	
Natural beers only	
Sediment - add two if sediment free	
(bottle conditioned beer exempted)	0 - 2
Head: - no head to most desirable	0 - 8
Aroma and Bouquet:	
Malt and hops	0 - 15
Taste:	
Head: no taste 0; gassy 2; foamy - creamy 6	0 - 6
Beer: balance between hops\malt\rice\bitter\sweet	
-poor to very good	0 - 14
Carbonation:	
Mouthtaste	0 - 5
Aftertaste:	
Lingering chemical 0; bitter stale 2;	
none 4; great 10	0 - 10
Production: Craftsmanship Bonus - Aging	
Large commercial	0 - 2
brewpub - micro brewery	2 - 5
Overall:	
Did you like it?	0 - 25

Comments:

Rating: Below 70, no mug
        70 to 74, good, a single mug
        75 to 84, very good, two mugs
        85 to 89, excellent, three mugs
        90 to 100, superior, four mugs.

GLOSSARY OF TERMS Brewing and Food

ADJUNCT:

Grains or sugars added in place of barley malt. Usually to cut costs.

ALE:

Beer made with top-fermenting yeast. (It is not unknown for some brewers to make "lagers" with ale yeast, strictly speaking this is not possible. Similarly I am suspect of a bottom fermenting ale yeast now used on the West Coast.)

Or the purists might prefer this definition of ALE from 1597.

ALE is made of malte and water; and they the which do put any other thynge to ale then is rehersed, except yest, barme, or godesgood, doth sofystical (sofisticate) theyr ale. Ale for an Englysshe man is a naturall drynke. Ale must haue these propertyes; it must be fresshe and cleare, it muste not be ropy or smoky, nor it must haue no weft nor tayle. Ale shuld not be dronke vnder.v. dayes olde. Newe ale is vnholsome for all men. And sowre ale, and deade ale the which doth stande a tylt, is good for no man. Barly malte maketh better ale then oten malte or any other corne doth: it doth ingendre grose humoures; but yette it maketh a man stronge. From Andrew Borde's "The First Boke of the Introduction of Knowledge." London, 1597.

BAGUETTE:

French bread.

BANGERS AND MASH:

Grilled sausages and mashed potatoes.

BEER ENGINE:

Hand operated draft suction pump.

BERE (Beer):

Bere is made of malte, of hoppes and water: it is a naturall drynke for a Dutche man. And nowe of late dayes it is moche vsed in Englande to the detryment of many Englysshe men; specyally it kylleth them the which be troubled with the colycke, and the stone, & the strangulion; for the drynke is a colde drynke; yet it doth make a man fat, and doth inflate the bely, as it doth appere by the Dutche mens faces & belyes. If the bere be well serued, be fyned, & not new, it doth qualyfy the heat of the lyuer. Once again from Andrew Borde, physycke doctor, 1597.

BITTER:

Well hopped English ale.

BLACK AND TAN:

Bitter mixed with stout in equal amounts. (There are numerous variations to this basic combination.)

BOCK:
>A bottom fermented beer (type of lager), usually darker than most lagers, with a higher alcoholic content.

BOTTLE CONDITIONED:
>Beer that continues a natural secondary fermentation in the bottle.

BOTTLED DRAFT:
>If draft is non pasteurized, well refrigerated, filtered beer, it is possible to have "bottled" draft! Then why the difference between bottled and kegged draft?

>Starting in the United States with "one way" bottles, the fashion came to Canada where the returnable bottles made the whole process more difficult. First tried on a large scale by Labatt's in Quebec in 1967; by 1992 Labatt Genuine Draft rated as Canada's fourth most popular beer along with Coors and Molson Special Dry.

>The difference derives basically from the degree of filtration according to Sleeman's Brewmaster Al Brash. Bottled draft is cold filtered with submicron filters that remove almost all the residual yeast cells or bacteria, producing a cleaner product. This "over" filtration, necessary for the longer shelf life bottle draft requires, reduces the chances of a good foam and diminishes the flavour and colour.

>In essence the less microscopically filtered keg draft may have more foam and flavour because it is not as "clean" as bottle draft and has not had as many impurities removed.

BREWSTER:
>A woman brewer.

CARAMEL MALT:
>Barley malt that has been cooked until the sugar crystallizes.

CASK CONDITIONED:
>Ale with yeast still alive in the cask. The cask has to settle several days after being moved before being tapped.

CHAMPAGNE LAGER:
>See Krausened.

COCK ALE:
>To make cock-ale take eight gallons of ale; take a cock and boil him well; then take four pounds of raisins of the sun well stoned, two or three nutmegs, three or four flakes of mace, half a pound of dates; beat these all in a mortar, and then put to them two quarts of the best Sack; and when the ale hath done working, put these in, and stop it close six or seven days, and then bottle it, and a month after you may drink it. From, "The Closet of the eminently learned Sir Kenelme Digbie Kt. opened: Whereby is discovered several ways for making of Metheglin, Sider, Cherry-Wine,

etc. together with Excellent Directions for Cookery as also for Preserving, Conserving, Candying etc." London, 1669.

You might wonder why this recipe has been included. See The Kingston Brewing Co., the recipe is not as archaic as you might like to think.

COLD FILTERED:

No one ever "warm" filters their beer. An advertising gimmick stating the obvious.

CORNISH PASTIE:

Flaky pastry filled with meat, potatoes and vegetables.

CREAM ALE:

A North American term, referring to a brew where ale and lager have been blended.

DRY BEER:

"The vinification and rarefication of taste to minimum liquid alcohol." Beer with the residual sweetness removed. Remember this beer was developed in Japan, and then think of the national beverage sake. Once again according to Brewmaster Al Brash, the super attentuation removes the residual sugars from the body removing the underlying sweetness provided by the malt. This removal of the fermentable sugars leads to the dryness. When I asked Al why this beer was made he said "This is not a brewer's beer, it is a marketing man's beer, it is not balanced." It was developed to remove the sweet aftertaste.

DUVEL COCKTAIL:

Gin and tonic with Duvel on top. Recommended by Kevin and Dora at Allen's.

EISBOCK:

Ice bock was first introduced by Niagara Brewing to Canadian palates in 1989-90. It is a bock beer that has been frozen. As water freezes before alcohol, the ice is removed leaving a more potent concentrate. See Ice Beer.

FIRE BREWED:

Traditional use of direct flame to heat the brew kettle, tends to offer a touch of carmelization. Most brewers use steam heat today.

FIZZY QUAFFER:

Beer drinker who swears by carbonated, sweet, pasteurized beer, preferably American, and in cans, but bottles will do. Represents the majority of the Canadian market.

GAMBRINUS:
  Legendary King of Beer, originally from modern day Belgium. Gambrinii
  are people dedicated to the appreciation of beer, and are engaged in the
  quest of finding the perfect beer.

HB:
  Hofbräu, or court brew associated with a Munich beer hall.

HIGH GRAVITY:
  The process many large brewers use in which they brew the beer to a high
  alcoholic content and then cut it with water.

HOMEBREWER:
  Anyone who is tired of subsidizing the government further by paying
  taxes for beer, and who is interested in making good beer. After the last
  Ontario provincial budget, which slapped a tax on brew your own
  operations it is more difficult to beat the tax man, but still possible to brew
  your own great beer. Look at the homebrewing section and consider
  joining the Canadian Amateur Brewers Assoc.

  Often people who enjoy a pint of homebrew claim that it has a less inebriating
  effect than commercial brews made with the same alcohol. This is a false
  perception. They often do not feel the effects of the alcohol immediately,
  as the high carbonation in commercial brews quickly enhances the feeling
  of elation most people associate with alcoholic consumption. For a
  comparison think of the quick effects of champagne. Watch out though,
  even though homebrew may take longer to hit you, the alcohol is still
  there in all its force.

HOPS:
  The flowers used from the female hop vine as a preservative, and to add
  bitterness to beer. (Aftertaste.)

ICE BEER:
  See Eisbock and the ads by Labatt's and Molson's. Ice Beer is nothing
  new, as early as 1946, Peller of Hamilton, unable to directly advertise the
  fact he sold beer ran an ad campaign that said "Don't forget the ice."
  Producing ice as well as beer, people soon realized that he was reminding
  them to pick up some ice for their freezer to cool down some Peller beer.
  And according to a story related to me by German brewmaster, Harald
  Sowade, Ice Beer was discovered by accident in Bavaria between the two
  World Wars, when a group of Nazi's transporting a truck load of beer got
  stuck in a storm, the beer froze. Not wanting to waste it, they siphoned off
  the remaining beer concentrate and bottled it. They enjoyed the higher
  alcohol and discovered a new style of beer. The style was again
  "discovered" by Allied Brewers in the United Kingdom in 1967.

IMPERIAL STOUT:
> Not actually made in Canada, it is medium dry, and 7 to 10% in strength.

KRAUSENED:
> The addition of a new wort to the fermenting brew to activate the yeast. Beer made in this manner may be called "Champagne".

KRIEK:
> Cherry flavoured Belgium beer. Developed before hops became the dominant seasoning.

LAGER:
> Beer made with bottom-fermenting yeast. (It is not unknown for brewers to make "ales" with lager yeast, even though strictly speaking this is not possible.)

LAGER - NORTH AMERICAN:
> This new style, suggested to me by brewmaster Michael Hancock, could aptly describe the best North American mainstream beers. Light in colour, light in taste, light in aroma. Sweet.

Originating in the last quarter of the 19th century, this lighter lager grew out of the twin demands of technology and temperance. Refrigeration and improved transportation networks made it possible to move beer across the continent. Pasteurization increased the product's shelf life, making this movement feasible.

Temperance advocates demanded a lighter product. The brewers responded with lager.

Introduced to Canada by E.P. Taylor of Canadian Breweries, the quality and standardization of the product received new impetus when Canadian troops acquired the taste for light, fizzy American beer during World War 11. With a ready market for this new product, lager grew in popularity until the 1960's, when the ad man enters telling us not only what to drink, but what we like.

LAMBIC:
> Unique to Belgium, "spontaneously fermenting" beer.

LITE:
> World Beer Guru Michael Jackson claims that this is an American term for a watery style lager, lighter in alcohol, calories and taste than the standard beers. I have to agree, just try lower alcohol German and English beers to discover that they do not have to be without character. Or at 4.5% try Dragon's Breath if you want taste in a lower alcohol beer.

MALT EXTRACT:
> Evaporated liquid from wort. Used for homebrewing, and in some brewpubs and micros.

MALT LIQUOR:
> Bottom fermented beer. The malty taste and higher alcohol content make it more like an ale than a lager.

OATMEAL STOUT:
> Stout made with pre-cooked rolled oats, try St. Ambroise's Oatmeal Stout.

PASTEURIZATION:
> Lengthens shelf life, but tends to dull flavour and flatten the taste. It stops further fermentation, and interferes with natural carbonation. Advances in micron filtration are making this process relatively obsolete.

PEROGY:
> A potato dumpling filled with cheese, meat, vegetables, or rarely, fruit.

Usually fried and served with sour cream and bacon.

PILSNER "PILS" (PILSENER):
> Originally from the City of Pilsen Czechoslovakia, the beer was not developed until 1842. In its purest form it possesses a hoppy aroma and dry finish. It is the inspiration for most popular North American mass produced beers today.

PLOUGHMAN'S - PLOUGHPERSON'S LUNCH:
> The ingredients vary to this most traditional English pub fare, but it should include some form of crusty bread, cheese, pickles or relish such as chutney, pickled onions are a rare treat, lettuce, tomatoes, and sometimes fruit. Cold cuts and soup do not really belong.

PORTER:
> Originally brewed in London, and enjoyed by porters, this ale is made with roasted unmalted barley. A creamy, sweet, nutty beverage. Some countries produce bottom fermented porter.

POUTINE:
> French fries with gravy and cheddar curds.

REAL ALE:
> For the purist this is an all natural unfiltered, cask conditioned, draft beer. In Canada, Wellington County's "County Ale" and "Arkell Best Bitter" qualify along with the products of the Granite Brewery in Toronto and Halifax.

> CAMRA Canada defines real ale as beer "...brewed only from malt, hops and water, fermented with yeast, naturally conditioned, stored and served without artificial carbonation.

REINHEITSGEBOT:

German Pure Beer Law. The Bavarian food purity law proclaimed in 1516 specifying that beer could only be made from barley malt, hops, and water. Yeast was not listed as the work it did had yet to be identified. In 1919 the law was amended to permit the use of wheat instead of barley. Still the law in Germany, beer made to these standards is of the highest quality and assures the imbiber that they will be getting a natural, unpasteurized, chemical free product. Unfortunately, the law does not apply to exported German beers.

SCRUMPIE:

This is the subtle knee-bending elixir my mother always warned me about. Described as the "natural essence of apples", scrumpie is made from fermented apple juice. While water is never added, refined sugar may be if the season has been too wet.

An old English word meaning "small apples", in Somerset England where it has a wide following, the term refers to the strongest or roughest of ciders.

SECONDARY FERMENTATION:

Beer that continues a natural secondary fermentation in the bottle.
It is often induced with the addition of new wort, or fermentables.

SHANDY:

Half beer or ginger-beer with lemonade.

STALE BEER or failed homebrew:

The kindest way to kill a slug is to lie a beer bottle on its side in your garden allowing the slug to crawl into the bottle, imbibe at leisure, and then fall into eternal slumber. It beats dousing the slug with salt, a painful and torturous death.

STOUT:

The successor to porter. An inky coloured beer, brewed with roasted malt and unmalted roasted barley, often with lots of hops.

TOAD IN THE HOLE:

Sausages in Yorkshire pudding.

VIENNA:

Today a much abused term, but originally an amber coloured bottom fermented beer, more than 5% and less than 6% from Vienna.

WHEAT BEER:

Wheat is used either on its own or with barley. There are a number of interesting variations.

WEIHENSTEPHAN:

Technical University of Munich Institute for Brewing Technology and Microbiology. The German brewmaster's University.

THE YEAST IS IN YOUR WORT:
The author's way of saying "the ball is in your court".

FLAVOUR PERCEPTIONS:

The Fox
"This of all things is to be avoided; for when once he creeps in it is difficult to hunt him out. It is an ill smell, and a worse taste, occasioned by neglect, uncleanliness, and bad heats. It is too often tasted in private breweries, as the vessels are thrown aside uncleansed and unattended to."

F.C. Accum. "The Art of Brewing", London, 1821.

FLAVOUR DETECTION:

Flavour is a sensory perception which depends on the detection equipment of the mouth and nose. This equipment centres on small detector cells which respond to particular molecules. The variation in response of these cells to the many molecules they encounter accounts for the perception we have of different tastes and flavours.

Nerve cells connect to the detector cells and relay Information to the brain where responses are interpreted as particular flavours.

THE TONGUE.

Most taste receptors are grouped onto taste buds situated from front to the back of the tongue. The four flavours that the tongue is sensitive to are:
a)SWEET, perceived at the tip of the tongue;
b)SALT, perceived along the side of the tongue near the tip;
c)SOUR, perceived along the side near the middle of the tongue, and
d)BITTER, perceived at the back of the tongue. Because the taste buds respond to particular flavours and they are located in four distinct areas of the tongue, it is important when tasting to swirl the beer throughout the mouth in order to make a complete evaluation of the flavour perceptions.

THE NOSE:

The nose plays a crucial role in the evaluation of beer quality. It is the first organ to enjoy physical contact with the product and provides an instant warning of an unsavoury sample. Since beer is an intentionally aromatic drink, a satisfactory 'nose" is essential in a quality product.

Aroma and taste are in many ways complimentary, providing information on different features and compounds. They are not necessarily mutually exclusive since many flavours can also be smelt. Moreover in many cases the aroma of a compound may be more pungent and impressionable than the flavour. Analysis, however, requires the use of both senses and tasting with a cold or other head infection can produce an imbalanced result.

HOW TO ANALYZE THE FLAVOUR:

Differences in abilities to detect flavour features are due to inherent genetic variability as well as to experience and training and technique.

Little can be done to rectify inherent differences and wide variation is found between individuals in their different sensitivities. It is also notable that while some people may be wholly flavour blind, others may only be deficient in particular areas. In full analysis of beer, a wide spectrum of competence is Important to avoid an unbalanced impression.

After inherent ability, experience is the next most vital requirement in developing good flavour analysis. As with any language, communications is Impossible without an understanding of terms, and for this, a first hand tasting of samples cannot be omitted. A glossary of terms can be found at the end of this discussion.

FLAVOUR THRESHOLDS:

The concentration at which a flavour compound can be detected may be simply taken as that where it becomes evident to the senses.

On closer examination it can be seen that thresholds occur at a number of levels. Initially a threshold may be noticed where the substance can be detected but not identified. Only at a higher concentration can recognition occur.

Above this point differences in concentration can be detected. The smallest change in concentration which can be detected is termed the difference threshold.

The persistence of flavours is important in beer assessment and varies for different compounds. Sweet tastes generally decline rapidly while bitter tastes increase for the first 20 seconds and may persist for 90 seconds. Astringency is most persistent and may be of great importance in after-impression of a beer.

BEER FLAVOUR GROUPINGS:

While the tongue and nose recognize certain basic flavour types, the assessment of beers requires recognition of major flavours produced by ingredients and by the brewing process. Each of these flavours may stimulate a variety of aroma and taste receptors and produce a particular overall impression.

The level of each of these flavours should be determined separately, even though others may be present. The ability to concentrate on one particular flavour is an important skill to develop and is equivalent to listening to one conversation in a noisy room.

Once determined, the level of a particular flavour can be judged as suitable or not for the beer style considered. If unsuitable, then a knowledge of the origins of the flavour can be important in identifying faults in production and in pin-pointing where to remedy the situation.

Flavours in beers may be either primary as arising from the brewing ingredients, or secondary as arising from the brewing process and subsequent fermentation.

PRIMARY FLAVOURS:

The identification of these flavours allows the brewing recipe to be investigated, although significant changes in some features can occur during brewing and processing. Hop features, for example, become less bitter during fermentation and volatile oils may vent away.

The two major raw materials contributing to flavour features are obviously malt and hops. In many beer styles these should compliment each other to produce a balanced range of flavours with no particular flavour predominating.

Malt and starch adjuncts provide notable grainy flavours as well as sweetness and astringency according to processing. Sulphury notes may arise from some malts but only incidentally.

Graininess is readily apparent from chewing malt. Cereal and floury flavours are initially evident but a distinct graininess appears later. With prolonged chewing and dissolution of the starch, husk features become apparent. While a given level of graininess is desired in most beers, huskiness, being harsher, is less encouraged. Excessive levels may give a beer an undue astringency and may result from over enthusiastic milling or prolonged sparging, particularly at high liquor temperature and PH.

With age graininess develops into papery and cardboard like flavours which indicate staling reactions, particularly associated with oxidation. Mouldiness is also a defect associated with grains and often results from mould growth on poorly stored grain.

Sweetness in beer is caused by unfermented sugars left after fermentation. Naturally-processed beers, kept in contact with yeast, become less sweet as the sugars are used up in slow fermentations and will vary in their profile over time. Pasteurized or filtered beers should be fully matured before processing, since little change will occur to sweetness after these treatments although note should be made of any effects of pasteurization on caramelising sugars.

Different sugars can provide sweetness according to their type and molecular size. Glucose, maltose and maltotriose are all common wort sugars but are used readily in fermentation. Lactose and dextrins are not fermented and can remain to provide sweetness and body in the beer.

Hops are added to beer as a major flavouring component and provide both oils and bitterness. Both of these features are very distinct and can be easily separated during beer assessments.

Bitterness develops on boiling by the conversion of alpha and beta acids in the hops to iso acids. A good boil of at least 30 minutes is necessary for this conversion although pre-prepared isomerised hop extract may be added in larger commercial breweries.

Hop oils, alternately, are very volatile and are driven off by boiling. A late addition towards the end of the boil is often practised to ensure that fresh hoppiness is present. Dry hopping the fermented beer may provide the same effect. Old hops may show staling flavours as hop oils oxidise. A good hop nose should be crisp and bright.

A good balance of bitterness and oil flavours is desirable in a beer and indicates good hop quality. Some varieties are bred for high bitterness and can give low oils.

SECONDARY FLAVOURS:

At a basic level, six main groups of secondary flavours can be recognized and should be easily identifiable to brewers and beer connoisseurs. In general, a common listing implies common causes but this may be complicated in many beers by infection with other microbes than the brewing yeast.

1. ALDEHIDIC.

These flavours are sharp and pungent at higher concentrations and are often characteristic of raw or "green" beers. They are produced by aldehyde and ketone compounds released by fermentation. Acetaldehyde is a common example and smells and tastes of fresh, green apples. It is produced directly from ethanol. Normal maturation will lower levels, higher concentrations can indicate too rapid processing or microbial spoilage. Cold storage or carbon dioxide washing may help and care should be taken to ensure that the fermentation completes its full course before the beer is processed.

2. FRUITY.

These may be pleasant flavours reminiscent of ripe fruits of various types ranging from bananas to coconut. They often result from the production of esters by the combination of acids and alcohols which are both produced by yeast fermentation. High levels may be due to high fermentation temperatures and they are encouraged in high gravity beers. Fruity flavours are more evident in ales and may be controlled by selection of the yeast strain and temperature. Levels in mature beers should be perceptible but not overt. They should also be of appropriate types, fruity esters will balance with sweetness in richer beers while solvent-like esters should be absent in most styles. Levels of esters decline with age as they become converted to fusel alcohols and acids with more solvent like features.

3. TOFFEE.

This flavour resembles butterscotch and is due to the compound diacetyl which is a by-product of fermentation. The flavour is less noticeable in ales than in lagers and a maturation period is usually necessary for active yeast cells to degrade the flavour. High levels may also be produced by microbial infection, particularly by **pediococci** or certain **lactobacilli.**

4. SULPHIDIC.

These flavours are naturally produced by yeast cells but excess can indicate poor processing or microbial spoilage. A number of types of sulphur flavours are known ranging from cabbage to rotten eggs and can be quite pungent. Good maturation allows levels to vent off. Carry over of yeast cells from early fermentation can lead to harsh sulphur flavours when the cells die and burst and careful racking should avoid this. One sulphur flavour of off beers is termed ribes and resembles tom cat or skunk aromas. It may result from the effect of light on hop alpha acids and may be most commonly encountered with sun struck hops in green or clear containers.

5. ACIDIC.

These flavours have a pungent aroma and a sour taste. Acetic acid is a common example and is characteristic of infected beers. Lactic acid also causes acidic flavours but may be added intentionally and has a smoother feel which is more easily balanced by other flavours. Acidity in beers most commonly arises from microbial spoilage by bacteria. An early detection during brewing can help avoid long term infection but most acidity problems develop during storage.

6. PHENOLIC.

These flavours are distinctive of problem brews. They frequently resemble TCP and can be instantly recognizable. Wild yeast infections or interactions between chlorine and plastics can be responsible. Water quality and the introduction of new plastic equipment should be investigated in any outbreak, occasionally some styles such as wheat beers may show a particular phenolic flavour resembling cloves. This results from special yeast strains and should be balanced with a slight acidity.

COMMON FLAVOUR DEFINITIONS

Alcoholic/Solvent.

> The general effect of ethanol and higher alcohols. Tastes warming.

Astringent.

> Drying, puckering feeling often associated with sour. Tannin. Most often derived from boiling of grains, long mashes.

Bitter.

> Basic taste associated with hops; or malt husks, like tonic water.

Clean.
>Lacking off flavours.

DMS. (dimenthyl sulfide)
>A sweet-corn like aroma/flavour. Can be attributed to malt, short or non-vigorous boiling of wort and in extreme cases bacterial infection.

Diacetyl/Buttery.
>Described as caramel-like, buttery.

Fruity/Estery.
>Similar to banana, raspberry, pear, apple or strawberry flavour; may include other fruity/estery flavours caused by iso Amyl Acetate. Often accentuated with higher temperature fermentations and certain yeast strains.

Hoppy.
>Characteristic odour of the essential oil of hops. Does not include hop bitterness.

Husky/Grainy.
>Husk or raw grain-like flavour.

Light-Struck.
>Having the characteristic smell of skunk caused by exposure to light. Some hops can have a very similar character.

Metallic.
>Caused by exposure to metal. Also described as tinny, coins bloodlike. Check your brewpot and caps.

Mild.
>Smooth, well blended, lacks harshness and lacks strong bitter.

Nutty.
>As in Brazil-nut, hazelnut or fresh walnut; sherry-like.

Oxidized/Stale.
>Develops as a beer ages or is exposed to high temperatures; winey, cardboard, rotten pineapple, vegetable-like odour. Often coupled with an increase in sour, harsh and bitter. The more aeration in bottling/siphoning, the more quickly a beer will oxidize. Cool temperatures inhibit oxidation.

Phenolic/Medicinal.
>A solvent/chemical flavour, resinous, Listerine, Iodine-like, similar to the odour of a hospital. Faulty cleaning of containers.

Skunky.
>See light-struck

Solvent-like.
>Flavour and aromatic character of certain alcohols often due to high fermentation temperatures.

Sour/Acidic.

Pungent aroma, sharpness of taste. Basic taste like vinegar or lemon; tart. Typically associated with lactic or acetic acid. Can be the result of bacterial infection through contamination or the use of citric acid.

Sweet.

Basic taste associated with sugars originating in malt.

Sulphur-like.

Rotten eggs, rotten corn, burning matches.

Watery.

Nose- indicative of a rice ladened (adjunct), high gravity brew.

Low in barley malt and hops. Think of American beer.

Taste- Sweet, thin, lacks malt and bitterness associated with hops and traditional brews. Ginger ale often has more character.

Yeasty.

Sulphur-like flavour. Often due to strains of yeast in suspension or beer sitting on sediment too long.

Acknowledgement

Information for this pamphlet was graciously provided by the Wellington County Brewing Company, and the Canadian Amateur Brewers Association.

THE TASTINGS

AMERICAN CONTRACT BREWS

The Entrants.   **Taster's Comments.**

Pabst, Blue Ribbon, 5%
(Lakeport Brewing Co.)

* colour - hint of amber; foam - hint of lace, longest tasting of the four; the aroma was a peculiar mixture of sweet corn, and I think hops; watery taste, I tried and tried but could not find any discernable character, except to say that it is refreshing and the foam was fizzy; mouthtaste - puckering; aftertaste - definite hops after the sweetness recedes, puckering.

President's Choice,5%
(Lakeport Brewing Co.)

*see BOTTLED DRAFTS

Schlitz, 5% (The Silver Creek
Brewery Sleeman's)
made with a slightly

* washed out honey colour; lightly laced foam; the sweetest aroma of the four, watery.a liquid cornfield; taste - sweet, candylike unbalanced;

higher alcohol content to appeal to Canadian tastes.	foam taste - creamy, dry; smooth mouthtaste; aftertaste - un- pleasant, chemical.
Stroh's, 4.4% (The Silver Creek Brewery)	* washed out honey colour; lightly laced foam; the aroma was so faint as to give this beer an advantage over the less agreeable smells found with the other beers; taste - watery, light bittering; foam - creamy; smooth mouth; aftertaste - light chemical, sweet, light puckering.
Lone Star, and the products from Molson's and Labatt's.	* Absent:

Bias:

This was difficult, as an ale drinker I tried to forget my preferences and rate these beers on their merits as beers, as you can see I was not too successful. As a Canadian beer drinker I wonder why so many of us are embracing American suds? I can only think that it is the price. For this reason I stood the American's against President's Choice, and found that PC, when compared to the Americans, stood head and shoulder above them.(See bottled Drafts)

Once Canadian beer was respected for its character, American's longed to get a hold of it and for good reason – it wasn't watery, syrupy and tasteless. Too bad its only the micros that have taken note of this.

Best American Contract Brew of the Day

Pabst (after PC) While Pabst's Blue Ribbon may have been America's best beer in 1893, they seem to have forgotten something over the last century.

Blind Tasting

One way to verify any tasting exercise is to conduct a blind tasting. Without the visual clues, it is just you and the individuality of each brew. I tried discerning the nose in a blind "smelling" and was only right 60% of the time. I constantly confused Pabst and Schlitz and could only identify Stroh's because of the lack of aroma. The blind tasting for "taste" was a little easier, and I was right 75% of the time. I wouldn't put any money on it though.

BEST BITTER

The Entrants	Taster's Comments
Arkell Best Bitter, 4% *(Wellington County)*	* Balanced hop/malt aroma with a fullness almost earthiness. Colour - brownish. Short foam, faint taste. Taste - malt up front, chocolate tones, light hops.
Conner's Best Bitter, 5%	* Terrific Belgium like head and retention. Orange in colour. Creamy delicious foam. Flowery nose. Warm well balanced mouth,with the assertiveness of the hops coming through. Slight residual sweetness in the nicely puckering aftertaste.
Publican's Special Bitter, 4.8%, (Upper Canada Brewing.)	* Light nose. Moderate head retention. Orange colour. Creamy foam. Smooth mouth, nicely hopped, not challenging. Bittering comes through in the aftertaste.

Bias:

Towards armloads of hops over malt.

Best Bitter of the Day

-Conner's Best Bitter. In a blind tasting it stood alone - sorry Jamie (MacKinnon) I can't agree with you "That this is a relatively simple beer..." A fine representative example of an English best bitter with the emphasis on balance.

BOCK

The Entrants	Taster's Comments
Brasal Bock, 7.8%	* Tawny cloak; laced, dense, rocky, foam; rich enticing, apricot nose; aero bar quality foam; full chewable, sherry like mouth, with a residual sweetness bordering on chocolate; smooth, gently carbonated mouth; sweet, nutty, puckering - warm aftertaste. Overall a "full" beer that hides its high alcohol subtly.
Brick Anniversary Bock, 1992, 6.5%	* Tawny cloak; laced dense, rocky foam; chocolaty malt aroma; silky foam; candy toffee like taste, an "adult" candy; smooth mouth; sweet, fresh aftertastewith a lingering bitterness, "lip-

smacking", the warmth permeates every pore in your mouth. Overall an enticing full, beer with an overwhelming toffee-like character.

Formosa Springs Bavarian Style Bock (Algonquin) 6%

* brilliant orange amber colour; aerated head, diminishes rapidly; aroma subtle at first, almost smoky, leading to a complex nutty - sherry like fullness; aerated foam taste; nicely balanced mouth, not too sweet, but fine - sherry-like; smooth mouth; pleasantly bitter, lightly puckering aftertaste, gently lingering. Overall a fine light introduction to the style, a perfect summer bock, charming, delicate - if only it had the foam!

Upper Canada True Bock, 6.5%

* rich red mahogany colour; laced, dense, rocky foam; vinous/ malty/ chewable chocolaty aroma; creamy whip cream tasting foam; complex taste, releasing a bittersweet depth; smooth mouth, sweet light growing to bitter aftertaste.

Bias:

A Bock should be an expression of the brewmaster's virtuosity.

BEST BOTTLED BOCK OF THE EVENING-Upper Canada True Bock.

This was extremely close and on the blind tasting Brick Bock came ahead. Who can distinguish excellence? All four are superb products!

BOTTLED DRAFT

The Entrants

Taster's Comments

President's Choice, Premium Draft, 5% (lager)

* Light golden pine colour; short head retention; fizzy, sweet, surprisingly refreshing foam; aroma - lightly hopped, sweet; to start with the sweetness in the taste is overpowering, but develops adding hints of fruitiness and hop character - not too much though - appealing to the mass market. I wonder if this was a European import, if this taste would be called subtle? The carbonation is smooth but backed by a pleasing "bite". While the aftertaste is watery, there is a light puckering.

Special Draft, (Conners',) *5% (ale)*	* Orange amber colour; rocky long lasting creamy - almost chewable foam; fresh, hint of yeast, malt and hops - in a word balanced aroma; taste- the malt can't be missed, followed by hops, reminds me of a bitter, a convincing draft taste - like a traditional Ontario beer; mouthtaste - smooth, dry; assertive malt - hop aftertaste. The warmer it becomes the more flavourful it gets.
Trapper Cold Filtered Draft, *(Niagara) 5% (lager)*	* Light golden pine cloak; light creamy tasting foam with a dryish aftertaste; a rich flowery, hoppy bouquet; sweet earthy taste, almost yeasty, and dry; smooth mouth; after-taste, earthy coming to a light bitterness.
Formosa Cold Filtered Draft	*Absent

Bias:

Towards distinctive, young flavours.

BEST BOTTLED DRAFT OF THE DAY - Special Draft.

Here the bias for ale came through, the President's Choice was a close second, and on a hot day, who knows?

BROWN ALE

The Entrants   Taster's Comments

Conners' Ale, 5%	* Tawny cloak, rocky fairly substantial foam with some lacing with a light whipped feel; nose - light, fruity; lively mouth, sweet; pleasantly dry aftertaste, warm; overall - promising nose but the taste is reminiscent of "a shower with your boots on."
County Ale, (Wellington County) *5%*	* At last a "real" brown ale; rocky, but short lived foam appropriate to the English style, the real action begins with the rich, complex, nutty, burnt sugar sweet, gently hopped, fruity, woody -autumn like nose. One taster even found hickory; the taste was "complete", aggressive, full malt, while the mouth was seductively smooth; and the good news followed through in the aftertaste which in turn was chewy, meaty,puckering, peaty, nutty, sweet - all of this in one beer? Overall a beer to savour and

talk about, not for the beginner, a taste of England.

Dark Ale,(Upper Canada,) 5%

* crystal clear brown colour; foam, rocky but short-lived and too airy in the mouth; aroma - sweet, thick, blackstrape molasses, healthy; taste - assertive, bittersweet, you either like it or you don't, fruity: aftertaste - fruity - sweet - sweet - warm. Overall: Once the most distinct ale brewed in Ontario, the taste has been modified. Still it is very much there.

Griffon Brown Ale, 5%, (McAuslan)

* ruby highlights in a traditional brown ale; laced, long lasting, rocky foam; aerated foamy head; aroma - balanced, but underlined with richness of the malt waiting in the wings; subtle nuttiness; tingly mouth; rich nut-like taste; aftertaste; sweet, pleasing, dryish. Overall: an all round understated, workmanlike ale.

Gritstone Premium Ale, 5.8%, (Niagara Falls)

* tawny; rocky lightly laced short lived foam with the texture of light whipped cream; touch of caramel in the nose, malty, nutty, sherry-like; intense malty yet balanced mouth, rich, barley wine like, a lot of taste for the content; smooth, lightly tingling mouth; after- taste: sweet - puckering - smoky - nutty. Overall: prelude to a barley wine.

Rousse (red) ale,(Boréale,) 5%

* rich tawny cloak; rocky, dense, laced, whipped cream foam; the nose is a hint of its former self, elusive raisins found after 40 seconds of sniffing; Belgium in taste and complexity, but light, slight vinosity, nutty, balanced; underlining refreshing aftertaste, warm dryness, fruity, - like dried fruit. Overall: lacks former distinctive fruity character, but still retains its capacity to excite.

Special Reserve, (Algonquin,) 5%

* orange, colour, a bit light, clear; what foam? Here and gone; head - taste "fairy cloud" like; nose - very subtle, earthy malt; taste -surprisingly complex - chocolaty apricot - followed by malt - pleasantly bitter; bubbly, inviting mouth-taste; aftertaste - chewable, not over- done, lingering. Overall a pleasant, complex brew. A good introduction to micro brews.

The Tasting:

Bias:

To English style creamy headed ales, think of England's Marston Pedigree.Unfortunately many of our fine ales lack longstanding foams.

BROWN ALE OF THE DAY - County Ale by Wellington County

This was extremely difficult particularly in the blind tasting, where Upper Canada's Dark Ale was found to be just as commendable.

The tasting was complicated by the fact that County along with Conners kept evolving and developing as they warmed up.

This exercise proved the old adage that "There are no bad beers, just better."

CREAM ALE

The Entrants:

Taster's Comments

Hart Cream Ale, 4.5%

* copperish cloak; rocky, peaked, laced, long lasting foam - exceptional; nose - flowery upfront, followed by malt, not balanced, but enticing; froth - light fresh whipped cream; taste -warmth from malt, rife with hops throughout; aftertaste - earthy, malty blossoms to fine bittering. Overall smooth, distinctive, more ale like.

Sleeman's Cream Ale, 5%

* Clear brilliant golden ale; creamy foam; aroma - warm malt, balanced with hops; taste - tingly mouth, again well balanced; aftertaste - fruity warmth, chewable, refreshing, nicely hopped.

Bias:

Towards Cream Ale as a non challenging refreshing brew, as a style, a fine alternative to mainstream lagers and ales.

BEST CREAM ALE OF THE DAY:

This was very close, while the Sleeman's was cleaner, and more balanced, and probably more within its style; the exceptional head and complexity of character exhibited by the Hart put it just ahead. Both terrific ales, you wouldn't go wrong with either.

LAGER

The Entrants	*Taster's Comments*
Brick Premium Lager, 5%	* golden crystal, hints of orange in the colour; aroma; flowery from the hops, full bodied almost earthy; head: fairly short, but continues to form; head: taste - foamy; taste: round malt, followed by flowery bittering, mouthtaste: tingly; aftertaste: flowery, pleasant bitter puckering.
County Lager, (Algonquin,) 5%	* clean golden colour; short foam with an aerated taste; light, subtle aroma; taste: malt in mouth, some balance; tingling mouthtaste; aftertaste: puckering, flat, sweet.
Extra Premium Lager, 5%, (Upper Canada)	* brilliant orange amber in colour; head: light lacing, well formed, certain rockiness and longevity with an almost cream taste, a great prelude; Aroma: an enticing flowery nose that envelopes your senses the moment the bottle is opened - balanced, fruity. Taste: a tingling mouth, full round balanced, honey like with an assertive bitterness. Aftertaste: full of taste, warm, sweet, almost burnt orange in quality, pleasant, longlasting.
Great Lakes Premium Lager, 5%	* light gold colour with a reddish tinge; short aerated foam; assertive flowery nose - almond - balanced; light bitter, chewy, earthy, nutty, smooth taste; refreshing, puckering aftertaste. Overall: Assertive nose, light mouth, refreshing palate.

Höpps Brau, (Brasal,) 4.5%

* crystal light amber gold brew; long lasting continuously forming, frothy foam; carefully hopped flowery - sweet nose; smooth, balanced sweet - dry, puckering taste; lingering, gentle, bittering - warm - sweet, like honey graham crackers aftertaste; Overall a liquid graham cracker, light refreshing, warm, pleasant.

Laker Premium Lager, 5%,
(Lakeport Brewing)

* Clean golden amber colour; short aerated, sweet foam; light nose; cane sugar in the refreshing sweet mouth, which is sharp and tingly; bittersweet coarse aftertaste.

Red Baron, 5% (Brick)

* crystal light, amber gold; a nicely laced creamy foam; very light nose; sweet mouth; puckering to warm, reassuring - sweet aftertaste.

Sleeman Silver Creek Lager, 5%

* clean golden cloak; short, but continuous and frothy foam; nose of spring flowers, balanced, green, warm; smooth mouth, malty - bitter; aftertaste: nicely bittered, warm, gently sneaks away leaving a fresh, puckering feeling for more. Overall: A complex nose, hallmark Sleeman foam - a traditional lager.

Wellington Premium Lager, 4.5%

* orange in colour; elusive foam; earthy, malty, sweet, light aroma followed by a good hopping as it warms up; full, fruity exceptionally finely balanced taste-complex, ale like; aftertaste nutty to a pleasing bitterness.

Creemore Springs Premium Lager.   *Absent:

(Almost too incredible to believe!)

Bias: Towards a well hopped full tasting lager.

BEST LAGER OF THE EVENING: Höpps Brau, second place was closely tied by Sleeman and Upper Canada.

LIGHT (LITE) BEER (YES I AM SERIOUS!)

## The Entrants	## Taster's Comments

Algonquin Light, 4%

* Light pine hue, short foamy head; sweet nose; smooth tingly mouth, balanced with sweetness and warmth; dry puckering aftertaste.

Formosa Springs Light, 4%, Algonquin

* almost oak complexion, the lightest of the lights; short foamy head; sweet nose, followed by a tingly sweet mouth, and a sweet aftertaste.

Light Lager, 4%, Upper Canada

* reddish amber, clean clear; nice head formation, even some rockiness; almost creamy foam; malty nose, missing a few hops; smooth enticing mouth; delicate balanced, very light taste; puckering, malty aftertaste. Overall: Looks right!

Refreshing, not unpleasant.

Premium Light, 4%, Laker

* honey pine; long lingering and continually forming foam!; foamy tasting head; balanced, light head. Fresh, sweet, hint of honey in the taste, and fruity; aftertaste light bittering, puckering to dry. Overall an extremely clean, refreshing brew with some surprising complexity.

Real Light, 3.1%, Brasal

* a clean amber lager; long lasting foamy head; the nose is malty, almost too much so, with an aroma often associated with non alcoholic beers, but saved by the fact that it is not as cloyingly sweet, and is much more like "beer"; taste - sweet malt, lightly hopped; aftertaste - sweet. Overall: A light beer with taste!

Sleeman Premium Light, 4%

* crystal amber; the foam continued to form throughout the tasting, and produced an almost creamy taste; the nose had a certain richness and balance; the taste was sweet, candy shop like, fruity; harsh, dry aftertaste.

Stroh's Light 4% * bleached pine in colour; aroma - cornfield; taste - ginger ale like, light to bitter; aftertaste sandpaper.

Bias:

Towards a refreshing clean taste, rather than something cut down offering a pseudo taste. That was until a light beer with real character came along, causing a split judgement.

BEST LIGHT BEER OF THE EVENING:

Premium Light, Lakeport - refreshing, clean, tied with Brasal's Real Light, which was loaded with taste and character.

MALT LIQUOR

The Entrants
Tasters' Comments

Rebellion, (Upper Canada,) 6% * Brilliant gold; rocky, laced head; rich, fruity-apricot, malty-dusky, light-bitter, vinous aroma; whipped cream foam; complex, chewable, malty bittersweet taste; astringent mouth; warm, puckering aftertaste; an assertive, vibrant, challenging brew.

Spécial, (Brasal,) 6.1% * warm copper colour; rocky, laced head; malty-rich-sherry-like nose, followed by light flowers; creamy foam; light, sweet-malt balanced taste; smooth mouth; puckering aftertaste. A refined, subtle brew -to try this in full bloom have Brasal's Bock.

Bias:

The microbreweries have shown that malt liquors do not need to be sweet, nasty, foul beers, with these two very different and palatable entries. It was very hard to make a decision here.

BEST MALT LIQUOR OF THE EVENING:

Rebellion.

NEAR BEER OR NON ALCOHOLIC BEER

The Entrants

Tasters' Comments

Clausthaler, 0.5%, imported by Brasal, (brewed by Binding, Frankfurt, Germany.)

* Smells like beer, hoppy nose followed by malt. Straw colour, creamy head. Taste: malty with bitterness. As it warms up the malt begins to dominate, with a residual sweetness. Notes of "ginger ale". Similar to a shandy in character. Nice puckering aftertaste.

Point Nine, 0.9%, Upper Canada Brewing:

* Orange amber. Light nose, very light all over.

Absent:

Too numerous to mention.

Bias:

I must admit I was pleasantly surprised by both brews, and dreaded the idea of having to stick my nose into a glass of either product after suffering the oppressively molasses like products found at the grocery store. I know that this opinion is out of date when moderation and drinking and driving are considered, but I did tend to agree with the findings of the New York City Department of Health in 1920 when they reported: "It is the general consensus of opinion that 'near beer' is utterly useless as a beverage, that it affords no pleasure whatsoever and that it is a waste of time to bother with it. The consumption of six or eight bottles gives them a sense of nauseated fullness with none of the stimulated sense of well-being that old-time beer gave after only two or three bottles." (A.D. Eames, "A Beer Drinker's Companion", Ayers Rock Press, Harvard, 1986, pg. 139.)

Put another way I asked veteran brewmaster Al Brash what the problem with non-alcoholic beer was and he simply stated the obvious, "lack of the right yeast"!

From these two products it appears the flavour my be changing for the better.

NEAR BEER OF THE MORNING - Clausthaler.

PALE ALE - The Psychological Tasting

The Pale Women. Frances Boire-Carriere (left) and Lor Pelton mentally prepare for the challenge ahead. Cornwall, Spring 1993.

The Entrants:

Dragon's Breath, Kingston Brewing Co. (Hart), 4.5%

Griffon, Extra Pale Ale, (McAuslan,) 5%

Hart Amber Ale, (Hart,) 5%

Tasters' Comments

* Colour: cloudy like frozen maple syrup; Aroma: flowery smooth, lightly spiced, perfume like rather than flowery, young green, spring like; Taste: jagged sharp as it goes down, fruity apricot fresh; Aftertaste: - well bittered, flowery, puckering; Potability: extroverted, almost aggressive.

* Colour: too yellowish, light copper; Aroma: sweet flowery, sunny, delicate, young spring flowers, hops up front, followed by malt; Taste: dandelion, tinny, thin, too flowery, not balanced. Aftertaste: sour, not unpleasant; Potability: the taste is disappointing because of the exceptional aroma.

* Colour: Clear, sparkling copper; Aroma: rich bouquet, well balanced, fresh, subtle but determined; Taste: orgasmic, thirst quenching, satisfying balanced; Aftertaste: ecstatic, progressive refreshing, open to possibilities, summer elixir.

St. Ambroise, Pale Ale,
(McAuslan,) 5%

* Colour: Perfect, crystal copper clear, clarity of vision; Aroma: gentle well balanced, light sunny, spring day, assertive with an aroma I associate with the best bitter pale ales; Taste: subtle grows to a wholeness; Aftertaste: exceptionally enticing, sweet and bitter, deserving another; Potability: an all purpose beer, simply satisfying.

Special Pale Ale, (Wellington
County,) 4.5%

* Colour: buckwheat honey; Aroma: warm, honey sweet, thick, friendly, hop bittering cut immediately by malt; Taste: round vowel solid taste, effervescent, well balanced, like graham crackers; Aftertaste: short, light bittering, unusual but pleasant, pre verbal; Potability: fine; a persuasive beer of substance, pleasant, mellow, smooth.

Upper Canada Pale Ale, 4.8%

* Aroma: more caramel than bronze, not in the metallic colour zone, too dark; Aroma: weak tea, few hops, very thin, lukewarm; Taste: malty warmth, like a crumpled bed, out of category, sharp then disappears, sad sack - crumples; Aftertaste: mild bittering, grows, Potability: suffering from bi-polar depression – too much identification with persona.

Boreale Blonde

*Absent:

Bias:

Our tasters included two men and two women; a transplant from PEI, a theologian turned civil servant, a writer and myself. While three of the four had spent years experimenting with beers for recreational purposes, this was their first "professional" tasting. This explains some of the violent reactions.

PALE ALE OF THE DAY

- three out of four chose St. Ambroise Pale Ale, with Hart Amber not too surprisingly, a close second.

The blind tasting confirmed just how close St. Ambroise and Hart really are!

STOUT

The Stoutmen: Left to right: Gord Holder, Ian Bowering, Phil Irwin, Jim Duffy. Lennoxville, February 1993.

The Entrants:

Brock Extra Stout, 5.8%,
        (Niagara Falls Brewing).

Colonial Stout, 4.8%,
        (Upper Canada Brewing).

Imperial, 5%,
        (Conners Brewing).

Imperial, 5.5%,
        (Wellington County).

Oatmeal Stout, 5.5%,
        (McAuslan Brewing).

Boreale and Hart

Tasters' Comments

* A sweet licorice nose. (Can a Stout this good be bottom fermented!)

* Very light, more like a porter.

* Chocolaty notes, nice hop finish.

* Uncharacteristically light nose, silky mouth, full roasted taste.

* Pronounced roasted nose, almost edible with lots of mouth feel and body. Loaded with character.

*Absent

The Tasting:
Bias:
    All of the tasters expressed a strong preference for full flavoured, you could say unbalanced - in the beer judge's sense - beer. Some of the beers though fresh when acquired, did not travel well.

Location: McAuslan Brewing.

It may sound a little peculiar to take beer to a brewery, but what better place to taste beer can there be? To make the tasting as even as possible, only bottled products were sampled.

STOUT OF THE DAY

Oatmeal Stout, St. Ambroise. If the bottled example was very good, the draft stout was simply perfect - with a smooth creamy head, and full, flavourful mouth.

The draft was so good that we were late for our appointment at Brasal.

STRONG ALE

The Entrants	*Tasters' Comments*
Iron Duke, 6.5%, *(Wellington County)*	* Rich mahogany complexion; rich nutty, fresh apricot, deep, malty, earthy nose; longlasting dense, laced, firm foam; dense, creamy, bitter tasting head; taste: round, chewy malty, but not too sweet. Overall: a meal in a bottle.
Olde Jack, 7.2%, *(Niagara Falls Brewing)*	* Crystal golden cloak; Aroma: deep, rich, sherry like, almonds, more balanced than Iron Duke; Foam: laced, dense, rocky, the longest lasting of the two; Foam taste: foamy, creamy, tart; Taste: more balanced than Iron Duke, the chocolate comes through and dominates; Overall: Smoother and less aggressive than Iron Duke.

Bias:

None to speak of.

STRONG ALE OF THE NIGHT:

Iron Duke.

How do you judge excellence? This was an extremely difficult tasting as both beers are so good. The blind tasting underlined this point - out of three tasters only one of them was correct 100% of the time.

And Jamie, I believe that Iron Duke evolves more as it warms up.

CHAPTER 10

Homebrewing

AMATEUR BREWING

In my opinion amateur - or home - brewing is one of the most diversified hobbies that exists.

It challenges your creative abilities — you try to develop a beer recipe that has a particular style or flavour you enjoy. It challenges your abilities to appreciate a variety of beer styles. It even induces a few of us to aspire to become beer judges.

Home brewing brings out the inventor in each of us as we try to create the equipment we need to improve our techniques. And we make new friends with similar interests from incredibly diversified walks of life.

In other words, brewing has something for everyone.

People get involved with brewing for a wide range of reasons. I, for example got involved because of the beer strike/lock-out in Ontario in the mid 80's.

Until recently most people started home brewing because they wanted variety, and/ or some of the traditional beer styles not readily available in Canada. But with the advent of the Microbrewery industry, this has become a secondary reason for brewers to take up the hobby.

These days most people start home brewing because it's less expensive than buying beer. Usually that's only the beginning. People tend to stay involved because it's a great hobby.

I think many of us go through a progression as we learn more advanced brewing techniques. It starts when we buy our first beer kit or when we first visit a brew-on-premise location.

That inevitably leads to some experimentation - we might dabble with the raw materials - bulk malt extract & hops, add a few natural grains to add complexity to the flavour, and finally, exclusively use grains and hops.

We may never travel through all the steps. We can create excellent beer at virtually any step in the process. But many of us do go through all the stages because it's the same process used by commercial brewers.

The hobby is certainly a social one so the amateur or homebrewer need never be alone in the quest for the perfect brew. Many homebrew clubs have been formed across the country, where members share ideas - and their beer - with each other.

The Canadian Amateur Brewers Association is another source of information for the homebrewer. The Association offers a forum for brewers to talk about techniques. It offers conferences, seminars and competitions.

We've included recipes for the first place entries in both the 1991 & 1992 Great Canadian Homebrew Competition here. We hope it gives you some food for thought and many hours of productive brewing.

Cheers!

Paul Dickey

President, Canadian Amateur Brewers' Association.

The Canadian Amateur Brewers Association Inc.

Objective: "The promotion of brewing: the education of members in brewing methods and history." The Canadian Amateur Brewers Association (CABA) is a Federally Incorporated non-profit organization whose purpose is to promote homebrewing as an enjoyable hobby through educational publications, events, and other activities.

CABA is dedicated to improving the skills and knowledge of its members. Members are invited to participate in the special events organized including the annual conference, frequent competitions and special seminars.

(Logo courtesy, The Canadian Amateur Brewers Association Inc.)

Annually, CABA sponsors; a Tasting/Judging seminar and Beer Judge Certification Program, a Seminar & Competition in Montreal in March; hosts the Great Canadian Homebrew Conference and Competition in Toronto, and holds the annual General Meeting in October.

Throughout the year the Association publishes a newsletter every two months which contains news of events, winning recipes, articles on homebrewing and member services. Members are encouraged to write to the HAPPY HOPPER for advice on brewing techniques or processes. One service which is available to members free of charge is the evaluation of beer samples by recognized and Certified judges. Judges will evaluate the samples provided and provide written advice on the appropriate class of beer for competition purposes, and comments on how brewing techniques or ingredients might be changed to enhance the product.

Another service that CABA provides is a "Brew-Buddy" program to link brewers of varying levels of expertise to learn from each other, and have a first hand chance to see more advanced brewing techniques from fellow amateur brewers in their own community.

Membership is $15 per year and can be obtained by writing CABA, 19 Cheshire Dr., Islington, Ontario, M9B 2N7.

Better Brewing With Beer Kits . By Mike Ligas

As you all know, brewing beer can be accomplished in various ways, from grain mashing, mash/extract recipes, extracts only, and from the use of prehopped 'kits'. You can brew excellent beer using any method as long as you pay attention to details, like thorough cleanliness, minimal use of adjuncts, healthy yeast, etc. Many new homebrewers start by brewing from kits and gain valuable experience this way. The quality and variety of kits available to homebrewers has improved drastically over the past few years and some folks brew exclusively from kits due to their convenience and tasty results. The choice to move into extract or mash brewing is a personal one, and is by no means necessary. Just do what suits you. Since many of you are new homebrewers and are using prehopped kits, we have prepared a step by step guideline to brewing beer from kits which will improve your results if you are currently employing the manufacturers suggestion of using corn sugar to raise the gravity of the wort.

All pieces of equipment should be cleaned completely and sanitized with a mild bleach solution prior to use.

Large pails and carboys can be soaked for 30 minutes in a mild bleach solution containing 1/2 teaspoon bleach per 5 gallons of water. They do not need to be rinsed but must be thoroughly drained before being employed. Everything must be cleaned well after brewing to avoid the growth of nasty microbes on brewing equipment during storage.

1. Bring 4 to 5 litres (1 Imp. gal.) of cold water to a boil in a stainless steel or enamel pot (NO ALUMINUM). Stir in 1.5 kg light (pale) unhopped malt extract (dried, syrup, or combination) and bring back to a boil. Boil for 15 to 20 minutes.
2. Stir in the contents of your can of kit beer and bring back to a boil. Boil for 5 more minutes. Remove from heat and pour into your primary fermenter.

Top up to 22.5 litres (5 Imp. gal.) with cold water and stir well. If necessary, cool to 19-22°C by immersing your covered fermenter in a tub of cold water and pitch yeast.
3. Ferment for 3 to 5 days and then rack into a clean glass carboy and seal with an airlock. Try to fill the carboy to 1 - 2 inches below the bottom of the rubber bung. If the beer foams for a few days after racking, just put a tube into the hole in the rubber bung and immerse the other end of the tube into a pail of water. When foaming subsides, replace the tube with an airlock.

4. The beer will continue to ferment slowly for 3 - 10 days, and maybe longer for high gravity beers or slow fermenting yeast strains. When visible signs of fermentation are nil (very few rising CO_2 bubbles) the beer is ready to bottle.

5. For bottling, dissolve 3/4 to 1 cup of corn sugar (Dextrose) in a small volume of water (1-2 cups) and bring to boil. Cool until warm and pour the sugar solution into your primary fermenting vessel. Siphon your finished beer into the same vessel, being careful not to agitate and thereby oxidize your beer. Gently stir to ensure that the dextrose is evenly mixed into the beer and fill your bottle to approximately one inch from the top. Secure caps and let the bottles stand for one to two weeks at room temperature in a dark place and then refrigerate.

6. You can start drinking your beer at this point but a few more weeks in the cold will help develop smoothness and flavour. You may wish to hide a few bottles away for a few months just to see if the particular style of beer you have made ages well.

Yeast must be treated with respect if you want a healthy fermentation. If you are not using a liquid culture, which is highly recommended, then you should rehydrate the dried yeast which is supplied with the kit. First, boil some water in a kettle and pour about one cup into a glass and cover with a plate. Let this stand until the water temperature is between 35 - 43 °C.

Empty the dried yeast into the warm water and let the yeast stand for 5 to 10 minutes. Stir the yeast slurry and pour into your wort and mix well.

It is never necessary to suck on a hose to start a siphon. This is a common source of contamination. Just fill your hose with water and clamp it shut so the water stays in the hose. Immerse one end in the beer, place the other end at a lower level in a cup and open the clamp to start the siphon. When the water has collected in the cup and beer is in the tube, clamp shut and transfer to your pail or carboy and commence siphoning.

(This article originally appeared in "The Sensitive Brewers Newsletter", vol. 1, no. 1 (June, 1990) from the Sensitive Brewers, Hamilton, Ontario. It has also been reprinted in "The Ithaca Brew News", vol. 3, no. 3 (Nov. 1991) from the Ithaca Brewers Union, Ithaca, N.Y., the Boston Wort Processors newsletter, Boston, Mass., and "The Newsletter" Canadian Amateur Brewers Assoc. Inc., vol 2, no. 1, (Feb., 1992). Reprinted with the kind permission of the author.)

NOTICE

While Homebrewing is an enjoyable and safe hobby for millions of people, neither the author, the publisher nor the Canadian Amateur Brewers Association accepts any liability or responsibility for any accidents or injuries that may occur to people who either overindulge or have an allergic reaction to alcoholic beverages and its various ingredients as a result of following these recipes.

THE RECIPES

The following lists the first place entries for the 1991 and 1992 Great Canadian Homebrew Competitions sponsored by the Canadian Amateur Brewers Association. The author would like to thank the CABA and all of the winning entrants for permission to print their recipes.

CANADIAN ALE

A mild, pale light bodied ale about 4.75% alc./vol. Full hop and malt flavour.
Example: Molson Export

1st Place - 1991
Canadian Ale
Erich Mann

Ingredients for 19 litres;
- 1.8 kg dried pale extract
- 750 gm rice extract
- 40 gm Saaz pellets (50 minutes)
- 12 gm Hallertauer pellets (5 minutes)

Water Treatment: 1/4 tsp calcium chloride

Yeast: Munton & Fison Ale yeast

Original specific gravity: not taken

Final specific gravity: 1.018

Age when judged (since bottling): 3 months

Brewer's Specifics: Boiled for 50 minutes. 5 days in glass primary and 17 days in glass secondary at 16°C. Bulk primed with 3/4 cup corn sugar.

Judges' Comments: "This is a very well made beer. Use less bittering hops and more aroma hops."

"Needs more malt sweetness. Add a bit more malt or less adjunct, if any used. I like this beer."

1ST PLACE - 1992
CANADIAN 66
ROBERT HALLIDAY

Ingredients for 23 litres;

- 3.5 kg pale malt
- 100 gm crystal malt
- 250 gm Munich malt
- 1/2 oz Cluster
- 1/2 oz Cascade

Water Treatment: n/a

Yeast: own top yeast

Original specific gravity: 1.044

Final specific gravity: 1.010

Age when judged (since bottling): 2 months

Brewer's specifics: Boiled for 60 minutes. One week in stainless steel primary at 68°F. Glass secondary used.

Judges' comments: "Clean aroma. Could use a little more hops to balance the sweetness. Faint phenolics; high temperature fermentation giving some undesirable alcohols."

BRITISH ALE

This class represents the classic pale ale. With original gravities of 1.043 to 1.053, these ales are usually malty and highly hopped, or bitter and hoppy. The brewing water is hard, being high in calcium carbonates and sulphates.

Examples: Bass Ale, Double Diamond, Dragon's Breath,Conners

1st Place - 1991
E.S.B. Bitter
Michael Nazarec

Ingredients for 20 litres;

- 1.5 kg John Bull E.S.B. extract
- 2 kg. DMX malt extract
- 60 gm Cascade (60 minutes)
- 60 gm Willamette (30 minutes)
- 30 gm Chinook (finishing hops)

Water Treatment: 1 tsp gypsum, 1/4 tsp salt
Yeast: 11 gm Edme ale yeast
Original specific gravity: 1.058
Final specific gravity: 1.020
Age when judged (since bottling): 2 1/2 months

Brewer's specifics: Boiled for 60 minutes. 24 days in glass primary at 18°C, 16 days in glass secondary.

Judges' comments: "Good malt balance - perhaps a little more bitterness needed. Beautiful head on this beer! Like a thick, creamy, tight mousse. Rich and amber colour. Nice hops and esteryness. Some cidery esters (due to the yeast used or perhaps the fermentation temperature.)"

1ST PLACE - 1992
JAY'S PALE ALE
JAMES TURNER

Ingredients for 48 litres;
- 6 kg Edme lager malt
- 3 kg Edme Ale malt
- 400 gm 6-row malt
- 400 gm crystal malt
- 100 gm chocolate malt
- 100 gm roast barley
- 60 gm Northern Brewer (60 minutes)
- 50 gm Cluster (30 minutes)
- 50 gm Goldings (15 minutes)

Water Treatment: n/a
Yeast: Whitbread ale yeast, 15 gm

Original specific gravity: n/a

Final specific gravity: n/a

Age when judged (since bottling): 2 months

Brewer's specifics: Boiled for 60 minutes. 1/2 weeks in plastic fermenter at 65°F.

Judges' comments: "Big time malt nose, inviting. Subtle aromatic hops, nice but please, a bit more. A commercial quality beer with however, some of a commercial beer's shortcomings - not enough bittering hops. Take more chances next time and I'll order a few cases."

BROWN ALE

Typically a sweet, dark brown brew from southern England, with 3 to 3.5% alc./vol. Drier and more reddish-brown than further north. 4.4 to 5% alc./vol.

Example: Newcastle Brown

1st Place - 1991
   Big Brown One
   Mark Larsen

Ingredients for 19 litres;
- 3.15 kg pale malt
- 220 gm crystal malt
- 220 gm dried amber malt
- 220 gm dried pale malt
- 84 gm chocolate malt
- 42 gm Willamette (90 minutes)
- 14 gm Willamette (5 minutes)
- Dry hopped with 5 gm Saaz

Water Treatment: none

Yeast: MeV #013 High Temperature Ale yeast

Original specific gravity: 1.048

Final specific gravity: unknown

Age when judged (since bottling): 5 months

Brewer's specifics: Mashed at 64℃ for 1 hour and 66℃ for 30 minutes. Sparged at 71℃. Boiled for 105 minutes. 3 1/2 weeks in glass primary and 2 1/2 weeks in glass secondary at 20℃. Primed with one level teaspoon per bottle.

Judges' comments: "Lovely malty aroma. Excellent head retention. A fine beer. Good malty flavour, well balanced."

1ST PLACE - 1992
BRADLEY'S BROWN
BRAD LEDREW

Ingredients for 30 litres;
- 11 lb 2-row malt
- 2 lb crystal malt
- 1 lb dextrin
- 3/4 lb Munich malt
- 3/4 lb flaked barley
- 4 oz chocolate malt
- 1 3/4 oz Northern Brewer (60 minutes)
- 1 oz Cascade (15 minutes)

Water Treatment: 1 tsp. NaCl

Yeast: MeV #072 Ale yeast

Original specific gravity: 1.050

Final specific gravity: 1.014

Age when judged (since bottling): 1/2 month

Brewer's specifics: Boiled for 70 minutes. One week in stainless steel primary and two weeks in glass secondary. Fermentation temperature was 40℉. Primed with one cup corn sugar.

Judges' comments: "Very, very drinkable beer. Great colour and clarity. Good balance on hop side."

ENGLISH BITTER

Gold to copper with low carbonation, this beer has a low to medium maltiness. A hop flavour or aroma may be present. These beers are generally served on draft in England. 3.5 to 5% alc./vol.

Example: Conners Best Bitter, St. Ambroise Pale Ale

1ST PLACE - 1992
CRYSTAL CASCADE AMBER ALE
RANDY DAVIS

Ingredients for 23 litres;
- 5 kg 2-row pale malt
- 454 gm crystal malt
- 454 gm toasted pale malt (350°F for 10 minutes)
- 14 gm Chinook (60 minutes)
- 14 gm Cascade (60 minutes)
- 14 gm Cascade (30 minutes)
- 28 gm Cascade (steeped for 30 minutes)
- 28 gm Cascade (dry hopped in secondary)

Water Treatment: 2 tsp gypsum

Yeast: Wyeast #1056 American Ale yeast

Original specific gravity: 1.052

Final specific gravity: 1.010

Age when judged (since bottling): 2 1/2 months

Brewer's specifics: Mashed at 124°F for 1/2 hour in 13 litres water, and at 158°F for 90 minutes in 19 litres water (added six litres). Sparged with 23 litres at 170°F. Boiled for 60 minutes. One week in plastic primary and four weeks in plastic secondary. Fermentation temperature was 18°C. Primed with one cup dextrose.

Judges' comments: "Deep gold colour, good head formation. Good carbonation level for the style. Very good hop and malt balance with a hop bite through the aftertaste.

BOCK

Originating in Germany, this style of beer is generally a strong, malty beer with an adequate but not assertive hop bitterness. Copper to dark brown, having at least 6.25% alc./vol.

Examples: Upper Canada Bock, Brick Bock

1st Place - 1991
 Heavenly Bock
 Steve Murdoch

Ingredients for 48 litres;
- 10.5 kg United Canadian Malt, pale extract
- 500 gm Carastan
- 250 gm roasted barley
- 160 gm Tettnanger (60 minutes)
- 40 gm Tettnanger (30 minutes)
- 50 gm Tettnanger (10 minutes)

Water Treatment: none

Yeast: 23 gm Edme beer yeast

Original specific gravity: 1.058

Final specific gravity: 1.012

Age when judged (since bottling): 5 months

Brewer's specifics: Crystal malt and roasted barley put in cold water and brought to a boil. When boil starts, remove grains and add malt extract. Boiled for 60 minutes. 1 1/2 weeks in plastic primary at 68°F. Carbonated by trickle method in 50 litre Sankey type keg at 40 psi at 2°C for 18 hours. Primed with 1 cup dextrose.

Judges' comments: "Floral aroma. Well done. An excellent example of this style. The banana esters were particularly authentic."

1ST PLACE - 1992
MANN'S SPRING BOCK
ERICH MANN

Ingredients for 19 litres;
- 2 kg pale malt
- 2 kg pale/wheat 60/40 extract
- 500 gm Munich malt
- 250 gm caramel malt
- 170 gm chocolate malt
- 28 gm Perle (60 minutes)
- 28 gm Hallertauer (60 minutes)
- 14 gm Hallertauer (15 minutes)
- 14 gm Hallertauer (1 minute)

Water Treatment: none

Yeast: Munton & Fison, 14 gm

Original specific gravity: n/a

Final specific gravity: 1.020

Age when judged (since bottling): 3 1/2 months

Brewer's specifics: Boiled for 60 minutes. Five days in glass primary at 58°F and 21 days in glass secondary. Primed with 140 gm corn sugar.

Judges' comments: "Very clean aroma but light in malt which one would expect from this style. Very nice beer; good alcohol content without being overpowering. Clean taste."

EXTRA STRENGTH

Any malt liquor above 6% alc./vol. These beers usually have a full flavour which can be predominantly malty or hoppy. Colours can range from pale to dark.

Barley Wine;

Coppery, tawny to dark brown in colour, these ales usually have residual sweetness full of esters and fruitiness, counterbalanced with medium to assertive hop bitterness and alcohol 6 to 13% alc./vol.

Example: Iron Duke, Wellington County

1st Place -1991
Too Hot Barley Wine
Craig Nichols

Ingredients for 21 litres;
- 6 kg (4 cans) Muntona Amber DMS pale dry malt extract
- 1.5 kg crystal malt
- 1.4 kg dextrose
- 210 gm Northern Brewer pellets (70 minutes)
- 28 gm Kent Goldings (70 minutes)
- 50 gm Styrian Goldings (40 minutes)
- 60 gm Fuggles (10 minutes)
- 50 gm Cascade (10 minutes)
- Dry hopped with 28gm Northern Brewer + 28gm Kent Goldings

Water Treatment: 2 1/2 tsp. gypsum and 1/8 tsp. salt
Yeast: 2 pkt. (10gm) Lalvin wine yeast + 1 pkt. (5gm) Red Star Pasteur
     Champagne yeast
Original specific gravity: 1.110
Final specific gravity: 1.024
Age when judged (since bottling): 7 1/2 months

Brewer's specifics: Boiled for 70 minutes. 16 days in plastic primary at 21°C, 25 days in glass secondary at 18°C. Primed with 1 cup dextrose.

Judges' comments: "Hops very assertive; perhaps could use more sweetness and fruitiness. First class head. Nose is perfect for style."
"Good residual sweetness. Carbonation a little light. Balance good."

1ST PLACE - 1992
WHAT DO YOU MEAN BY THIS?
MICHAEL NAZAREC

Ingredients for 18 litres;
- 2 kg Ironmaster light extract
- 2 kg DMX
- 400 gm crystal malt
- 200 gm toasted 2-row malt

- 100 gm chocolate malt
- 500 gm brown sugar
- 28 gm Centennial (60 minutes)
- 14 gm Centennial (30 minutes)
- 28 gm Cascade (20 minutes)
- 14 gm Centennial and 28 gm Perle (finishing hops)

Water Treatment: 1 tsp. gypsum and 1 tsp. mag. sulf.

Yeast: Champagne yeast, 7gm

Original specific gravity: 1.090

Final specific gravity: 1.025

Age when judged (since bottling): 3 1/2 months

Brewer's specifics: Boiled for 60 minutes. 3 1/2 weeks in glass primary and two weeks in glass secondary. Fermentation temperature was 18°C. Primed with 600 ml original style.

Judges' comments: "Very alcoholic. Beautiful hop nose, clean flavour. Slight oxidation at finish. Appearance very attractive and inviting. Well balanced with hops; nice conditioning. Very good beer."

FRUIT BEER

Any beer made using fruit as an adjunct added to the primary fermentation or later to produce secondary fermentation. The result should have the fruit qualities distinct yet harmonious with the total flavour.

1st Place - 1991
Kristmas Krieg Lambic
Craig Nichols
Ingredients for 21 litres;
- 3 kg (2 cans) Brewferm Kriek Malt Extract
- 1.4 kg 60/40 malt/wheat extract
- 21 gm Hersbrucker pellets (60 minutes)
- 7 gm Hersbrucker pellets (10 minutes)

Water Treatment: 3/4 tsp gypsum

Yeast: 2 pkg. Brewferm ale yeast

Original specific gravity: 1.057

Final specific gravity: 1.021

Age when judged (since bottling): 2 months

Brewer's specifics: Boiled for 60 minutes. 11 days in plastic primary at 18°C; 9 weeks in glass secondary at 15°C. Primed with 1 1/8 cup dextrose.

Judges' comments: "Really nice cherry flavour, just the right amount. Could have a bit more malt character."

"A little thin. Clean and well brewed."

1ST PLACE - 1992
VERRY CHERRY
MARTIN SEWELL

Ingredients for 20 litres;
- 2 kg pale malt extract
- 500 gm dry malt
- 12 pounds of frozen pitted sour cherries
- 35 gm Hallertauer (55 minutes)
- 15 gm Hallertauer (5 minutes)

Water Treatment: none

Yeast: Red Star lager yeast

Original specific gravity: n/a

Final specific gravity: n/a

Age when judged (since bottling): 2 1/2 years

Brewer's specifics: Boiled for 55 minutes. At end of the boil the cherries were put into the primary along with the wort. Two months in plastic primary and 2 weeks in secondary at 72°F.

Judges' comments: "Pleasant sour note. Lactic acid flavour resulting in some fruity and nice tartness warming; very good. Cherry fruit aroma. Good job integrating fruit without losing beer character. Good summer drinking beer.

CANADIAN LAGER

Pilsener beer, originally brewed in Pilzen, Czechoslovakia, is probably the most copied beer in the world. The best Canadian imitations have a very light character and are delicately hopped. Not aggressive bitterness but enough for a clean, dryish finish. Well but not over-carbonated and 4 - 4.8% alc./vol.

Examples: Labatt's Blue, Molson's Canadian

1st Place - 1991
   Party Pilsner
   Dave Willis

Ingredients for 23 litres;
- 2.3 kg 2-row malt
- 2.3 kg 6-row malt
- 12 gm Northern Brewer pellets (70 minutes)
- 17 gm Hallertauer pellets (70 minutes)
- 22 gm Saaz pellets (30 minutes)
- 14 gm Saaz (15 minutes)
- 14 gm Saaz (10 minutes after boiling)

Water Treatment: 2 gm gypsum to mash

Yeast: #26 HiTemp. Lager yeast

Original specific gravity: 1.045

Final specific gravity: 1.010

Age when judged (since bottling): 3 months

Brewer's specifics: Boiled for 70 minutes. Made 1 1/2 litre starter for yeast. The pH was 5. Step infusion mash at: 45°C for 15 minutes, 54.4°C for 15 minutes, 60°C for 15 minutes, 65°C for 30 minutes, and 63-65°C for 60 minutes. Sparged with 22 litres water at 77°C. The pH of the last of the runoff was 5.5-6.0. One week in glass primary at 50-60°F; one week in glass secondary. Primed using Cornelius keg.

Judges' comments: "A little strong on hop aroma for the class, but very appealing. Great beer."

"Good colour. Well conditioned. Very clean. Perhaps a tad too full for the style."

1st Place - 1992
Gator Beer
Kevin Backshall

Ingredients for 50 litres;
- 2.2 kg Edme MEQ
- 3.2 kg EDME Lager malt
- 3.6 kg maltose
- 40 gm Northern Brewer (50 minutes)
- 35 gm Hallertauer (10 minutes)

Water Treatment: none
Yeast: Edme yeast, 12 gm
Original specific gravity: n/a
Final specific gravity: n/a
Age when judged (since bottling): 1 month

Brewer's specifics: Boiled for 50 minutes. Two weeks in plastic primary at 65°F. Carbonated by CO2 injection.

Judges' comments: "DMS corny sweetness. Very clean. Unbalanced towards malt. Needs more hop aroma. Appearance perfect for this style. Very drinkable, congratulations."

Lager

Continental Lager

The European copy of the original pilsener. True to style with a little more of everything than the Canadian Lager. About 5% alc./vol.

Examples: Upper Canada Lager, Brick Lager, Granville Island Lager, Lowenbrau, Grolsh, Creemore.

1st Place - 1991
Czech-It-Out
Jay Turner

Ingredients for 48 litres;
- 3 kg 2-row malt
- 3 kg Munich malt

- 1 kg wheat malt
- 1 kg Carastan
- 0.5 kg DMX extract
- 2 kg honey
- 50 gm Hallertauer pellets (60 minutes)
- 100 gm Saaz (60 minutes)
- 80 gm Saaz (30 minutes)
- 70 gm Saaz (15 minutes)

Water Treatment: 2 tsp gypsum and 1 tsp Epsom salts

Yeast: 25 gm Konig lager yeast

Original specific gravity: 1.040

Final specific gravity: 1.009

Age when judged (since bottling): 1 month

Brewer's specifics: Mashed at 146-153°F for 2 1/2 hours. Boiled for 60 minutes. Six weeks in plastic fermenter 46°F; filtered and primed by CO2 injection.

Judges' comments: "Needs more residual sweetness; finishes too dry. Nice continental hop nose, smells like Hallertauer. Some Saaz finishing hops may improve this even more. A touch dark for the class."

"A touch of fruitiness. Good balance of malt sweetness/hop bitterness. Excessive carbonation causes the body to appear thinner than it really is."

1st Place - 1992
   Domestic Bliss
   Mark Larsen

Ingredients for 18 litres;
- 3 kg 6-row malt
- .45 kg crystal malt
- .45 kg dextrine
- 28 gm Hallertauer (45 minutes)
- 14 gm Tettnanger (30 minutes)
- 14 gm Tettnanger (5 minutes)

Water Treatment: none

Yeast: Wyeast #2206 Bavarian lager yeast

Original specific gravity: 1.050

Final specific gravity: n/a

Age when judged (since bottling): 1/2 months

Brewer's specifics: Tap water boiled and cooled, and then syphoned off the precipitate. Boiled for 65 minutes. Nine weeks in glass primary and 8 weeks in glass secondary. Fermentation temperature was 4.5°C.

Judges' comments: "Slight fruitiness in aroma, not appropriate for this style. Could use more hop aroma. Appearance perfect. Good hop balance. Slight astringency. Well made beer, no obvious defects."

Lager

Continental Dark

Less sweet, hoppier and more carbonated than a Brown Ale. Characterized by a clean, subtle, crisp delicateness that can only be obtained by a significant period of cold storage. 4-4.8% alc./vol.
Examples: Heinekin Dark

1st Place - 1991
> **Fall Back**
> **Mark Larsen**

Ingredients for 18 litres;
- 4.5 kg lager malt
- 56 gm crystal malt
- 220 gm Munich malt
- 42 gm Hallertauer (90 minutes)
- 21 gm Tettnanger (30 minutes)
- 7 gm Tettnanger (5 minutes)
- Dry hopped with 7 gm Saaz

Water Treatment: none

Yeast: MeV German lager 001 yeast

Original specific gravity: 1.054

Final specific gravity: 1.012

Age when judged (since bottling): 5 months

Brewer's specifics: Mash in at 38°C; protein rest for 15 minutes at 54°C; mash for 95 minutes at 68°C; sparge at 77°C. Boiled for 105 minutes. 4 1/2 weeks in glass primary at 18°C; 3 1/2 weeks in glass secondary at 16°C. Primed with 1 level teaspoon of corn sugar per bottle.

Judges' comments: "Slight DMS in aroma, but fades when poured. Appearance right on for the class. Nice balance of malt and hops. Good clarity and head retention."

1st Place - 1992
Linda's Fest Bier
Linda Taylor

Ingredients for 22 litres;
- 6.8 kg Munich malt
- 340 gm wheat malt
- 26 gm Perle (60 minutes)
- Dry hopped with 30 gm Tettnanger

Water Treatment: none

Yeast: Brewers Choice #2206 Bavarian lager yeast

Original specific gravity: 1.061

Final specific gravity: 1.018

Age when judged (since bottling): 3 months

Brewer's specifics: Mash in at 2.5 litres per kg.; protein rest for 20 minutes at 50°C; saccharification for 90 minutes at 66°C; pH of mash was 5.3; pH of sparge was 5.7. Boiled for 90 minutes. Two weeks in plastic primary and one week in plastic secondary. Fermentation temperature was 9°C. Carbonated by reverse CO_2 in stainless keg.

Judges' comments: "Clean malty nose. Colour too light. Carbonation level a bit low. Good malt flavour. Clean and pleasant. Maybe could use a slight more bitterness and flavouring hops. It's a little fruity and shouldn't be. Try longer cold aging. I like this beer."

Porter

A dark English medium-bodied ale originating in London. Its darkness comes from the use of black malt, rather than roasted barley as in stout. High hopping lightens the mouth feel to give a clean, quick finish to an otherwise heavy beer. Varying in style from bitter to mild and sweet, dark brown to black, London style porter can be from 5 to 7.5% alc./vol.

Examples: Labatt's Velvet Cream Porter

1st Place - 1991
    Dark Machination
    Rob Lauriston & Don Moore

Ingredients for 19 litres;
- 5.45 kg 2-row pale malt
- 1.34 kg Munich malt
- 150 gm wheat malt
- 265 gm chocolate malt
- 300 gm Carapils malt
- 75 gm roast barley
- 84 gm flaked barley
- 42 gm black malt
- 45 gm Northern Brewer (90 minutes)
- 5 gm Northern Brewer (30 minutes)
- 45 gm Perle (at end of boil)

Water Treatment: none

Yeast: lager yeast

Original specific gravity: 15.1 degrees Plato

Final specific gravity: 4.1 degrees Plato

Age when judged (since bottling): 1 month

Brewer's specifics: Mashed in 25 litres of water at 45°C; raise temperature and rest at 53°C for 10 minutes, 68°C for 30 minutes, and 76°C for 10 minutes. Sparge to collect 30 litres. Boil for 90 minutes. Two weeks in stainless steel primary at 8-14 °C; six weeks in stainless steel secondary at 0-4°C. Carbonation method unknown.

Judges' comments: "Very good nice malt but could us more hop aroma. Perfect appearance. Very close to a Samuel Smith Taddy Porter; just increase the finishing hops a bit."

1st Place - 1992
Mann's Porter
Erich Mann

Ingredients for 19 litres;
- 3 kg pale malt extract
- 500 gm caramel malt
- 150 gm black patent malt
- 135 gm chocolate malt
- 90 gm wheat malt
- 60 gm roasted barley
- 35 gm Cascade (60 minutes)
- 8 gm Cascade (15 minutes)
- 12 gm Cascade (1 minute)

Water Treatment: none
Yeast: Munton & Fison yeast
Original specific gravity: n/a
Final specific gravity: 1.018
Age when judged (since bottling): 4 1/2 months

Brewer's specifics: Boiled for 60 minutes. Four days in plastic primary and eleven days in glass secondary. Fermentation temperature was 62°F. Primed with 1/2 tsp. of corn sugar per bottle, along with one drop of hop oil.

Judges' comments: "Nice aroma; can pick up both malt and hops. Nice flavour; a little too malty-sweet; more hops should be used to balance. Congratulations. Reminiscent of Sierra Nevada Porter."

Specialty

Any beer using herbs, spices or fermentable ingredients other than or in addition to malted barley which create distinct qualities in the beer.

Herb Beer

Any beer using herbs or spices other than hops to create distinct qualities can be classified as a herb beer.

Unique Fermentables

Any beer brewed using fermentable ingredients other than or as well as malted barley as a unique contribution to the overall character of the beer.

Examples include honey and maple syrup. Examples do not include fruit or herbs, although they can be used to add to the character of other uniquely fermentable ingredients.

Example: Maple Wheat Niagara Brewing

1st Place - 1991
     Caraway Ale
     Gordon Holder

Ingredients for 24 litres;
- 3 kg extra DMS
- 1 kg clover honey
- 82 gm caraway seed
- 28 gm Fuggles leaf (before boil)

Water Treatment: none

Yeast: Williams Ale yeast

Original specific gravity: 1.072

Final specific gravity: n/a

Age when judged (since bottling): 6 years

Brewer's specifics: Boiled for 60 minutes. Diluted high gravity brew (four gallons to six gallons). 317 weeks in plastic fermenter. Primed with sugar and bottle conditioned.

Judges' comments: "Great summer drink. Peach overtones. Clear dry warming finish. Nice drink for a summer afternoon. Possibly could use a little more residual sweetness."

1st Place - 1992
      3-Bag Ale
      Philip Jones

Ingredients for 50 litres;
- 8.6 kg Edme dark extract
- 800 gm crystal malt
- 250 gm black patent malt
- 250 gm roast barley
- 300 gm ginger root
- 150 gm licorice root
- 9 jalapino chile peppers

Water Treatment: none
Yeast: Whitbread ale yeast, 25 gm
Original specific gravity: 14 Ball.
Final specific gravity: 3 Ball.
Age when judged (since bottling): 1 month

Brewer's specifics: The total boil was for 50 minutes, with the herbs boiled for 20 minutes. Two weeks in plastic fermenter at 65°F. Carbonated by CO_2 injection.

Judges' comments: "Old peculiar style with a hot spicy finish; good beer. Some diacetyl but nice. A little sweet; great effort; very complex. Ginger dominates; jalapinos may be there. Perfect appearance. Excellent balance."

Stout

The generous use of highly roasted grain is fundamental to this extra dark to black style of beer. There are two subcategories of stout.

Dry Stout

Slight to heavy hopping and the use of roasted, unmalted barley create a clean, bitter, roasted coffee-like character with little hop flavour or bouquet. This is the Irish stout style and is 3.5 to 6% alc./vol.
Example: Guinness, Murphy's Beamish, Boréale, St. Ambroise, Conners' Imperial, Brock's Extra Stout.

Sweet Stout

Sweet or "milk" stout is an English style sweetened with sucrose and given more body with lactose sugar just before bottling. Pasteurization stops further fermentation, resulting in a very sweet black beer. 3 to 7% alc./vol.
Example: Dragon

1st Place - 1991
    Draft Irish Stout
    John Stockmann

Ingredients for 15 litres;
- 3.3 kg pale malt
- 300 gm Carastan malt
- 120 gm roast barley
- 120 gm Black Patent malt
- 150 gm flaked barley
- 25 gm CJ4 hops (60 minutes)
- 10 gm Northern Brewer pellets (60 minutes)
- 20 gm Northern Brewer pellets (20 minutes)
- 10 gm Goldings (10 minutes after boiling complete)

Water Treatment: 1/2 tsp gypsum, 1/8 tsp potassium chloride, 1/8 tsp salt
Yeast: 7 gm Munton and Fison yeast
Original specific gravity: 1.041
Final specific gravity: 1.019
Age when judged (since bottling): 2 months

Brewer's specifics: Add salts to 9 litres water at 31°C, add grain, heat on stove to 53°C, and rest for 20 minutes, heat to 67°C and rest for another 30 minutes. Heat to 76°C. Sparge in grain bag with 160°F water to collect 15 litres.

Boiled for 60 minutes. 17 days in plastic primary and 13 days in glass secondary at 65°F. Primed with 100 gm Demerara sugar.

Judges' comments: "Although a little more body would have helped, this was an excellent brew. Excellent colour, although it could be a shade darker."

1st Place - 1992
    Her Majesty's Stout
    Rob Rosen

Ingredients for 19 litres;
- 3 lb DMX
- 1.7 kg Coopers Stout kit
- 360 gm crystal malt
- 220 gm black patent malt
- 220 gm roast barley
- 200 gm chocolate malt
- 2 oz Northern Brewer (60 minutes)
- 2 oz Centennial (60 minutes)
- 1 oz Willamette (30 minutes)
- 100 gm espresso coffee

Water Treatment: 2 tsp gypsum
Yeast: Coopers kit yeast
Original specific gravity: 1.066
Final specific gravity: 1.015
Age when judged (since bottling): 2 months

Brewer's specifics: Boiled for 60 minutes. Three weeks in plastic primary and two weeks in glass secondary. Fermentation temperature was 72°F. Primed with 3/4 cup DMX.

Judges' comments: "Nice dry stouty flavour - similar to Guinness. Cut back on bittering hops. Very coffee-like. I like the mouthfeel of this beer; aftertaste dry/astringent, body somewhat thin."

Trappist

Each of the Belgian Trappist ales is different and distinctive in the manner of Belgian ales. 'Trappist' is an appellation which only the Trappist monasteries may use; other Belgian breweries produce this style of beer as well, but they may not refer to their beer as a Trappist. These beers range from light to dark in colour, have a high alcohol and a phenolic flavour, and have a unique flavour attributable to the use of candy sugar and the yeast used. *Examples:* Chimay, Orval, St. Sixtus.

1st Place - 1992
Hello Brussels
Peter Mullowney

Ingredients for 20 litres;
- 4.2 kg 2-row malt
- 2 kg amber dried malt extract
- 120 gm crystal malt
- 20 gm Northern Brewer (90 minutes)
- 100 gm Goldings (90 minutes)
- 30 gm Goldings (at end of boil)
- 20 gm Goldings (after 15 minutes)

Water Treatment: none
Yeast: Wyeast ale yeast
Original specific gravity: 1.072
Final specific gravity: 1.014
Age when judged (since bottling): 2 1/2 months

Brewer's specifics: Boiled for 90 minutes. Four weeks in stainless steel primary and two weeks in glass secondary. Fermentation temperature was 18°C. Bottle conditioned.

Judges' comments: "Very clean aroma, nice colour and head retention. I like this beer; a Trappist ale should be a little more complex. Reminds me of Stella Rosa - not a Trappist but very good."

Wheat Beer

Wheat beers are top fermenting and very lightly hopped. Their fruity palate is also very malty, yet remains sharply refreshing, often with a taste hinting of cloves. The southern German style has at least 50% wheat malt. The yeasts used produce a tart, spicy palate distinct from their lactic cousins. About 5% alc./vol.

1st Place - 1991
Weizen-Up
Dave Kimber

Ingredients for 19 litres;
- 1.5 kg B.M.E. 67% wheat extract

- 1.4 kg dried malt extract
- 54 gm Hallertauer (60 minutes)
- 27 gm Tettnanger (15 minutes)
- 27 gm Tettnanger (at end of boil)

Water Treatment: none

Yeast: MeV liquid Wheat Beer yeast

Original specific gravity: 1.050

Final specific gravity: 1.012

Age when judged (since bottling): 2 months

Brewer's specifics: Boiled for 60 minutes. 3 weeks in glass primary at 65°F; 2 weeks in glass secondary at 55°F. Primed with 2/3 cup DMX extract.

Judges' comments: "Nice Spring aroma. Clean with a touch of sourness. Excellent; wonderful beer. All in great balance. Colour perfect for a dunkel weizen."

1st Place - 1992
Cheshire Wheat
Paul Dickey

Ingredients for 50 litres;
- 5.4 kg pale malt
- 3.2 kg wheat malt
- 500 gm crystal malt
- 100 gm Hallertauer (60 minutes)

Water Treatment: 5 gm gypsum and 5 gm calcium chloride

Yeast: Whitbread yeast, 10 gm

Original specific gravity: 1.042

Final specific gravity: n/a

Brewer's specifics: Boiled for 60 minutes. Two weeks in stainless steel primary and one week in stainless steel secondary at 19°C.

Judges' comments: "Clove aroma comes through with fruitiness. Nice clove flavour comes through."

CHAPTER 11

SO YOU WANT TO BE A TASTER!

The Tour

"There is nothing which has yet been contrived by man by which so much happiness is produced as by a good tavern or inn."

Dr. Samuel Johnson.

THE 1993 IRON GUT TOUR!

How often I have been told I would like that job of yours! And questioned "How do I become a beer taster?"

When I started out on the tour to do the research for this book, I was only looking for beer, brewpubs and copy. Instead I discovered small town Ontario, and a few weeks later Quebec's Eastern Townships.

After spending some two days on the telephone and $100. in long distance charges to make appointments and contacts, the following entries from my daily journal relate my discoveries.

Day 1

Start Cornwall: 9:20 - finish London, motel 7:30 p.m. - 672 kms, by car, walk 8 kms.

Take Highway 401 to Mississauga, non stop to Marconi's Brewpub, for a quick tasting and rating of their three products. Try to arrange an interview or to talk to anyone, not interested.

Arrive at Sleeman's in Guelph, at 3:15, 15 minutes early. Meet P.R. person, Krista Arbuckle, who speaks with at true "midwestern Ontario twang". Brewmaster Al Brash comes to see me in the tasting room, produces the brewery's five products and says "Let's taste." Interview Al. John Sleeman drops by for a few words. 5 p.m. leave for London to find a motel. Locate in the east end so I can visit Mash McCann's, a former brewpub. Once I am settled in the motel, I head back downtown, feel hunger and enter a Vietnamese grocery and buy a bag of shrimp chips. In a few blocks I am at Mash McCann's. While the brewing vessels are still in the front hall, this leather bar, is too tough for me. Men and women are equally scary. I talk to the owner who asks that I not recommend him. No problem. After a quick pint I head back and see the "Abyssinia" an Ethiopian Restaurant at 670 Dundas St. More or less empty except for the staff and a few friends playing taped music and speaking Ethiopian I head for the counter. And then for some unknown reason I ordered a

Miller Draft. Ginger ale has more character. Not having a clue what to order from the menu, I guessed and ordered Saro, split pea, flour cooked with onions, tomatoes and season and served on injera bread, a huge pancake like object, which acts both as a plate and a eating utensil, all presented on a painted tin platter. The idea is to eat the dish you order and then sop it up with the bread, when you are done there are no plates left. A great idea, it eliminates knives and forks, and of course dishes. If I had been with someone else, everything would have been served on a common platter, the thinking being this, "If you share from a common dish, you will never betray one another." Offering vegetarian and meat dishes, they also had honey Ethiopian wine, Tusker, Guinness and you know what else.

Back to the room for the night.

Day 2

Start London: 8 a.m. - finish Kitchener, Walper Terrace Hotel 10:50 p.m. - 154 kms, by car, walk 12 kms.

Donut and coffee for breakfast while watching the "Avengers" and then reading the "Toronto Star". Leave motel at 10 a.m., visit two second hand bookshops, one antique store, one flea market, and two coin dealers, while listening to CBC radio between stops. Photographed a museum, which was typically closed. Saw a cop giving a parking ticket to a bicycle linked to a tree, (remember this is February), CBC's Murray McLaughlin's show aptly played a song titled "Me and Stupid" while London's finest did its best. Found a parking spot far away from this law enforcer and photographed the armouries.

Kuntz House, 167 King Street South, Waterloo, built circa 1878, now owned by Labatt's and just a stone's throw away from Brick.

Visited the CEEPS Brewpub and sampled three pints. Interviewed the publican. Reminisced about my first year at Western. On my way to the newly opened Thames Valley brewery I visited the Royal Canadian Regiment's Museum. Then onto Thames Valley, no one was there, so I took a few photographs. I had already sampled the lager at the CEEPS.

Almost out of London, I checked the map for my bearings at Crumlin. Stopped at an antique store, where the proprietors were older than the antiques.

Onto Woodstock to photograph the armouries (I have been working on a book about Ontario's armouries for the last five years, there are some 200 of them.)

On my way, I got stuck behind a horse drawn cutter, finding myself in the middle of winter fair festivities. To add to the fun there was a person dressed as a walking Duracell Battery. Already out of film, I reloaded the camera, and photographed the armouries, now the Board of Education Office, and while I was at it, took the old jail, now used by the Oxford Board of Health. The airwaves were pierced by the local radio station, 102.3 FM on remote, while kids were attacking cups of hot chocolate and plates of cookies.

Next stop New Hamburg, where I stopped to photograph the brewery. Then to Baden, where I followed Brewery St., passing Mennonites in their buggies. The brewery was gone.

At 5 p.m. I reached Heidelberg where I stopped at the Olde Heidelberg Brewpub and Restaurant for their beer, and a plate of pigtails, sauerkraut and mashed potatoes. Still hungry I ordered a side order of tails. Finished, I visited one last antique shop.

Then to Waterloo, I knew when I was there as it must be the only municipality in Ontario where the synchronized lights work.

Decided to stay at the Walper Terrace, remembering the time I stayed there years ago with my parents. I got caught in the middle of a wedding party as I was unloading the beer samples I had already been given, to prevent them from freezing. 6:30 p.m.

Decided to visit Huether's, walked over. Dave Adlys noticed I was nosing around and asked what I was up to - I told him and at 10:30 p.m. and after four more beers, I went back to the hotel.

Day 3

Start Kitchener: 8 a.m. - finish 9 p.m., motel Guelph - 75 kms by car, walk 4 kms.

Up at 8 a.m. to the "Bowery Boys", checked out at 10 a.m., bitterly cold, blustering, took a photograph of the Oktoberfest Headquarters. Coffee at "Seven -11". Got lost on the one-way streets looking for Woodside the home of Prime Minister Mackenzie King. Winter storm watch announced on the radio, stopped off at another "Seven-ll" for a burrito.

Finally found Woodside and toured it. Left at 12:30, the radio was playing "Psychotic Reaction".

Decided to head to Elora. A keen east wind was whipping across the fields, while I was slowed down by a traffic jam created by galloping Mennonite carriages, heading for home after Sunday service. Filled with bright pink faced, black clad adults and children huddled at their feet under the wooden dash or in a hutch in the rear wrapped in light blue scarfs for colour, a full road of these carriages were dashing headlong for home.

In Elora I visited three antique shops. Went to the Elora Inn, met with Tim Taylor of the famous Taylor and Bate's Brewery. He offered me lunch, I had to refuse to get to Guelph before the storm worsened. Arrived in Guelph at 2:30 p.m. and found a motel.

Walked to the Woolwich Arms to meet entrepreneur Bob Desautels. With his wife and daughter we talk about beer, of course it was now time to have some beer (four Wellington County), and eat. I had the "Arm's Classic", a hamburger with jalapenos and sweet mango chutney. I thought it was more than enough, but after walking back to the motel through the snow at 8 p.m., I wandered over to Pat and Marios and had a plate of calamari and a bourbon.

Room 9 p.m.

Day 4

Start: Guelph: 8 a.m. - finish 9:15 p.m., parent's home Oakville -159 kms by car, walk 3 kms.

First visit Brick Brewing Waterloo, arrive early at 9 a.m. when planned to be there at 9:30. Interview with Jim Brickman, a typical modest brewer, tour plant, collected samples.

Head back to Guelph to visit Wellington County, again too early so I took a break, purchased more film, and then went to Burger King for zesty fries.

1 p.m. back at Wellington County with a 2 1/2 hour interview with the new brewer Mike Stirrup. Tried the Extra Special Bitter, before it arrived in the stores.

Photographed the former Sleeman mansion, now a "peeler's

The Sleeman Mansion, now turned into a "peeler's pub" and motel. At one time overlooking the Silver Creek Brewery, the sidewalk is said to have been lined with upended beer bottles.

pub" at 3:30. Arrived at Sleeman's Brewery to complete taking historic photographs at 3:45. Finally knew where I had met Krista Arbuckle, it was her accent, she grew up in Brantford as I did, and her sister-in-law shared some of the few classes I made in high school, with me.

Had a lager at 5 p.m. At 6:30 went to a German restaurant for a dinner of pickled pork hocks, and a pint of Hacker-Pschorr on tap.

Day 5

Start Oakville: 9 a.m. - finish Bowmanville, Flying Dutchman Motel 9 p.m. 289 kms.

To St. Catharines, stopped at 10:30 and visited a grocery store where I purchased some calarmari salad for a snack, onto Conners where I tasted the new lager, while interviewing Liam McKenna.

Next stop 1 p.m., the now defunct Pacific Brewery, tasting, interview with manager, and brewer and tour.

Next stop Mississauga and Brax n' Brew where I enjoyed the Winter Warmer Ale. And while in the vicinity, I went to CC's and was pleasantly surprised. After this I went on to Bowmanville, the brewpub was closed and had not been in operation since October 1992.

Pacific Brewery located in the old Potter Distillery Plant. Thriving with its canned Pacific Real Draft, the brewery was "murdered" according to manager Steve Smith when the province introduced its tax on tinned beer.

Day 6

Start Bowmanville: 7 a.m. with the movie channel, finish 8:30 p.m. parent's home Oakville - 482 kms.

A Boston Cream donut, and the news Brian Mulroney had resigned. Throughout the day I was incredulous how every one who had criticized him now suddenly thought he was a fine chap.

Travelled to Brighton for the official Grand Opening of Ontario's First Cidery by Northumberland Brewers Inc. at 9:30. After enjoying several apple snacks, and glasses of cider, I engaged in a tasting at 12:30. Coffee followed.

On my return to Niagara Falls for an interview at Niagara Falls

The Concord Hotel, Ferry Street, Niagara Falls. On the site of the old Drummondville Brewery and possibly containing elements of the brewery which was badly damaged by fire in 1886, the Concord is yet another "peeler's pub". Is there some historic affinity to strip clubs and breweries?

Brewing at 4 p.m. I listened to more Mulroney malarkey.

Tasted two brews and chatted with the brewmaster. Told that the old Drummondville Brewery, now the Concord Hotel was still standing, went and photographed it. Arrived at my parents in Oakville at 8:30, had a meat pie for dinner with a Bock and bed 10:30 p.m.

Day 7

Start Oakville: Left at 8:30 - finish 1 p.m. at my in-laws in Toronto - 145 kms, walk 6 kms.

Cold meatloaf for breakfast, load up the car with beer.

Started off to Hamilton via the Burlington Skyway and predictably got lost in the rabbit warren of expressways, Mack Trucks and Dofassco. As I was going to be late for my appointment, I called. It turned out I was only one turn away, and arrived at 9:45 and had an interview with Bill Sharpe, President of Lakeport Brewing, located in the old Peller Brewery. Picked up beer, Bill gave me historic photographs of the plant.

The Art Deco influenced Peller Brewery, 1946.

Headed for Mississauga for my 1:30 interview at Algonquin, picked up beer, left at 2:30.

Arrived at Great Lakes Brewing at 3 p.m., interview with Anetta Bulut, and had a short tasting with Bruce Cornish, the brewmaster. Wonderful, like fresh Pilsner Urquell.

Next stop Upper Canada for 5 p.m. for a short chat, and to pick up more tasting supplies.

7:30 drove up Bathurst to Lawrence took 30 minutes to my in-laws for the night at 7:30.

8 p.m. met Kevin Keefe the proprietor of the Granite along with T.V. producer Conrad Beaubien to talk about a T.V.

(Photographs courtesy, Lakeport Brewing Corp.)
The Amstel Brewery now Lakeport Brewing Corp., 201 Burlington St. East, Hamilton on Hamilton Harbour. Greatly expanded by Amstel, the core of the old Peller Brewery can still be seen in the tower in the lower left.

special to be called BREW. Ate, drank, went on to sample Vinefera's brew and then ended at the steroid haven known as the Spruce Goose.

Day 8

Start Toronto: load up at 9 a.m., left 9:30 - finish Cornwall 4:30 - 462 kms

Only stopping off in Kingston to visit a publisher and have a coffee and chat at the Kingston Brewing Co., I carefully made my way home to give myself and my liver a well earned rest. With a briefcase full of notes, a car load of beer, a wallet packed with visa bills, and seven rolls of film - all I had to do now was write the book.

The booty, 17 cases of beer, eight days, and 2,438 kms later.

Realizing I couldn't possibly sample all of their products and live to write about it, all the breweries involved generously provided me with samples.

BEER AND FOOD

"The Baker says, 'I've the staff of life,

And you're a silly elf!'

The Brewer replied with artful pride,

'Why, this is life itself!'"

From the "Baker and the Brewer" sign,

Birmingham, 19th Century.

Whatever the season there is a beer and food combination to suit your tastes, and rest assured, there are no wrong choices - just better. Let your imagination be the final judge.

SUMMER -

Any lager, Wheat Beer, Dry Beer, Cream Ale, English Bitter, or Light Beer - pizza, pasta, salads, fish, barbecues.

Bitters - curries, Mexican - the malt acts as a fine antidote to the spices found in these foods.

Wheat Beer - hot dogs, sausages.

FALL -

Microbrewery ales, bitters or Oktoberfest lagers - perogies, steak and kidney pie, chicken pie, shepherd's pie, pig's tails, sauerkraut, fish and chips.

Porter or Stout - Jamaican meat patties, oysters.

WINTER -

Strong Ales, Malt Liquors - roast beef or stew. Eisbock or Maple Wheat - old cheese, desserts.

SPRING -

Brown Ales, Amber Ales, Dark European or March Lagers - fried or grilled foods, phoughperson's lunch, soups.

Bock or Stout - cheese or cakes.

COOKING WITH BEER.

Beer not only aids the digestion of food, but is an ideal ingredient. The following recipes have been provided, courtesy of the Granite Brewery, Toronto, Halifax.

BEEF AND BEER STEW

1 •. Dice in 1/4"
- 4 carrots
- 4 large peeled potatoes
- 1 turnip
- 2 large Spanish onions
- 1 1/2 pounds (700 g) mushrooms
- 3 tbsp (50 ml) chopped garlic

2 •. In two to three litres of water
- 2 tbsp (25 ml) red wine vinegar
- 1/4 cup (50 ml) brown sugar
- 1 tbsp (15 ml) thyme
- 1/3 cup (75 ml) beef bouillon
- 2 tsp (10 ml) Dijon mustard
- 12 oz (341 ml) bottled ale
- 1 tbsp (15 ml) black pepper

3 •. 2 pounds (1 kg) browned diced beef

4 •. 1/2 cup (125 ml) flour
- 1/2 cup (125 ml) vegetable oil

Preparation:

A. In a large pot combine the veggies, stock and seasonings, including beer - cooking until the veggies are tender.

B. Add beef, and continue to cook 10 to 15 minutes.

C. Add flour and oil to mixture to thicken.

Serves 4 - 6.

STOUT CAKES

1   •. 2 1/2 cups of flour
- 1 cup sugar
- 3 1/2 tsp baking powder
- 1 tsp salt
- 2 tsp cinnamon

2   •. 1/2 cup orange juice
- 3/4 cups of beer (stout)

3   •. 2 eggs
- 1/8 cup of vegetable oil

4   •. Zest from one orange
- 1 cup of raisins

Preparation:

A. Sift all of no. 1 together, hold aside.

B. Combine no. 2 together, hold aside.

C. Whip eggs then add oil and whip.

D. Combine B and C together and whip.

E. Add wet mixture to dry mixture and combine thoroughly.

F. Add no. 4 to mixture and mix well.

G. Pour mixture into an 8" well oil spring form pan.

H. Bake in 375° oven 30 minutes. Check by sticking a toothpick in the centre of the cake, if it comes out clean, its ready, if not cook another 5 - 10 minutes, until the toothpick comes out clean.

I. Let it cool and ice.

ICING

1. 4 ounces creamcheese

2. 1 ounce of butter

3. 1 1/2 cups of fine sugar

4. 5 ml. vanilla

5. zest from one orange

Method

1. Combine all the ingredients together, mixing well.
        And if that isn't enough you can try these menus.

MENU

"I recommend...bread, meat, vegetables and beer".
Sophocles on Moderate Diet.

Lunch

Food: soup - mulligatawny

Beer: Cream Ale, Pale Ale
"I do like a little bit of bitter with my bread".

A.A. Milne.

Food: bread/bannock/cornbread
Ploughperson's lunch (the ingredients vary, but should include crusty bread, cheese, pickles and relish such as chutney and pickled onions, lettuce and tomatoes, and sometimes fruit - cold cuts do not really belong.)

Beer: Best Bitter.

Food: Dessert: fruit/custard/rice pudding

Beer: Maple Wheat, Morte Subite, La Chouffe, Wheat Beer.

Dinner

Why then the world's mine oyster,
Which I with 'church key' will open.
Shakespeare, adapted.

Food: First course: oysters/pickles

Beer: Stout

Food: Second course: boiled white fish

Beer: Wheat Beer.

Food: Third Course: grilled chops or roast beef and Yorkshire pudding.

The waiter's hand that reach
To each his perfect pint of stout
His proper chop to each.
Lord Tennyson.

Beer: Despite Tennyson's recommendation - Brown Ale.

Food: vegetables - fiddleheads/peas/boiled potatoes/greens.
Beer: you could add a microbrewery lager here.

"Wine is on every lip: beer in every stomach. Those same writers who prate
about priceless wines, drink beer".

A.D. Eames, "A Beer Drinker's Companion", Ayers Rock Press, Mass.,
1986.

Food: Dessert: trifle-blue cheese-nuts-fruit.

Beer: Eisbock, Chimay, Iron Duke.

CHAPTER 12

THE BEER AFICIONADO

Brewing literature and organizations.

Knowledge of a subject enhances enjoyment; and serious beer drinkers like to know and debate the merits of what they find in their mugs. To meet this demand for information a small, but dedicated corps of beer writers has appeared across North America, along with a number of beer clubs. This short list of beer publications and beer related organizations will provide you with an idea about what is available and where to join.

The list, however, is not complete and does not include any American groups, but only the most effective Canadian organizations now in existence, that I know of, and a selection of the current beer literature.

Beaumont, Stephen. Bi-weekly Saturday column about beer in the "Toronto Star", Associate Editor for "The Celebrator", an American beer tabloid, which is interesting if you visit the U.S., but is more likely to make your mouth water needlessly if you don't. Subscription: P.O. Box 375 Hayward, CA, 94543. As for Stephen, he has turned beer journalism in Canada into a profession, his columns are always informative, entertaining and a welcome alternative to wine.

"The Beer Sellar", Brewers Retail Incorp. Marketing Service, Mississauga, 1992. An in house publication outlining the history of the Ontario brewing industry with profiles of current Ontario brewers.

Berberoglu, H. "Brewing, Canadian Breweries and Home Brewing". Food and Beverage Consultants, Toronto, 1987. Written for students enrolled at the School of Hospitality and Tourism Management, Ryerson, Toronto. Good description of beer styles, handling and appreciation. Bias towards German lagers.

Bowering, Ian. "The Art and Mystery of Brewing in Ontario". General Store Publishing House Inc., Burnstown, Ontario, 1988. The beginning - the first serious look at the history of brewing in Canada. Includes over 125 archival photographs, description of every major Ontario brewer, historic brewery architecture.

Bowering, Ian. "In Search of the Perfect Brew. A guide to Canada's Brewpubs and Microbreweries". General Store Publishing House Inc., Burnstown, Ontario, 1990. Canada's first beer guide. You have just read the update.

Brewers Association of Canada, Heritage Place, 1200-155 Queen Street, Ottawa, Ontario, Canada K1P 5C9. The brewers' national association. They produce a newsletter, that usually outlines the problems with government over taxation, and provides statistics.

"Brewing in Canada". Brewers Association of Canada, Ottawa, 1965. An overview of the brewing industry.

Canadian Amateur Brewers Association, they were formed for "The promotion of brewing; the education of members in brewing methods and history." Apart from running training seminars for brewing and judging, they also produce a newsletter. Membership: CABA., 19 Cheshire Drive, Islington, Ontario, M9B 2N7. 416-237-9130.

The Canadian Brewerianist. These people produce a printed historic profile of the brewers in the locality they hold their annual meeting. Along with a yearly convention and sale, they collect and preserve historic beer memorabilia. Memberships: 19 Lambert Road, Thornhill, Ontario, L3T 7E6.

(This is the National organization.)

The Canadian Brewerianist, "Golden Horseshoe Chapter". Along with a newsletter this group based around Toronto also holds sales. Membership: P.O. Box 191, Station G, Toronto, Ontario M4M 3G7.

D'Eer. Mario. "Guide de la bonne bière". Editions du Trécarré St. Laurent, Quebec, 1991. A review of Quebec's better beers with discussions about everything from beer styles to bière et sexualité.

Donaldson, Gerald and Lampert, Gerald, editors. "The Great Canadian Beer Book," McClelland and Stewart Ltd., Toronto, 1975. A silly book that glorifies the beer belly and the dubious art of chugging.

"Facts on the Brewing Industry in Canada". Dominion Brewers Association, Ottawa, 1948. An overview of the industry in 1948.

Filer, S. Patricia. "The Winemaker - the autobiography of Andrew Peller, founder of André Wines Ltd" Private Publ., 1982. Along with the story of the winery, the book traces the history of the Peller Brewery, Ontario's first independent after World War 11. Not able to advertise beer in the media, Peller promoted ice to attract attention to his product.

Gervais, C.H. "The Rumrunners - a prohibition scrapbook". Firefly Books, Scarborough, 1980. An entertaining look at brewing and distilling around Windsor during prohibition.

Jackson, Michael. "The Simon and Schuster Pocket Guide to Beer," revised, third edition, Simon and Schuster Inc., To., 1990. A must for all beer aficionados, and it even includes an adequate description of Canada's beers.

Jennings, Paul, reprint editor for Hackwood, F.W. "Inns, Ales and Drinking Customs of Old England," Bracken Books, London, 1987. 392 pages of the British enjoying their national beverage. A must.

"Kegs and Cases," published by Brewers Retail Inc. Printed "...for the Ontario hospitality trade." Published three times a year. Editor Dennis McCloskey, 1 City Centre Drive, ste 1700, Mississauga, Ontario L5B 4A6. 416-949-0429. Articles about the Ontario beer industry.

MacKinnon, Jamie. "The Ontario Beer Guide. An Opinionated Guide to the Beers of Ontario". Riverwood Publ. Ltd., Sharon, Ont., 1992. The title says it all, this is a blow by taste description of every Ontario made beer Jamie had the pleasure and sometimes misfortune to taste. This book is sure to fuel the flames of any conversation about beer and the Ontario industry. A good read, whether you agree with the statements or not.

McCloskey, Dennis. "365 Beertime Stories", General Store Publishing House Inc., Burnstown, Ontario, 1989. You will never run out of something to say over your favourite pint with this book around. And just in case your stories are wearing a little thin Dennis will be producing a companion piece to be called "Mugshots".

Rich, H.S. "100 Years of Brewing," H.S. Rich Publ., Chicago, 1903, (reprint Arno Press, 1974). A classic primarily describing the developing lager tide in North America and then worldwide at the turn of the 19th century.

Robertson, James D. "The Beer Log". Bosak Publ. Co., CA., 1992. Rating some 3,000 beers around the world, Robertson gives Canadian brews a more than passing taste. At $37.50 U.S., plus postage though, I am not sure you need this in your library unless you are really unsure of your judgement. Jackson is a far better buy. And as this tome is served up in a three ring-binder for notes and expansion, Jackson is far handier.

Rohmer, Richard. "E.P. Taylor". McClelland and Stewart, Toronto, 1978. Here is wheeler-dealer, Edward Plunket Taylor in all his manifestations.

Sandwell, K. Bernard. "The Molson Family". Privately printed, Montreal, 1993. 500 copies only. This is the first of a trilogy of Molson books including "The Barley and the Stream", by Merrill Denison, and "The Molson Saga", by S.E. Woods Jr. In style they are all the same. If you want a thorough, illustrated discussion of the beer that made Molson famous, you will not find it. The books do, however, provide readable overviews of the history of Canada's oldest brewery and brewing family.

Shea, Albert, A. "Vision in Action. The Story of Canadian Breweries Limited From 1930 - 1955," Canadian Breweries Ltd., To., 1955. The unabashed story of E.P. Taylor's brewing empire. Unfortunately, just as the book was released, the Combines Investigation's people started hearings to determine if Canadian Breweries were wilfully eliminating competition to create a monopoly. To prevent fuel from being added to the fire, the book was withdrawn. Fortunately the Ontario Archives does have a copy.

By the way, even though Canadian Breweries had acquired 23 breweries in 23 years, and closed 12 of them, reducing 150 brands to 9, and had captured 60% of the Ontario industry, it was determined by the Commission, that they were just following modern business practice through centralization.

Sweet, Richard, L. "Directory of Canadian Breweries". Privately printed, Saskatoon, Sk., 1990 and subsequent updates. For the collector of beer memorabilia Richard's works are a must. Listing as many of Canada's breweries as he can verify, and all of their corporate reincarnations, Richard's work is the cornerstone to any new research on Canadian brewing history.

Vaillancourt, Emile. "The History of the Brewing Industry in the Province of Quebec," G. Ducharme, Montreal, 1940. This slim volume may not be that accurate or detailed, but it is all we have. Vaillancourt places the start of the Quebec brewing industry squarely on the needs of the Jesuits in 1634, while Jacques Cartier and his brave band of men, and incidentally the Province itself were saved from scurvy by drinking Indian spruce beer.

Yenne, Bill. "Beer of North America". Bison Books, Greenwich Ct., 1986. An incredibly wide topic, handled competently, well illustrated and still found in remainder bins. Well worth owning.

BEER FESTIVALS

Every fall Canadians let out a collective yodel, squeeze into their lederhosen, dance the polka, and down vast quantities of beer to be able to join in with the Gemütlichkeit of Oktoberfest. Celebrated by everyone who loves beer throughout Canada, Kitchener-Waterloo holds the second largest Oktoberfest celebrations in the world. This world class event starts on the Thanksgiving weekend and runs a week. For a room in town you need to book at least six months in advance.

Information

K-W Oktoberfest Inc.,
77 Ontario Street S., P.O. Box 1053,
Kitchener, Ontario, N2G 4G1,
519-576-0571;   FAX: 519-742-3072

Logo courtesy, K-W Oktoberfest Inc.

P.S.   Just Published: "Beer Magazine", quarterly, subscription: $16.20,
102 Burlington Cr., Ottawa, Ont., K1T 3K5.

Canada's only national beer magazine.

Index

ABOUT THE AUTHOR

Illustration by Lor Pelton

Ian Bowering is a professional historian, museum curator, dedicated beer enthusiast, and author of "The Art and Mystery of Brewing In Ontario", a history of Ontario's brewing industry from the arrival of the United Empire Loyalists to the present, and "In Search of the Perfect Brew", the brewpub and microbrewery guide to Canada.

While Ian professes to believe that "no one's taste is wrong", he has been on a crusade to convert people to real beer, and to turn them away from the light, homogenized, designer products that threaten to turn us into a nation of fizzy quaffers. He proselytizes through speaking engagements and beer tastings all over Eastern Canada.

Apart from telling beer drinkers that the taste should reside in the bottle and not the label, Ian writes extensively about beer, teaches antique appreciation courses, and is currently writing about Ontario's history and the fur trade.

While Ian enjoys hiking, opera, deep sea fishing and hoarding practically anything, his real hobby is finding that perfect brew in the ideal setting in the company of good friends.

He is married to artist Lor Pelton, has two children, Anna and Mac, and Babooshka the cat.

OTHER BEER BOOKS FROM GSPH

THE ART & MYSTERY OF BREWING IN ONTARIO	$14.95
365 BEERTIME STORES	$ 9.95
MUG SHOTS	$ 12.95